FIRST FIND YOUR CHILD A GOOD MOTHER

Paul Riesman

First Find Your Child a Good Mother

The Construction of Self in Two African Communities

With a Prologue by Suzanne Riesman

Editorial Committee:
David L. Szanton
Lila Abu-Lughod
Sharon Hutchinson
Paul Stoller
Carol Trosset

Rutgers University Press
New Brunswick, New Jersey

Library of Congress Cataloging-in-Publication Data

Riesman, Paul.
    First find your child a good mother : the construction of self in
two African communities / Paul Riesman ; with a prologue by Suzanne
Riesman ; editorial committee, David L. Szanton . . . [et al.].
        p. cm.
    Includes bibliographical references and index.
    ISBN 0-8135-1767-2 (cloth)—ISBN 0-8135-1768-0 (pbk.)
        1. Fula (African people)—Kinship.   2. Fula (African people)—
Psychology.   3. Children—Burkina Faso—Djibo.   4. Children—
Burkina Faso—Pétéga.   5. Parenting—Burkina Faso—Djibo.
6. Parenting—Burkina Faso—Pétéga.   7. Fula (African people)—
Social life and customs.   8. Djibo (Burkina Faso)—Social life and
customs.   9. Pétéga (Burkina Faso)—Social life and customs.
I. Szanton, David L., 1938–   . II. Title.
DT555.45.F85R54   1992
306.8'08996322—dc20   91-18209
                                                            CIP

British Cataloging-in-Publication information available

CONTENTS

LIST OF ILLUSTRATIONS

Photographs

(All photographs except #9 were taken by Paul Riesman and all were developed and printed by Amanda Riesman.)

PREFACE

David L. Szanton

At the time of Paul Riesman's death in June 1988, he was working on a book-length manuscript growing out of his long-term research among the Fulani of Burkina Faso. Pained by his loss, and the potential loss of his work to the field, a small group of friends, colleagues, and family members formed an ad hoc editorial group. Our purpose was to complete Paul's 320+-page manuscript as best we could and ready it for publication. Paul had essentially completed the present chapters 2 through 8, part of the Introduction, and several outlines of the book which indicated its intended shape and conclusions. He had also written several essays in recent years that suggested the nature of the analysis he was bringing to the ethnographic data.

With this material in hand, the editorial group met for a day in Cambridge, Massachusetts, in May 1989. It was evident that Paul had already produced an extremely rich and provocative document that, even in its unfinished state, made a major contribution to several domains of anthropology and African studies. A number of questions remained, but Paul had done enough and left enough clues so that we felt we could bring the volume to closure.

To transform the manuscript into a book, a number of tasks seemed essential. The Introduction was incomplete; what Paul had written for it was supplemented by Lila Abu-Lughod, a past student of his. In addition, Paul Stoller (whose own anthropological

career among the Songhay was in some ways directly inspired by
Paul Riesman's work and approach) drafted a section on the historical and ethnographic place of the Fulani in West Africa. I com-
bined three divergent drafts of chapter 8 into a single statement.
Although Paul had sketched several outlines for the Conclusion,
he had not written any of it. Sharon Hutchinson, another ex-stu-
dent of Paul's, agreed to construct chapter 9 based on his notes,
several of his earlier publications, and her own related fieldwork
among the Nuer. And in lieu of a theoretical chapter, which is indicated in Paul's outlines but for which he made no notes, Carol
Trosset, also a former student of Paul's, wrote a brief essay discussing the theoretical implications of his work and its significance
for psychological anthropology.

Going beyond the draft manuscript itself, there were several
other things that needed to be done. Paul was a superb photographer, and his daughter Amanda went through some sixty rolls of
film and produced the photographs that grace this volume. We
also felt it would be helpful and appropriate to provide some additional contextualization, some of which Paul might well have
written himself. His wife, Suzanne Riesman, wrote a Prologue
describing the fieldwork that led to the book. Lila Abu-Lughod
wrote an introductory discussion of Paul's contributions as a reflexive anthropologist.

While each of us took primary responsibility for our respective
materials, we have tried to listen for and maintain Paul's voice as
best we could. As much as possible, we incorporated extended
quotations from his other writings. In an attempt to ensure continuity, Carol Trosset and I did most of the text editing of the book
as a whole. As Paul's college roommate, anthropological colleague,
and close friend for thirty-two years, I coordinated our efforts, ne-
gotiated collective decisions, and organized our contributions into
a unified manuscript. Carol Trosset also worked closely with Rutgers University Press on the final editing and proofreading, and
compiled the index.

There is no way that we could have completed the book as Paul
would have done. But it has been a labor of love. We can only hope
that we have come close enough to what he would have written so
that readers will be able to sense his insights, to be enriched by his

observations, and to work with the ideas of a man who still had so
much more to say.

A Note on Transliteration:

Capitalized letters in the middle of words indicate an immediately
prior glottal stop. The letter *c* in Fulfulde, the language of the
Fulani, is pronounced like the *ch* in cheese.

ACKNOWLEDGMENTS

Paul often spoke with gratitude and great warmth toward the people of Petaga and Djibo, Burkina Faso, both for their willingness to open the meanings of their lives to him, and for the numerous self-discoveries which they occasioned. The book is dedicated to them.

Funding for the field research was provided by the National Science Foundation, and by a Ford Foundation grant administered by the Joint Committee on African Studies of the Social Science Research Council and the American Council of Learned Societies. A year at the Institute for Advanced Study in the Behavioral Sciences, Palo Alto, and a sabbatical year in Paris supported by Carleton College, provided the freedom and encouragement to draft the manuscript.

The editors especially wish to thank Suzanne and Amanda Riesman for their crucial contributions to the completion of the manuscript at a time of deep personal pain and loss. Likewise, David and Evelyn Riesman's continuing encouragement for the effort has been greatly appreciated. We are also very grateful to Arthur Kleinman and Robert LeVine who helped think through the plan for completing the manuscript, and to Waud Kracke who provided a critical reading of the near-final version, which helped considerably with the final polishing.

Finally, we must thank the Institute for Intercultural Studies, New York, for underwriting the costs of producing the photographs, as well as the several publishers of Paul's essays used to complete the volume, the University of Chicago Press for permission to use the map from *Freedom in Fulani Social Life,* and most especially, Marlie Wasserman and Rutgers University Press, for their understanding and support for this unusual project.

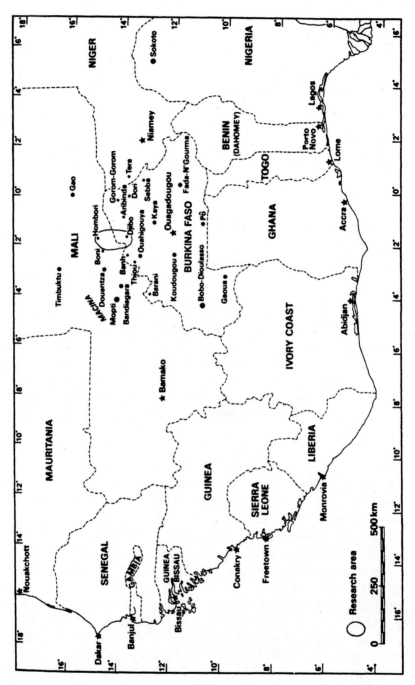

Map of West Africa, from Riesman 1977.

PROLOGUE
BURKINA FASO, 1974–76:
A PERSONAL MEMOIR

Suzanne Riesman

Most of this book was in manuscript form in Paul's briefcase when he died in June 1988. He had written it during a recent sabbatical year we spent in Paris. It came out of fieldwork we did as a family in 1974–76 in the small town of Djibo, in Burkina Faso. When we returned to the United States, Paul became immersed in teaching, to which he was devoted, and was preoccupied with tenure, health problems, family life, and requests to write articles and attend conferences on subjects that interested him, such as aging and development, but which were not his main research project. He managed to write several articles related to his main interests, in particular on the person and the life cycle, and on the irrelevance of child rearing to personality formation, but as time passed he grew more and more frustrated. He felt he had been writing too many theoretical articles and wanted to get down to the more ethnographic writing of the book to back them up.

Much of the year before the sabbatical was spent organizing his materials into a data base and he actually started writing on his computer at our apartment on rue Montbrun in the 14th arrondissement in Paris, in late fall of 1986. He had hoped to finish the whole book by the end of the sabbatical year and felt very disap-

FIRST FIND YOUR CHILD A GOOD MOTHER

pointed that he did not. He had completed the ethnographic sections but had only begun to discuss their theoretical implications. He was good at both. Sensitive to detail as well as to its relation to the larger culture, he always used his own culture as a point of comparison. Paul saw himself as an anthropological tool, whom the reader needed to know in order to interpret the material presented in his ethnography. Therefore, he tried to put as much of himself and his relationships to his children and other family members into his work as inhibitions and discretion permitted. Even though he embraced it in theory, self-revelation was hard for him. He was considered among the Fulani, and those who knew the Fulani well, to be as refined, self-restrained, and controlled as they were.

The central idea of this book germinated during our first field trip in Petaga, Burkina Faso (at that time, Upper Volta) during 1966–68. Steeped in psychoanalysis, both intellectually and as an analysand, Paul observed that both the FulBe and their former slaves, the RiimaayBe, used the same child-rearing practices—birthing, breast-feeding, body contact, toilet training, discipline—yet the personalities of the members of the two groups were strikingly different. He felt it would be an ideal setting in which to study child rearing in depth in order to dispute the Freudian theory that personality is determined by certain child-rearing practices during the early years of childhood.

During our first field trip, Paul had done a participant-observation study of village life for his doctoral thesis under the direction of Georges Balandier at the École Pratique des Hautes Études, Université de Paris. The thesis was later published in French and then translated and republished as *Freedom in Fulani Social Life*. The central question that informed that study came out of his own preoccupation, his studies in psychology and philosophy, and his close friendship and dialogue with his mentor, Dorothy Lee: What does freedom mean to the Fulani? To try to answer it we spent two years in a small village of thirty-three huts in the northwestern part of Upper Volta. We were in our mid- to late twenties and did not yet have children. We had intended to return there a year later after Paul finished writing his thesis. However, as often happens with theses, this one seemed to have a life of its own; instead of spending one year, Paul spent two and a half years writing it. At the same time the world economy declined and many governments reduced their support for projects in Africa. Paul had hoped to work in "development" in Africa as a way of repaying the generosity of the people who had helped us during our first trip, including the government of Upper Volta, the research center in Ouagadougou, and the chiefs and people of Djibo and Petaga. But by 1969, the number of jobs in development were few and not to Paul's liking. At the same time he was advised to get back into teaching in the United States, because that job market also showed signs of drying up. We thus left Paris in early December 1969 with a four-week-old baby and a two-week-old thesis, boarding the transatlantic liner *Le France* for its final crossing of that season. In New York we drove our new car off the ship and headed toward Northfield, Minnesota, where Paul took up a teaching position at Carleton College.

We still planned to return to Africa and wanted to get back before our children reached school age. Again there were delays. It was hard to get away from a small department: Paul was one of two anthropologists teaching in a sociology-anthropology department of five. When we were finally able to leave in 1974, our daughter, Amanda, was about to turn four and our son, Benjamin, was eight months old.

Leaving for the second trip was much harder than for the first. Taking two small children to a remote area had to be taken seriously. We realized we were taking risks, and many of our friends thought we were simply crazy or irresponsible. Our families were extremely anxious. It was also harder to leave because we felt we were starting from farther away, from "the bush" of Minnesota rather than from Paris. Furthermore, we were uncertain we would be able to stay where we had planned because Burkina Faso had suffered a severe drought and famine during the prior six years. We went with minimal necessities, leaving trunks to be sent as soon as we knew where we would be able to live.

Leaving was emotionally difficult. While hurriedly packing, Paul bruised his shin against a piece of furniture; because of his hemophilia and his unwillingness to take time to care for it right away, he bled internally. His leg swelled and he was on crutches for a month. It was not good for morale to start out that way. My mother died just weeks before we left, after wasting away gradually for fifteen years from multiple sclerosis. And we had to say good-bye to Dorothy Lee, a close friend and great source of strength to both of us and to our children. She was in the final stages of cancer, and we knew we would never see her again.

We wanted to settle in the same area as before, to reestablish ties with old friends from our village, but we also wanted to be in a town, such as nearby Djibo, where more food would be available for the children. During the first trip, Paul and I had eaten mostly the local food: millet, fresh milk and yogurt, with chicken and goat meat a rare addition, but no fruits or vegetables. In the town we could count on being able to buy meat most of the time for the children. Fruits and vegetables, grown near the town reservoir, were available for half the year. Furthermore, an Australian doctor had set up a hospital in Djibo during our absence. Last, for his study Paul needed a large number of families with small children. Djibo seemed to offer what we needed.

Upon our arrival we were relieved to learn that the Djibo region had received enough rain that summer and seemed to be recovering from the drought. We felt we could stay without being an unnecessary burden on the people. The chief of Djibo generously gave us a house in a courtyard he owned, placing us across from a Mossi family in which the husband was a military officer working for the customs service. (Djibo is near the Malian border.) Also living in the courtyard were distant relatives of the chief.

We spent fifteen hard months there. I think it surprised us just how hard they were, since we had lived in the region before. We discovered that children are not as adaptable as we thought; they only appear to be flexible because, ultimately, they can be dragged along with their parents. They would not eat local food at the beginning and we had to go to the local market daily to buy unnourishing French bread made from white flour, local peanut butter, and German jam. Also available in town was *lacciri*, a cereal similar to couscous, made from millet. At first we ate it with fresh milk and sugar, but after a month I felt compelled to boil the milk out of fear of tuberculosis or undulant fever. This made it taste awful and the children refused to drink it. They, would, however, eat it on lacciri and drink the yogurt that we made each day from fresh milk.

Nevertheless, the children were hungry for the first five months.

At last they started eating millet, heavy in carbohydrates, and which took a long time to digest but kept them feeling filled up. Even so, we continued to supplement their diet with bread and peanut butter during our entire stay. I had an oven built from mud bricks and baked bread with relatively nutritious millet flour. Since we rose with the sun along with everyone else—at 6:00 A.M. the year round, because we were so close to the equator—the children had had a full day by 4:30 in the afternoon. Living in a new culture and trying to learn a new language, added to exhaustion from the heat and a lack of accustomed food, meant that Amanda had a temper tantrum at that time every day for the first four months (and me along with her), until I could get supper ready and food in her. At sunset at 6:00 P.M., spent after a full day, she fell asleep on the mat spread out under the overhanging roof of our mud brick house.

I was surprised by another reaction I had upon returning to Africa. Paul and I had been pretty relaxed about sanitation during our first stay; we had accepted local customs without being personally much affected, although we always filtered our water. But returning with a crawling baby, I could not bear to put him on the ground of the courtyard, where chickens ran about, goats were tethered, and cows came in frequently to be milked. Therefore our son, Ben, had to be carried around by me or my helper or Amanda, except when he was in his playpen bed. We put up with this for about two months, until we built a large sandbox which ran the entire length of the patio underneath the overhang of our house and in which he could crawl around freely. More generally, the town seemed a lot dirtier and much less sanitary than our small village in the bush. Not only were more people crowded into the town, but they used uncovered holes for toilets. In the bush, people had walked for a mile before getting to a tree to defecate; as a result, there were fewer flies near the village.

The heat, as usual, was hard to adjust to. We arrived in October, just after the rainy season, which is followed by the "cooler" months of November and December. Even then, the less severe heat in the 90s and 100s took its toll. Ben had heat rash for the first nine months of our stay. Also, beginning in October, we all got colds, the kind that last two weeks and are accompanied by fevers. It seemed that everyone in the town had colds. The doctor said that people living on the edge of the desert are very susceptible to respiratory illnesses, and we got colds regularly for six months, until the hot season came.

We were a lot sicker that second trip, although we were fortunate that on neither trip did we have anything serious or life-threatening. The most serious illness that Paul had was a mild bout of hepatitis for five weeks, but even that was an eye-opener as to what a disease can do. Paul, who rarely slept more than five or six hours a night, now slept three hours in the morning, three in the afternoon, and went to bed with the sun. In between, he could barely eat anything but tomatoes and guavas, which fortunately were in season, but which he normally did not like. He had to force himself to eat, and took deep breaths to appease the nausea between bites. His weight, already down from 165 pounds to 150 from the initial adaptation, dropped another 15 pounds to 135.

As a result of the arduous conditions, Paul felt he had achieved very little at the end of the first year. He was glad to have another seven months. Every day he went out to visit and observe families, sometimes accompanied by Amanda. Occasionally, people would come by and visit us. Because of household demands, I didn't have as much time to receive visitors or to visit other people as I had during our first trip. In the evening, by kerosene lamp, Paul would write up his notes and we would listen to the BBC. Whereas, during our first stay, young men visited practically every evening to drink Arabic tea with us, during the second trip almost no young men came. Because we now had children we were in another age category. Instead, we had more contact with people in our own situation—adults with children—and with those considered to be of comparable status to visiting Westerners, local dignitaries, and officials.

We were often nostalgic for our first stay and felt we were getting to know the people much less intimately and making fewer lasting friends during the second stay. But we had set high standards for ourselves—to come to know the people well enough to be able to understand and explain what it meant "to be in the skin" of a FulBe and RiimaayBe. Perhaps, because we were unable to give more of ourselves on the second trip, we came to know them less well than we desired.

Death caught Paul suddenly in the midst of life. His family, friends, and many colleagues knew he was shaping his research materials into a new book. After his death, several of us joined together to combine his manuscript and several relevant articles into a book that would be as close to what he had intended as we could make it. Amanda developed the photographs. We hope to have at least partially completed the work of a man for whom we cared deeply, and for whose intellect and sensitivity we had the highest regard.

Paul's loss is tragic. His linguistic ability was extraordinary; he was an accomplished musician who also enjoyed and recorded music extensively in the Djibo area; he was an excellent photographer. He had a great gift for observing people in other cultures and for describing and interpreting those cultures elegantly to people in his own. The people of Petaga and Djibo were amazed and honored that he spoke Fulfulde with such fluency and sensitivity. He was known widely in West Africa as the "white man who spoke Fulfulde" and who acted nobly like a Fulani. This book is dedicated to the people of Petaga and Djibo who so kindly accepted the strange "whites" in their midst and opened their hearts and minds to us. May Paul join those who have passed before him, around the fireside, speaking Fulfulde while sipping Arabic tea.

FIRST FIND YOUR CHILD A GOOD MOTHER

REFLEXIVITY
IN HUMANISTIC
ANTHROPOLOGY

Lila Abu-Lughod

It is now widely accepted in anthropology that our knowledge of other societies as presented in ethnographies is the product of a complex set of interactions in the field and "at home" rather than the result of a simple process of investigation. Paul Riesman was an early pioneer in the exploration of some of the many ways this is true. Like many who followed, he questioned the strict separation that previously had kept serious ethnographies in an objective mode distinct from "confessional" fieldwork accounts in a subjective mode. For him, reflexivity was an essential aspect of anthropological work.

He made two important methodological breakthroughs in his first book on the Fulani of Burkina Faso (then Upper Volta), which was published in French in 1974, several years before the works generally associated with the development of "reflexive anthropology" were to appear (e.g., Dumont 1978; Rabinow 1977; Crapanzano 1977, 1980). Arguing that "few ethnographic works give a sufficient account . . . of how the material they report was collected," he tried systematically to share with the reader how he had gotten specific bits of information, describing the sorts of encounters in which conversations and questions had occurred in the field (Riesman 1977:2). In *First Find Your Child a Good Mother* he takes this further; the text is rich in stories of the closely observed interactions through which he develops his understanding of the quality and meaning of parenting and children's experiences in Fulani society.

More original than this careful attention to the encounters through which we come to know about others was his attempt to use reflexive introspection as an anthropological method. As he stated many years later, regarding his first field experience with the Fulani, "In the field my goal was to understand the world of the Fulani from within as much as I could and to discover particularly the significance of freedom, in both their terms and mine, for the way they lived and perceived themselves and society" (Riesman 1986:104). To achieve this goal he made use of what he called "disciplined introspection." He described this procedure as follows:

> I compare my feelings and reactions in particular situations with what I think the Fulani feel in those situations. And because the main problem is to know how they feel in those situations, I try to show the reader as best I can how I got the evidence that leads me to my conclusions. Ultimately, I hope to learn as much about myself as about the Fulani with this approach, for in using it I participate in both Western and Fulani cultural patterns, each of which has its particular effects on me. (Riesman 1977:2)

Many insights emerged from this use of himself and his self-reflections as an instrument for simultaneously understanding self and other.

What distinguishes Paul Riesman's use of reflexivity from that of several other anthropologists (e.g., Dwyer 1982, Rabinow 1977) who share his sense of its significance is that the self he draws on in reflecting on his own reactions is not simply his Western self, and certainly not just his anthropologist self, but the self of his whole life's experience. Although, as described below, he is highly conscious of his identity as a Westerner and of anthropology as being a project of cross-cultural understanding, the dimension of fieldwork he stresses is not so much its nature as a hermeneutic process of intercultural communication, but its capacity to generate transformative personal experiences. He was frank about the personal concerns that motivated his work and shaped the way he came to terms with various aspects of Fulani society. But beyond that, along with several other anthropologists with a psychodynamic perspective (Crapanzano 1977, 1980; Devereux 1967; Kracke 1987), he recognized the emotionally charged nature of fieldwork and explored the workings of such processes as transference and repression in his developing relations with his hosts.

In a bravely honest reflection on fieldwork, he traces his desire to do anthropology to a personal malaise, a sense of being trapped in his culture, unable to be himself with people but also unable to be himself when alone. He admits this was a common malaise among his peers in the mid-sixties. He writes of this fusion of the personal and the intellectual in his anthropological quest:

> When I first went to Africa to carry out fieldwork I was well aware that I was seeking to be jostled. . . . What I thought I needed, and what I hoped I would get through fieldwork, was a chance to be with people whose perceptions of the world and whose expectations about me would be totally different from what I was used to. This would relieve, at least temporarily, the conflict I was experiencing between my need to be with people and the feeling of being trapped while with them. (Riesman 1982:1–2)

Given this set of personal concerns, it is not surprising that freedom in the relationship of the individual to society was the central theme of the book he was to write based on this experience.

His second book is a meditation on the meaning and importance of relatives. One can see in it the working out of the questions of a more mature person who had become the devoted father of two children and who was also, perhaps, beginning to come to terms with being the son of a distinguished academic. His family of origin appears sometimes in the pages of his oeuvre, as he draws contrasts between Fulani involvement with relatives and his own early denials of the significance of family ties. Given his conclusion that the key to the development of the noble personalities he so admired among the FulBe (as opposed to their ex-slaves) lay in their sense of belonging to an important lineage, to suudu baaba (their father's house), it is a pity that he did not have a chance to comment on how this might have affected the way he thought about his own family situation.

Throughout it is clear that he took personal involvement to be an essential part of anthropological fieldwork. Sometimes that posed limitations. He admits the ways in which some of his own convictions made him less capable of examining certain aspects of Fulani society than others. He confesses, for example, that as an atheist he found it difficult to explore the meaning Islam had for his Fulani hosts. In both books, in fact, he hardly discusses Islam, despite evidence of its centrality to Fulani identity and experience of life.

Yet, more often when he encounters values among the Fulani that run counter to his convictions, he seeks to clarify why he holds his and what it must be like for them to hold theirs. For example, in chapter 4 he describes his violent reaction against authoritarian attitudes and the exercise of power; yet one of the central problems he has set for himself in the book is to understand why people accept a system of caste-like hierarchy. Instead of morally condemning the system as oppressive or evil, he asks how it works and why people come to think it makes sense. "To my mind," he once wrote, "a truly critical—and radical—psychological anthropology is one which seeks not just to identify evil, but to understand how it arises as a human process" (1987).

The most unusual part of his personal involvement was his insistence that fieldwork was for him a process of personal transformation. This is a rarely explored form of reflexivity in anthropology. He writes about how living with the Fulani changed him and analyzes how that process of transformation occurred. In a letter to the man with whom he had undergone psychoanalysis he describes one of the changes as being toward greater emotional openness: "I feel more able to stand being loved, and I think that living in the village has had something to do with this." He concludes, "I was discovering that in this society I could admit to a need to depend on others and still maintain my integrity." He was enabled to change not only by exposure to a society in which the "recognition of dependence in human relations was the norm," but by being forced to take the role of a child in a process (fieldwork) that resembled both psychoanalysis and initiation (1982:9–10).

The premise of Paul Riesman's reflexive methodology and reflexive goals for anthropology is a profound humanism—the conviction that we are all made of the same human material, react through processes that are universal, but are subjected to different forces and conditions. Sometimes he even questions the existence of differences. Reflecting on his reaction to reading about another society, for example, he writes, "I catch myself and wonder whether the difference that I am tempted to call 'cultural' is not perhaps an artifact of the way I have my knowledge of those people; in other words, maybe one of the most fundamental differences is not between myself and them, but between how I know myself and how I know them" (1986:104). In general, however, he takes differences seriously and seeks to learn from them.

The twist is that he wants to see not only what we can learn about humanity from these differences but what we can learn from those who are different from ourselves. Writing about his central anthropological concern with the self and personhood, he says, for example, that

> being a person and understanding what a person is are the same sort of process. In fact, the very reason why you and I are struggling with these thoughts today is so that we can be whoever we are more fully. Just as Newton hoped to discover God's design in the order of the cosmos, and thus be better able to further that design, so are we, as we study personhood in African societies, hoping perhaps to find a design for living that will imbue our own lives with greater meaning than they now have. (1986:112)

This final kind of reflexivity, in which one learns from others not just on a personal level but a cultural one, is also an important element of Paul Riesman's anthropology. In addition to his unusual appreciation of the personal dimension of anthropology, he was aware from the start of anthropology's Western origins and identity. He wrote that his first book should be seen as "a resultant of the encounter of a man belonging to Western civilization, and haunted by questions which life there raises for him, with a radically different civilization which he investigates with those questions constantly in mind" (1977:1–2). Anthropology, for him, was a means of thinking critically about our own culture. Like his teacher and friend, Dorothy Lee (1959, 1976), he was following out a strand of American anthropology with a long history, a strand that Marcus and Fischer (1986) have recently called "anthropology as cultural critique" and advocated taking up once more.

The contrasts he draws are stark. At times he thinks about the differences between how life, self, and human relationships are experienced in Western industrial society and Fulani society as the result of the very different conditions of existence. At other times he seems to think that there is a common human truth about society that Western ideology (in the form of ordinary people's thinking as bolstered by the notions of professional psychologists and other academics), with its stress on separate isolated selves, actually masks. The consequence of our ideology is "a dulling or repression of any awareness that we mutually participate in one another's selves" (1983:123).

In the longer unpublished version of the review of the literature on the person and the life cycle in Africa that appeared in *African Studies Review* in 1986, he proposed that we should not so much learn *about* Africans as *from* them. The most important lesson we could learn from them was their "common . . . idea that persons exist in relation to others; they not merely need them for survival, but also derive a sense of identity from those to whom they are related" (1986:97). From living with and trying to understand the Fulani world, he was able to develop a critique of both the way we, as Western middle-class people, live and the ideologies that correspond to and make possible that way of life.

Reflexivity in anthropology is based on respect for people in other societies. To take up disciplined introspection as a method requires assuming a common humanity; otherwise how could one use the self to understand the other? To become so personally involved that one could be transformed and enriched by the experience of living with others requires a basic humility. And, finally, to regard other cultures as having something to teach us as a civilization requires a total rejection of ethnocentrism.

Paul Riesman would not insist that this respect could solve the larger problem of Western domination of the non-West and anthropology's participation in that venture. Sensitive to this problem, he remained critical of attempts to finesse these political and ethical dilemmas and yet hopeful that some human good could come of this encounter between people of different cultures. Admitting that the interpretations of the Fulani he worked out "could only be the product of my interests, problems, and questions, as applied to the thoughts, feelings, and actions of my Fulani hosts" (1986:104), he criticized some of the new proposals for a dialogic or polyvocal anthropology in which the subjects with whom we work would somehow be made more equal partners (e.g., Clifford 1988; Dwyer 1982; Tedlock 1987; Tyler 1987). "There remains," he concludes, an inherent contradiction between treating the natives as equals and using the knowledge they give us for goals they would never imagine themselves. The dilemma is real; no amount of agonizing will make it go away. We have to face the fact that we are using other people for our own purposes all the time. Rather than try morally to purify ourselves to the point where we cease to use ethnography, it is my contention . . . that through an intense fieldwork experience we can go beyond ethnography, as it were, to a relationship with others that broadens everyone's sense of what it means to be human. (1982: 19–20)

I

INTRODUCTION

We hold without question two basic assumptions in the West about the personality of individuals.[1] The first is that one's personality influences the whole life course, for at every moment, it affects one's chances of success or failure. The second is that one of the most important factors shaping the personality is the way the parents raise the person from the very beginning of childhood.

There have been countless anthropological studies relating childhood, personality, and culture. In nearly all of these the researcher has assumed that early child care, toilet training, and all other normal experiences that children in a given culture undergo should be considered, from a sociological point of view, as the socialization process of the society. In this perspective, the problem for society is to transform the raw material—that is, a newborn infant—into an adult member of the society, and thus nearly everything that happens to the child is interpreted as if it had some role to play in that transformation. It follows from this idea that since different societies need different kinds of people—agricultural societies need farmers, pastoral societies need herdsmen and warriors, commercial societies need intrepid traders—the socialization required to produce these kinds of differences would also have to vary.

While doing fieldwork among the Fulani of West Africa in the years 1966 to 1968, I accepted these assumptions without question. I was quite Freudian in my thinking about the human mind and the importance of early childhood for the formation of personality. Fulani children seemed happy, adults seemed stable and self-confident, and it seemed quite likely to me that the explanation for these qualities lay in the way Fulani mothers dealt with the early "crises" of human development as described and analyzed by Erik Erikson.

What was more difficult for me to see was how those child-rearing practices might be responsible for those qualities of personality that distinguish the Fulani as an ethnic group from many of their neighbors. I felt that there must be some basis in early childhood for those qualities, but did not come upon any parental practices or typical childhood experiences that were obvious candidates. In fact, one observation I made raised a serious question in my mind as to whether such shared personality characteristics could or should necessarily be traced to early childhood. In close association with the Fulani live the RiimaayBe, descendants of the slaves that ancestors of the present Fulani captured or bought. These people speak the same language and cultivate millet like the Fulani, but do not normally herd cattle. In addition, they have a markedly different typical personality from the Fulani as displayed in everyday interaction and other ways. In my limited observations of how RiimaayBe mothers treated their children, however, I did not detect any notable differences from the way Fulani (hereafter, FulBe) mothers treated theirs. This surprised me because the differences in adult personality between the two groups seemed so striking.

Thus in 1974 I returned to Burkina Faso for a nineteen-month stay in the hope that I could investigate more closely the way RiimaayBe mothers took care of their small children and thus determine whether there was indeed no clear difference in mothering practices between the two groups during the early childhood years. If that turned out to be the case, I also hoped that my research in a culture so radically different from my own would not only lead me to new insights on personality formation there, but also would help me to rethink the whole question of what the personality is.

This book is the fruit of that investigation, and of much reflection since then. I have discussed elsewhere (Riesman 1983) the problems I see with many Western theories of personality formation and the studies that derive from them. Here I aim to accomplish two things. First, I will present as fully as possible what I have learned about early childhood among the FulBe and the RiimaayBe, as well as the people's own ethnopsychology of the formation of character. I will discuss the circumstances of life for the Fulani, in terms of perceived differences between members of the two groups, their economies, and the life plans of both men and women. I will then present a detailed analysis of the treatment of infants and small children, showing that FulBe and RiimaayBe child-rearing practices are essentially the same. After discussing Fulani ideas about personality, I will consider certain social processes that contribute to the development of a particular sense of self. We shall see that "finding a good mother" has less to do with choosing appropriate parenting behaviors than with linking the child to a particular type of social connectedness and set of relationships. A focus on the connections between different dimensions of the FulBe life experience will help to show how the FulBe's distinctive sense of who they are grows out of the totality of their experience rather than from a single formative aspect of it.

Second, I will use these materials as a basis for reexamining the question of what personality is and for shaping a clearer vision of the relationships between self, social structure, economy, and ideology. Through a systematic comparison of the circumstances of life, the child-rearing practices, and the personalities of the FulBe and the RiimaayBe in the Jelgobe region of Burkina Faso, I hope to develop an alternative theory of the way personality is formed, a sociocultural theory that takes seriously the point that being a person and understanding what a person is are the same sort of process; that being a person is essentially a process of making meaning. This theory treats as crucial the *sense* of connectedness that individuals come to have to others, especially relatives. This consideration of a different kind of connectedness than that which we usually perceive will also enable us to begin to understand why we in the West share the conviction that there is a causal connection between parental practices of child rearing and the formation of personality in our children. It may also enable us to think about what consequences this belief has for our own personalities. This book is about an African people but, like all anthropology, it is also about ourselves and has of necessity been shaped by the questions we are asking.

The Fulani in West Africa

Before we proceed with our investigation of personality, let me say a few words about who the Fulani are.[2] To begin with, they are the only cattle-raising people in West Africa.[3] Unlike the cattle-raisers of East or Southern Africa, the Fulani are scattered over a vast area, living not only in every West African state, but also in Cameroon, the Central African Republic, Chad, and the Sudan. Today, less than half of the Fulani still raise cattle, but there are millions who do, concentrated in the poorest countries of the region: Burkina Faso, Mali, Niger, and Senegal.

Some Fulani cattle-herders are still fully nomadic. Most are semi-sedentary and also depend on millet agriculture. Once Fulani have given up cattle-raising for other occupations they rarely go back to it again, yet both Africans and Europeans often continue to associate them with a romantic image of nomadism, cattle, and the freedom of the bush. Many Africans think of the Fulani as a hardy nomadic people who prefer to live their social lives in remote regions without the encumbrances of material objects. European notions of persistent Fulani nomadism are underscored by photo essays such as Carol Beckwith's *Nomads of Niger* (1983).

Presently numbering some nine or ten million people, the Fulani are one of West Africa's largest groups, on the same order of magnitude as the Hausa, Igbo, and Yoruba of Nigeria. They are not a majority in any West African state, but form large minorities in all of the Sahelian states, minorities that have historically played important roles in the region's sociopolitical development. By far the largest single group (4.8 million in 1972) reside in northern Nigeria. Most of them are sedentary and no longer speak their own language Fulfulde (called Fula by linguists) but instead speak Hausa, the language of a people they revolted against in the first decade of the nineteenth century. The word "Fulani" itself is a Hausa term.

Most of the rest of the Fulani—including the Jelgoji Fulani of Burkina Faso, with whom this book is concerned—live in countries that were former colonies of France. In those countries the most common name for the Fulani is *Peul*, the word used by the Wolof (the dominant population of Senegal) and by French-speaking writers. The Manding word *Fula* is used to refer to Fulani in parts of Guinea, Sierra Leone, Gambia, and Senegal. And in the inland delta region of the Senegal river, Mauritania and Senegal, there is a large population of sedentary Fulani called *Toucouleur*. The Toucouleur speak the same language as the other Fulani but call the language Pular rather than Fulfulde, and they call themselves *HallpularEn* (Pular-speakers).

Fulfulde is mutually comprehensible by speakers from nearly all areas, suggesting that the Fulani's geographic expansion was both fairly recent and fairly rapid. Modern linguistic and historical research connects the origin of the Fulani with the banks of the Senegal River some time during the first millennium of our era. Assuming the Fulani herded cattle then as they do now, small family groups probably broke off periodically to look for new pastures or to escape unpleasant political situations. They evidently moved eastward and lived among whatever agricultural populations would accept them in the Sahelian zone. As they became numerous in an area, they sometimes became threatening to the local people and were driven out. In other cases they took over the land themselves. One of the first such takeovers was in their apparent region of origin, the Futa Toro, in what is today central and eastern Senegal. Very little is known about the history of that region, but it is clear that Fulani dynastic rulers have dominated the area since the late fifteenth century.

In West Africa and the Sahel, many Africans place Fulani in the same category as Arabs and Tuaregs—"red-skinned" people—nomadic warriors who have used Islam as a vehicle of conquest and rule. In the mid-eighteenth century, Fulani became the rulers of large stretches of Sahelian territory. Organized as a holy war (jihad), the first successful uprising took place in the Fouta Djallon region of Guinea. A second Fulani uprising, the only one not in the form of a jihad, took place in Burkina Faso. Then in the early nineteenth century there was a series of religiously inspired Fulani revolts, sparked by Usman dan Fodio in northern Nigeria, and followed by Fulani in Liptako (in the Dori region of Burkina Faso), Cameroon (in the Adamawa region), Macina in Mali (the inland delta of the Niger River) and Torodi in Niger. The most politically powerful states formed by these movements were those of Usman dan Fodio in Sokoto, Nigeria, and Sheku Hamadu in Macina, Mali.

Prior to the formation of these Fulani states, Islam had been largely limited to West African cities. After the Fulani established themselves in power, Islam became a central thread in the fabric of West African social life, and rulers dispatched *marabouts* (religious adepts) to convert the nonbelievers living in remote areas. A combination of military power and religious zeal spread Fulani influence throughout West Africa in the nineteenth century. Even as far away as the Cameroon grassfield states such as Bamun, the rulers adopted Fulani dress and customs. The Fulani states of West Africa continued to function until the colonial conquests of the late nineteenth and early twentieth centuries. The size and dynamism of Fulani populations have long made them central actors in West African history, politics, and culture.

2

GLOBAL FULANI SOCIETY

In the Djibo region of Burkina Faso, on the southern edge of the African Sahel, Fulani society is divided into three classes of people: Fulani, artisans, and people of captive or serf ancestry. In Fulfulde, the Fulani are called *FulBe* (sing. *Pullo*); hence for greater clarity and ease of expression from now on I will use this term when I wish to specify that part of Fulani society. I will use the term Fulani as a noun or adjective only to refer to the larger society that includes the FulBe and the others as well. In the local dialect of Fulfulde there is no commonly used generic term for artisans. They, like the FulBe, are free (*rimBe*, sing. *dimo*, which also means "noble"), but they form a kind of endogamous caste since they do not marry people of other social categories. In the Djibo region they amount to a few percent at most of the total population, and consist of three principal craft groups: the *wayluBe* (sing. *baylo*) where the men are blacksmiths and the women potters, the *maabuuBe* (sing. *maabo*) where both men and women are bards, genealogists, and storytellers, and the *lawBe* (sing. *labbo*) where the men are woodworkers. The terms used to designate people of captive or serf ancestry are *maccuBe* (sing. *maccuDo*) and *riimaayBe* (sing. *diimaajo*). The nuance of meaning between these words is that the first means "captive," hence people captured in wars or raids and perhaps bought in a market, while the second refers to the original inhabitants of an area who continue to live and work there after having been conquered by FulBe invaders. The two categories of people are not distinguishable in any evident way, and today, in any case, both are free by law. Most of the time I shall use the term RiimaayBe to refer to both groups.

In the 1960s and 1970s, there were no special economic or political obligations between RiimaayBe and FulBe. FulBe traditional chiefs ruled the area, but this did not give them any particular power over RiimaayBe. The symbolic value of being Pullo or Diimaajo was often brought out in songs, stories, and in certain rituals such as marriage or naming a baby, but on a daily basis most FulBe and RiimaayBe lived apart from each other and did each other occasional services on a basis of reciprocity or payment.

Though the FulBe no longer have any rights over the RiimaayBe they used to own, the memory of the old relationship is still very much alive in both groups. Individuals vary considerably in how they feel about the past, but it is fair to say in general that FulBe regret the coming of the French, their loss of sovereignty, and the "theft" of their RiimaayBe labor force, while the RiimaayBe are glad of it. Old RiimaayBe experienced or heard about much hardship and cruelty at the hands of the FulBe. When the French came the FulBe then passed on to them any corvées that the colonists demanded of them, but even that was better than the situation that had existed before the colonial period. There are a few RiimaayBe who are servants and right-hand men of village or regional chiefs; these people are proud of their position and of their connection with important families. A larger number, possibly the majority, don't like the FulBe much, make fun of them behind their backs, and yet are not ashamed of being descendants of captives. They see that time when their fate was decided as a terrible epoch, when the law of the jungle prevailed, when the strong ate the weak and the ruthless ate those with scruples; what was done then cannot be undone now. The subservience of their ancestors and their own inferior social status are simple facts of existence. By a kind of Lamarckian evolution, they inherit their servitude just as the FulBe inherit their nobility or the blacksmiths inherit their special connection to their craft.

But these "simple facts" are actually far from simple, because the self-evidence on which they rest is a structure of ideas that people maintain in numerous ways in everyday life. For example, the differences between FulBe and RiimaayBe are supposed to be obvious. When I was still a newcomer to the area, people would ask me, "Can you tell FulBe and RiimaayBe apart? (*ADa waawi sendude Pullo e MaccuDo na?*)" Sometimes the question would be put to me upon my arrival at a gathering of people whom I didn't know, and I would be asked to point out the FulBe and the Mac-cuBe, or to say which was which between two men seated next to each other. At the time, I thought of this as a test of my knowledge, since people knew I was studying the language and life of the people. But on reflection I see that it was also a test of themselves, a test which was meant to confirm that even to a fairly ignorant foreigner the FulBe and the MaccuBe were easy to differentiate as types.

The main differences I was supposed to notice were visual. The ideal is that FulBe are tall, slim, and light-skinned; they have thin, straight noses and their hair tends to be long and curly. In contrast, the RiimaayBe are stocky, tending toward corpulence, dark-skinned, with flat, "squashed" noses, and short, kinky hair. The everyday clothing worn by FulBe is usually easily distinguished from that of the RiimaayBe. Jelgoji FulBe youths wear a distinctive tunic made from homespun cloth that they sew and dye themselves, while RiimaayBe of the same age generally wear machine-woven cotton sewn either by tailors in markets or by themselves. Women of both groups wear brightly colored cotton wraparound skirts, with or without halters, but the FulBe wear colors of more limited range and pattern, and they often wear bright red bandannas on their heads. RiimaayBe women tend to wear darker patterns for everyday clothing, and when they want to dress up they use a wider range of colors and styles than the FulBe do.

Another set of differences between the two groups appears in speech. I was constantly asking people the meanings of new words and writing them down. Whenever there were FulBe and Riimaay-Be synonyms or variants for the word in question, people would gleefully point these out to me. FulBe and RiimaayBe would both quiz me from time to time on my ability to distinguish their different ways of saying things. There are only a few such variations in vocabulary, and by and large they concern words that are rarely used. Thus it is especially significant that people would so frequently point them out and make sure that I learned them. My interpretation of this behavior is that maintaining and calling attention to all these distinctions is a part of the overall process by which the FulBe and RiimaayBe make it appear to themselves that the qualities that differentiate them are self-evident and somehow indelible aspects of their being.

Now, we Westerners are tempted to ask just how self-evident these qualities are. In particular, are the members of the two groups that readily distinguishable through their physical features alone? While I was in the field I was troubled by what seemed to me to be Fulani racism. Therefore I was on the lookout for "objective" data that would confound people's prejudices. It was my impression that the physical stereotypes fit the reality clearly in only a minority of cases, that many people were hard to identify as Pullo or Diimaajo by their physical characteristics, and that a certain number were quite contrary to the ideal physical types of their groups. I would even argue with people, pointing out to RiimaayBe, for instance, that some of them were actually lighter than some FulBe were. While they could see what I meant, at the same time they would continue to assert that the FulBe were really lighter than they were. What does this mean? On rethinking this paradox now, I think I must have been assuming, in line with my antiracist views, that for a racist people's biological qualities somehow determine their human and spiritual ones as well, whereas "we all know" that skin color or hair type vary independently of such qualities. But I was mistaken to attribute to Fulani the modern idea of biological determinism. We shall attempt later to analyze how the Fulani conceive of the person and of individual personality development. Suffice it to say for now that the discrepancies that seemed striking to me between the stereotypes and the actual people were overlooked or considered irrelevant by anybody I questioned about them.

Another way in which FulBe and RiimaayBe are supposed to differ is their behavior. Characteristic ways of acting for members of each group are described or alluded to in many stories, epic recitations, sayings, and proverbs. The most important qualities, in their own eyes, can be summed up by saying that FulBe have a strong sense of shame that guides them at nearly all times, and manifest a high degree of self-control and self-restraint. The RiimaayBe, in contrast, have little sense of shame, and are loud, brash, and uncontrolled in their way of interacting with others. In short, the FulBe are thought of as displaying dignity, nobility, and refinement in their bearing, while the RiimaayBe are humble, crude, and direct.

As I met more and more people in each group during my field trips I found that FulBe and RiimaayBe on the whole appeared to be of personality types that embodied the characteristics attributed to them in folklore. I had many opportunities to see people not only in their relations with me, but also as they interacted with members of their own and the other group. FulBe men and women generally talked and acted in a restrained and sensitive manner, while RiimaayBe tended to be loud, boisterous, pushy, and aggressive. For example, a group of RiimaayBe women pounding millet together was always cheerfully bantering and laughing, while the equivalent FulBe group would be much quieter. Among men, one could note the same kinds of differences in situations of greeting, casual conversation, or meetings where political, legal, or other issues were being debated. In my own conversations with men, FulBe tended to be soft-spoken, timid, or evasive until they got to know me, guarded in the expression of their feelings, and yet very alert to whatever emotions I might be revealing. RiimaayBe would talk in much louder voices and express their feelings much more readily than the FulBe. RiimaayBe men who didn't know me had just as much reason to be apprehensive as did FulBe, yet their manner was either hearty and direct or, occasionally, of an exaggerated servility, a kind of humility with a vengeance.

Now, if it will be granted that my observations are accurate and fairly reported, do they amount to sufficient evidence to generalize about the kinds of personality typical of the FulBe and the Riimaay-Be? There are several issues here. One is: Is what I saw really typical, and to what proportion of the people does it really apply? Another is: Am I possibly reading my own meanings into these behaviors, so that for the people themselves the gestures I noted have rather different meanings from the ones that seemed evident to me? A third is: How do I know that in describing these ways of behaving I am really talking about people's personality?

We will examine the third question in detail in chapter 8. Some would argue that before you can even talk about personality you have to define what it is. However, since the goal of this book is to rethink the very nature of personality, anything but a very vague definition of it would hamper that reflection at this point. What I hope to do is get along with our commonsense ideas until we reach the point where they obviously no longer serve us. By that time we shall have the materials in hand to draw on for thinking through the nature of personality.

Let us now examine to what degree my description represents the way people typically behave, and whether the emotional tone and meaning of the behaviors as I perceived them are in fact those felt by the Fulani. The question of typicality is a difficult one to answer in a fully satisfying way. My only "technique" for gathering data on people's personalities was my own observation of or interaction with groups and individuals. I attempted during my first field trip to administer some psychological tests designed to reveal configurations of personality in members of Western society, but this experiment gave me no usable data on the Fulani. The most important thing I learned from it was, in fact, that the information I wanted could only come from the interaction of my subjects with other people, including myself, since what really interested me was how the personality of people was expressed in everyday situations. The attempt to give projective tests also made even more starkly clear a problem that plagues such tests in our own society, namely the difficulty of knowing what the relationship is between the responses people give to the test and their behavior in other situations. So, when I say that acting in a hearty manner, for instance, is typical of RiimaayBe (but not of FulBe) I am conveying the sum of my impressions of many incidents of behavior. I have not put these observations in quantitative form, and I think that to attempt it would be misleading at best, since my observations were not systematic in the first place. I feel justified in asserting that RiimaayBe act hearty and outgoing where FulBe act reserved and even retiring on the basis of my long acquaintance with a limited number of people of each group rather than on the basis of an extensive survey.

Now, it is precisely because I knew people under a wide variety of circumstances in their lives that it is necessary to qualify my description of their personality. As is to be expected, there are individuals in each group who do not well exemplify the group's patterns. This is most obvious among the FulBe, since acting "out of character" would, in their value system, be seen as a kind of failure. Indeed, certain individuals who got on my nerves by acting truculent and insensitive were people who were disliked by many of those I lived with for the same reasons. On the other hand, the RiimaayBe I knew who acted out of character by being quiet, dignified, and subtle were either beautiful women or young men. The women, through their beauty, could aspire to be noticed by and associate with the most popular men of all castes; the young men were those who either were moving out of the local stratification system by greater involvement in trade or manufacture, or were pursuing religious studies and thus seeking to rise within the local system. Interestingly enough, in this connection, some of the younger FulBe who struck me as acting out of character were men who also may well have been sliding out of the traditional system into commerce.

These cases could be thought of as exceptions that prove the rule. There is another category of exceptions that we must examine, however, namely those circumstances when it is normal for people to deviate from the patterns I have described as typical for their group. Perhaps the most striking example of this deviation is the behavior of adolescent boys in groups. FulBe and RiimaayBe boys generally dress differently from each other, and they have certain different musical styles that they do not share (though there are others that are held in common), but in the area of decorum they are both about equally lacking and at times take delight in flouting the usual standards of behavior. They sing, dance, shout, whoop, horse around, and taunt one another with insults, all in a very uninhibited way. It is significant too, however, that FulBe boys would not do these things in the presence of their parents or others of that generation, while RiimaayBe youth do not have the sense that they are offending their elders by such cutting loose in their presence. The FulBe feeling is succinctly expressed in the common saying "*waannde goro goggo.*" *Goro goggo* means the husband of your paternal aunt, a person to whom you must be most respectful. The noun *waannde* derives from a verb meaning "to stymie, to cause total failure." Thus *waannde goro goggo* is what happens when your uncle shows up at a time when you are acting uninhibitedly—you get extremely embarrassed and freeze up. Among the FulBe, young people's gatherings for music and dancing normally take place outside the village and at a considerable distance from any houses, while RiimaayBe hold their celebrations in an open space in or right beside the village.

What are we to make of this normal, expectable behavior that is at such variance with the personality that FulBe exhibit in most other situations? This is not a case of occasional deviance, but a regular pattern. Should we revise our general description of FulBe personality and say that in fact it is not simply one pattern, but two? While this position might appear tenable from a strictly objective point of view, the fact remains that the lively, expressive behavior of young men in certain situations is thought of by people as simply the way young people are, full of beans and uncouth. The more sedate, refined pattern of behavior, on the other hand, is what everyone feels truly marks one as being Pullo. We must be very careful, however, not to take this to mean that in Fulani thinking one or the other behavior pattern is the "true" self, is more basic than the other. Thus we must examine what the Fulani understandings are of these different ways of behaving.

What about the meanings of FulBe and RiimaayBe personality characteristics? Using the most apt and vivid English words I could find, I have sought so far to portray how the typical personalities of FulBe and RiimaayBe adults struck me. It is the very perceptible difference between the two that is the starting point for my further investigations and reflections. We have seen that my perception of difference seems to be corroborated by the Fulani themselves, who frequently allude to specific characteristics of each group in conversation, song, and story.

For me, the striking dimensions along which their personalities differ were, as we have seen, coarseness versus refinement or heartiness versus self-restraint. Do the Fulani describe people's personal characteristics along these dimensions? What are the main ideas they use when describing typical FulBe or RiimaayBe behavior? FulBe, MaccuBe, and members of other castes, such as MaabuuBe, JaawaamBe, and WayluBe, often figure as characters in stories and proverbs. Sometimes their stereotyped qualities are taken for granted in the story, and the people are not described other than by their labels; in other instances, however, the teller discusses at some length a character's qualities, often in comparison with those of other figures. When giving a one- or two-word comment about a character, the most usual point of difference between FulBe and MaccuBe is intelligence: the FulBe are smart and the MaccuBe are dumb. One proverb sums it up this way, suggesting that MaccuBe have no powers of foresight: *"YeeNa meema jippoo faDDa—MaccuDo"*—literally, "Climb, touch, descend, throw—MaccuDo." This means, "Climb a tree, touch the fruit, climb back down, throw something at it—that's a MaccuDo for you," or, "How dumb can you get?" Another quality often hinted at in proverbs is the MaccuDo's lack of independence. Here are two examples. "*Si bumDo wi'i dawan fuu Dowoowo muuDum narri* (If the blind man says he'll be off at dawn, it's from his guide he's heard that)." "*Juungu nyiiwa wonaa kam hulYini Do dobii Don hulYini* (It's not the elephant's trunk that's frightening, it's what's attached to it that is)." These two proverbs could apply to any situation where one person controls another, and the traditional master–MaccuDo relationship is the main exemplar of that.

The longest direct comparison of FulBe and MaccuBe I know of in Fulani oral literature comes in Tinguidji's recitation of "Silamaka et Poullori," transcribed, translated, and published by Christiane Seydou (1972). The bard describes in detail how several incidents in the relationship between the Pullo Silaamaka and his MaccuDo Pulloori expressed the inequality between them, despite their affection and loyalty to each other. A major theme of the story is Silaamaka's nobility. Pulloori is not noble, but he approaches nobility through his loyalty not only to Silaamaka's person, but to the latter's ideal self. At the beginning of the story the bard describes how the men would eat together. Ever since childhood, Silaamaka would take three mouthfuls of food, Pulloori six; when they drank milk, Silaamaka would take three dipperfuls, Pulloori six; then ten cola nuts would be brought, of which Silaamaka would take three and Pulloori seven. This description implies both a lesser need of material sustenance and a greater ability to control his needs on the part of the Pullo. Later in the story, Silaamaka dies but his people want to hide the news from Pulloori. They dress up another Pullo in his clothes, but they forget to tell him Silaamaka's way of eating. When the two men eat together the Pullo goes on eating after Pulloori has finished! Pulloori is completely shocked and ashamed. He believes Silaamaka has gone mad and kills the Pullo after the following speech: "Since Silaamaka has gone mad I won't wait for anyone else to tie him up, I will kill him so he won't have to be tied. For I doubt that there are any hands in this world that could tie up Silaamaka while I am still alive" (Seydou 1972: 148–49). The false Silaamaka tries to escape by taking off his clothes and running, but Pulloori is too angry and grief-stricken to restrain himself. He stabs the impostor with his lance, then grabs him by the leg and drags him to the garbage pile outside the house, saying, "This is the place for a dog to die! This is the place for a pagan to die! No Pullo will take Silaamaka's place so long as I am alive!"

Though this epic was recorded in Niger, the story is known in the Jelgoji also, and many others with similar themes are a part of people's general sense of their past and of the meaning of life. It is clear from the episode just summarized that the Pullo must constantly demonstrate his superiority to the MaccuDo in order to justify the latter's subjugation and loyalty. This attitude was still very evident among the people I lived with, both FulBe and RiimaayBe. Members of both groups are afraid of shame, but the FulBe much more so than the RiimaayBe, and the consequences are more far-reaching and long-lasting for them. For example, one story I recorded about events that had taken place some fifty years earlier described one man as running from cattle raiders and hiding among the women washing their clothes at the well. His descendants continue to live in the shadow of that shame today. Among MaccuBe, such behavior would also be laughable, but unremarkable. I tried to get knowledgeable people to tell me about certain episodes of local history, but some of them wouldn't dare. One man told me that if members of the royal family of the area found out that he had told me the story they would kill him. Early in my second stay, before I realized that the subject was so explosive, a good storyteller was entertaining a group of people, including myself and one member of the royal family, with one tale after another. One of the stories he told dealt with the Mossi, who were also involved in the black pages of Djibo's history. So it was perfectly natural of me to ask about those episodes at that point, or so it seemed. The man, caught up in the pleasure of hearing himself talk, began to launch into the story. But almost immediately the prince interrupted him, saying he didn't know what he was talking about. He turned to me and said I shouldn't write down what the storyteller said because it was just empty words, not what really happened. I think he phrased his remark that way because he realized that I didn't know what I was asking about and would accept the argument that the information I was getting would be false. The storyteller became very upset and got up to leave. He said he didn't claim to have any knowledge of those episodes, but only about the other ones he had been recounting earlier.

At a more mundane level, many proverbs and stories, not to mention countless daily events, emphasize over and over the importance of maintaining the ideals of FulBe behavior. And the guiding thread of those ideals is self-control. Here are three proverbs that express this most forcefully. *"wo hakkillo haarata wonaa reedu* (It's the mind that reaches satiety, not the stomach)." Notice the connection established here between intelligence and self-control, and the implication that "dumber" people would consequently have less ability to control themselves. The second proverb is self-explanatory: *"pornde wootere hantataa fuudo kaa na semtina dimo* (One fart does no harm to the asshole but it still shames the gentleman)." The third proverb goes: *"tati njaasi e mawDo: min fewi, min riiDi, min wujji—Dee njaasi e mawDo* (Three things are indignities for a respectable person: I lied, I farted, I stole—these are all indignities for a respectable person)."

The common point between these three proverbs is worth exploring in a little more detail. To begin with, the term "lie" has a broader meaning in Fulfulde than in English. "To lie" in Fulfulde means to say anything that is incorrect, even if unintentionally. People were always annoying me by calling "lies" what I thought were "mere mistakes." Farting appears again and again in proverbs, sayings, and everyday comments as a particularly shameful thing for the Pullo. Unlike either lying or theft, which are consciously initiated acts, a fart just happens to one, often by surprise, and is for that reason a particularly severe test of a person's self-awareness and self-mastery. Finally, what makes theft shameful is not its undeniable threat to society, but the fact that the thief fails the test of mastery on two counts: first, he is poor, which implies that he has failed to manage his own life circumstances. Prior to the colonial period poverty in a noble also indicated cowardice, since a brave person would remedy his impoverishment by rustling cattle from enemies or by attacking them for cattle and slaves. Such actions are conceived of very differently from theft and are described by terms meaning "war" or "raid." Second, the thief fails to control his own appetite, for in most cases what is stolen is food, and in any case whenever a person uses a good for his own benefit Fulani say that he has "eaten" it.

This analysis of the meanings of lying, farting, and stealing suggests that in Fulani thought the boundary between self and other, self and world, is located not at the skin, or even within it as we usually think, but somewhere out in the world. Not only should the noble master his own needs, but such an achievement necessarily implies that he master to some degree the world around himself, such that his words correspond to the way things are and his resources suffice to fulfill his needs. Two brief examples offer further support for this interpretation. I once asked an old man if it was true, as others had told me, that he was going to prevent a certain marriage from taking place. He replied angrily that he had never said such a thing, and never would, because he didn't have the power to stop that marriage. If he said he was going to stop it and then failed to do so, that would be a shame for him (cf. Riesman 1977:241). The second example is that people call diarrhea an affliction that shames one. To be seen defecating is a great shame. FulBe normally go a considerable distance away from their huts into the bush to relieve themselves. They usually do this early in the morning, or combine their trip with one for some other purpose, such as getting tree leaves or water. To be seen constantly going to the bush, or worse, to be seen defecating nearby because you failed to get far enough before having to let go, is a shame. Hence people with diarrhea will usually spend the whole day out in the bush away from their huts to avoid this risk. I think it is significant that in a matter of shame what we would call extenuating circumstances make no difference to the FulBe. Any weakness that is exposed, regardless of the reason, is cause for shame; in fact it is the mark of a true Pullo to feel such shame deeply, while members of other groups would not.

Many stories and true incidents as well provide ample evidence of the extremes to which FulBe will go both to demonstrate their sensitivity to shame and to prove their superior powers of self-control. For example, there is the well-known case of the chief of Firigindi, a FulBe village near Djibo. This man had the custom of visiting Djibo nearly every day, but he would never eat food or drink water in that town. He would even stop before reaching Djibo to fill his little ablution pot so that he would not be obliged to use Djibo water for his prayers. To be seen eating is as great a shame for a Pullo as to be seen defecating. In addition, it is even a shame to be known to have eaten in certain places, because that act puts the person in a dependent relation to the source of food—ultimately the dominant family of the region—and implies in addition that he and his group lack the means to take care of their own needs.

One day in the French colonial period the local gendarmes arrested this man and jailed him while he was on his daily visit to Djibo. The reason for the arrest was not any wrongdoing on the man's part, but simply that the gendarmes wanted his testimony in some case. The point of the story as people told it, however, was that this Pullo refused to break his custom of never eating or drinking in Djibo. He died in the Djibo jail, and his self-starvation is cited with approval. Many FulBe whom I know personally would act the same way in a similar situation, or would at least make a gesture in that direction.

But FulBe also can laugh at themselves for these very same traits. The following story is a wonderful example of this capacity and presents in extreme form a situation which is a variant of everyday life for any Pullo. Unlike festive gatherings in the United States, where eating and drinking together are central to the fun of the event, in FulBe society the presence of people from many different families would make common eating a most shameful thing. Thus while young men and women sing, dance, and flirt, they never eat or drink together, and strive to avoid completely any gesture that would betray their need for nourishment. If visitors to a celebration have family or close friends in the village, they can occasionally sneak off to eat and drink at those people's huts, but otherwise they simply have to go without until they leave the place altogether.

Once there were two young men who were great friends. A wedding was taking place at a certain spot, and the two set out to go to the celebration. As they were going along they came upon an antelope that had died; it was carrion just lying there. One said to his friend, "Hey, let's see if we can't use this for something. Let's make a secret plan. Why don't we skin this carrion antelope, grill the meat till it's cooked through, eat what we can and then pack the rest. What we'll do is bring it with us to a place near the ceremony and store it up in a tree, since we can't eat in that village."

The other replied, "How can you say that! God preserve us from the sin of eating carrion! I'm still of sound mind, I have not farted in public or gotten in a fight with the king. Sure as can be I'll never eat carrion."

They left. But not before the first one skinned the antelope and grilled enough of the meat to last him for three days. He took the meat with him and when they got near the celebration he hid it high up in a tree. He and his companion then went on to the party together. They swelled up their chests and strutted about. The one swaggered about without eating; the other, if he got hungry, would sneak away and go eat his carrion to his heart's content, then come back to the party.

Came a time, then, when the first one was getting very worn out. He got so weakened that he could hardly do anything, couldn't even see well any more. The woman he loved lived in the host village, and he went to pay a call on her. He reached her hut and the woman invited him in. As he sat there he couldn't stop glancing out of the corner of his eye at the calabashes full of milk, the pots full of water. Soon came the hour when the cows were returning from grazing, so the woman got up to go and milk them. She would come back with the milk from each cow and pour it into a calabash sitting on the floor in front of her boyfriend. When she would go back out to milk the next cow he would just stare at the milk. Now it happened that he was sitting on a flimsy little bed of the kind FulBe use in bush camps. When the woman had gone out, the young man said to himself that he would just lean over that calabash and dip his lips in the milk. For if he were to tip the calabash to sip from it people could see the trace of the milk along the side. So now he would dip his lips in the milk the way he would drink water from a stream or pond. He would just drink enough to regain a little strength, and then stop. But just when he leaned over the calabash the little bed upended him. His head went splash right into the milk. His head went completely in. What could he do? He pretended to have gone crazy. He was bellowing, bellowing like a cow. "Moo! Moo!" People came running up. His beloved began to wail like a mourner. The man in the hut was going wild. "My God, he's spilled all your milk!" people cried. He was kicking pots, breaking them, wrecking everything in sight. People finally got hold of him and pinned him down, but he wouldn't stop bellowing, bulging out his eyes, crawling around.

At this point his friend reached the crowd and told everybody not to worry, that he knew how to handle this. He told people to get back. Everybody pulled back. He whispered to his friend, "Wouldn't eating carrion have been better than this?" The other replied, "Oh, much, much, much." The first one said, "Wouldn't eating carrion have been better than this?" The other said, "Oh, much, much, much." The first one was pretending to say a charm over his friend's head, saying, "Wouldn't eating carrion have been better than this?" The other kept saying, "Oh, much, much, much."

Finally he got up. His friend grabbed him and held him as he staggered along, until he could get him out of the village. They went home. That's the end.

What emerges from these stories and anecdotes, and the way people think about them, is that FulBe qualities are those of free or noble people. To have self-mastery implies that no one else has mastery over you (cf. Riesman 1977:140). FulBe are constantly called on to express their nobility by demonstrating that they control both their own bodies and their immediate circumstances. RiimaayBe, on the other hand, regard themselves as owned by others. In some cases they can be proud of this, as when their master is worthy like the legendary Silaamaka, or powerful like the current chief of Djibo. At other times they resent it, but even then few of them deny it. Let's look for a moment at what is so dumb about the so-called "typical" MaccuDo who would climb a tree, touch the fruit, come down again and then throw something at the fruit to bring it down. Obviously, the Pullo, the smart person, would climb up and just bring down the fruit. Better yet, he might trick someone else into doing it for him. But here's the rub. Why is the MaccuDo getting the fruit in the first place? Probably because somebody told him to. It's no skin off his back if it takes him twice as long to do it, or if the fruit is damaged in the process. In short, the MaccuDo's behavior in this little saying is the behavior of a person under orders, a person who is not thinking for himself, or who is at best working to rule.

I spent many hours talking with the RiimaayBe of Djibo trying to find out what their own conceptions of their status were. I was surprised by two things: first, to find that they and the FulBe both spoke of the meaning of being a MaccuDo in very much the same terms, and second, that they talked about these things very openly and matter-of-factly, as if the situation were strictly objective and were not a matter for embarrassment or shame. Here is the partial record of a conversation I had with a man of about fifty whom I talked with fairly often.

> I asked him what he would reply if someone asked him whether he was a maccuDo or a dimo (free person). Without hesitation he answered, "maccuDo, of course."
>
> "But why?" I asked. "Hasn't *maccungaaku* (slavery) been forbidden ever since the French?"
>
> "Oh, they say it has," said Iisa, "but it's not really over." He added that the European (*tuubaako*) has said that no one is to own people any more, but now it is he who owns us all. There cannot be two chiefs in the same place.
>
> I told Iisa that there were some MaccuBe who felt that to call a person MaccuDo was an insult (*yennoore*).
>
> "That's not true," said Iisa. "It is not a yennoore since that is what we are, MaccuBe. Maybe sometimes if one person calls another 'MaccuDo' he will answer, 'Did your father buy me?'"
>
> "What this means," Iisa explained, "is that you can still be a MaccuDo without being owned by anyone in particular. It is like stray cows," he went on. "If a cow goes astray and wanders into someone else's herd, everyone knows that the cow does not belong to the herdsman—but it does belong to somebody. Even if the cow has calves and those calves have calves, they do not belong to the herdsman; they belong to whoever is the cow's rightful owner."

It is striking that exactly the same comparison is used by FulBe to explain slavery, inheritance of slaves, and the relation between master and slave. The opinion that there cannot be two chiefs in one place is widely held, and is expressed in many proverbs. One of these goes "*ngonndi tolata de ngonndi luwo* (One [bull] has to lose its horns before the next one will grow them)."

Most mature RiimaayBe share the views, but not necessarily the vehemence, of one old lady I talked to from time to time, and who always expressed her opinions most forcefully. One day she was railing against a certain local administrator. This man was acting badly, and the obvious reasons were, first, that he was a bastard—his mother had given birth to him even before she married her husband—and second, that his mother was a *kongitirikoN*, a slave of a slave. This word, *kongitirikoN*, is rarely spoken because it is a grave insult. I only heard it a few times, often in whispers, while in Djibo. Thus this man was bound to be no good. He was *tuundi reedu* ("filth of the womb," another expression for bastard), and nothing could be expected of him. Not only that, the old lady who was angry about what he was doing felt that the son of a kongitirikoN was in any case incapable of exercising power well because nobody would respect him, nobody would take orders from him.

All the people I talked with, whatever their station, were absolutely convinced of the necessity of hierarchy in social life. Riimaay-Be didn't like being ruled by the FulBe, but it was less bad than being a kongitirikoN. It was the way things were, and it was possible to live a respectable life within that social framework. But people found it disturbing when people tried to act otherwise than their traditions ordained. The Pullo who eats too much or the MaccuDo who starts acting as if he were a prince is severely criticized and may even suffer sanctions. The proper way for all to act is to follow their *tawaangal*, their tradition. People commend each other by saying, "*a waDi ko tawDaa* (You did what you found)." For the MaccuDo, this means accepting as a given the fact that he is owned. The traits of character that MaccuBe are supposed to display do, in fact, convey the idea that they are not really their own masters.

3

ECONOMY

Life in the Jelgoji is and always has been hard. There is a single rainy season that permits crops, trees, and grasses to grow and sustain animals and people, but the amount and location of rainfall in the area is totally unpredictable; even in years when the overall rainfall is adequate, many micro-regions can fail to get enough, and people can lose most or all of their crop. Droughts are fairly frequent. In recent decades there have been several so severe that many cattle died, some people starved, and many people had to emigrate temporarily or permanently just to survive.

Not only is starvation a danger many years, but people experience hunger every year. Hunger is taken on voluntarily during Ramadan, the Muslim month of fasting, and there are often times when for one reason or another people fail to eat for a day or two. Endemic diseases cause enormous suffering through pain, incapacitation, and death. The parasitic afflictions malaria and schistosomiasis are among the worst in this regard. Though smallpox has been eradicated, measles, whooping cough, and scarlet fever sometimes wipe out all the young children of a family, or many of those in a single community. Cerebrospinal meningitis can be arrested if the victim can be given the right treatment in time, but this is often impossible in the bush, far from the nearest clinic. We don't usually think of childbirth as a disease, but it is probably the leading cause of death for women of childbearing age in this area. Because people greatly desire to have children, pregnancy is also an occasion for satisfaction and hope, but an undercurrent of anxiety and fear is inescapable.

How FulBe Survive

The FulBe economy is based on the combination of millet farming with cattle herding. For all people in the Djibo region, millet is the staple food. As the FulBe are the dominant ethnic group in the area, and as they no longer control any slaves, there are not enough non-FulBe farmers to grow sufficient millet for the whole population. Thus in addition to taking care of the cattle they own, nearly all FulBe have to cultivate and harvest a millet crop large enough to feed their families.

The consequences of these two tasks for a FulBe family vary according to circumstances. FulBe women do not do agricultural work and do not own land. While land is plentiful in the sense that there are many unoccupied areas that anyone may move into and make a field in, previously farmed land is individually owned and passed down in the male line. As sons divide family land the plots get smaller, and within about two generations of cultivating in one area some men of any family will have to seek land elsewhere. Now, in an area dedicated to farming rather than cattle raising, it wouldn't be necessary for sons seeking new land to move farther away than the next arable location. The FulBe, however, need to maintain pasture and water sources for their cattle in addition to millet fields. This means that when a family gets too large to live off a single field, the person who has to leave must establish his new field at a considerable distance from that of his parents or brothers. It is very common for several families cultivating adjacent fields to need to send off younger brothers at about the same time. When this happens the emigrating families will often go together and cooperate in clearing the bush for their new fields.

But a common difficulty with this solution is that an area which is suitable for a field in the rainy season may be without water in the dry season, especially water enough for a herd of cattle. Many FulBe, in fact, spend the year in at least two different places, sometimes quite distant from each other, because their millet fields and rainy season pasture areas are far from their dry season water holes and grazing grounds. The growing season begins with the first successful planting, which is frequently not the first attempt to plant. The millet may start to grow as early as May or as late as July, and will be harvested in September, October, or November, after two weedings. FulBe store their harvest in granaries of mud bricks set on rocks to keep termites from getting to them, or on platforms on stilts, protected from birds, animals, and the weather by a hemispherical thatch shelter just like their houses.

It would be almost impossible for a family with only one working man successfully to exploit these resources. The unit that normally works together in FulBe society is not sharply delimited either by kinship or function. Families who live together and help each other in agricultural tasks may pasture their cattle separately and water them at different wells. Other pairs of families who cultivate fields far apart may still pasture their cattle as one herd and send young men of either family or both to take the cattle on the annual transhumance for salt and other minerals. Over time, as young men grow up in the family, friendships and enmities will develop, arrangements will gradually or abruptly shift, and new working partnerships will form, though almost invariably in the framework of identifiable kinship relations. To my knowledge there was no man who lived for any length of time alone with one or more wives and no other able-bodied men to help him. As we shall see, this degree of independence and isolation might be a Western goal, but would be seen as failure rather than success by the Fulani.

In the rainy season the double task of caring for crops and cattle requires not only division of labor, but sometimes the actual splitting up of the family. If the field has no fence around it—and at times even if it does—someone must take the cattle away from the growing crop every day to pasture, for cattle are very tempted by millet at nearly every stage of its growth. When people have made their fields out in the bush this may mean that they have to guard their stock most of the time so as to protect them from wild animals or even rustlers and to prevent them from damaging people's millet fields and from straying or returning to places where they had lived previously. When people are living in an older village it is often sufficient simply to drive the cattle out into the bush in the morning; they will wander there by themselves during the day and find their way back home in the late afternoon.

FulBe agree that for the health of their cattle, and to ensure that they reproduce as often as possible, it is best to take them at least once a year to salt earth areas where they lick or eat the earth and thus obtain important nutrients lacking at home. Such a transhumance takes a minimum of fifteen days: five days to get to the salt earth area, five days there, and five days to come back. The herdsmen who take the animals on such a trip live exclusively on their milk during the whole time. Handling cattle on transhumance is very demanding and tiring work, but one of its attractions is precisely that each herdsman gains total independence of other people. If a herdsman wants to stay away longer than the minimum time there is no material obstacle to prevent him. Some men wander out in the bush with their cattle for a month or even a whole rainy season at a time. Though women almost never go on the transhumance to the salt earth areas, they sometimes join their husbands for prolonged stays at distant bush camps.

Fulani say that millet grows best with two weedings, one after the shoot is a few inches out of the ground, and the other when the plant has grown a foot or so. From then on it seems that, with good weather, the millet can sufficiently dominate any competitive weeds. In this region people use no animal traction in plowing at all, but do the entire job by hand, with a long-handled hoe made by local blacksmiths. It is quite possible for one person to weed a whole field whose harvest in a normal year would feed a family of six for the year, but to do that would require pretty steady work throughout the rainy season, with almost no time for care of cattle, visiting, ceremonial activities, or getting sick (malaria is widespread and crippling at this time of year). In reality, such a work arrangement is rare. It will most likely arise not when a younger brother goes out to the bush to clear a new field, but rather when a person is working closely with just one other man—such as a brother, cousin, father, or son—and when the two men agree to divide up their tasks such that one does most of the weeding while the other does most of the cattle-herding and other miscellaneous tasks. Often the most important of these tasks will be to keep the household supplied with millet, in the event that last year's grain stores are at some distance from the field being cultivated this year.

FulBe and RiimaayBe both try to make the work go faster and

less painfully by working in groups. Sometimes a man will just notify his nearby brothers, cousins, and nephews, so that for a day a group of about six men will work very hard and get a large chunk of the field done. The person calling the work party does not pay the workers, but gives them a good meal and perhaps some cola nuts. In addition, the person is expected to go to any work parties called by people who came to his (if he doesn't, people will stop coming to his when he calls them in the future). Occasionally a person will call a really big work party (one or two dozen people or more). Such a gathering might enable him to finish his weeding in one day, but it will cost him a couple of goats, sheep, or a bull, which will be killed and fed to the people who come. Work parties of great size (a hundred or more people) are organized now and then by religious leaders. In this case, the leaders themselves do not feed the workers, but the mothers, wives, and sisters of the men bring food to the gathering, and the religious leaders give shouts of encouragement and bless all those who help in any way, saying they will reap the benefits in heaven.

It should be easy to see by now why one man alone could not do all the pastoral and horticultural tasks that are required to maintain a household in the FulBe economy. Men who work together do not necessarily specialize all the time, but may just as well take turns in a given season doing all the operations in alternation with the other partner or partners. Which tasks do the FulBe find the most difficult or thankless? To my surprise, I did not find a consensus on this question. Though many FulBe, particularly young men, claimed to disdain working the soil, they nonetheless were willing to spend more time farming than herding their cattle on transhumance or other distant trips. At the time of my fieldwork among the Fulani it seemed to me that a change in values was occurring as a result of the loss of sovereignty and of the opportunity for gaining (or losing) livestock by means of raids and warfare. The consequence of the new political situation (new for a generation) has been that people find little connection between the effort invested in care of cattle and the benefits to be gained, while there is a more obvious connection in the case of agricultural work. I will discuss at greater length below the nature of the benefits conferred by cattle, for they are chiefly other than economic. If we take a materialist perspective, however, we can see that keeping cattle is an effective way of maximizing the very spotty fertility of the land that results from unpredictable rainfall. Also, the FulBe's relatively high intake (compared with the RiimaayBe and other neighboring peoples) of protein, animal fat, and calcium through milk could confer on them better general health. The people themselves do not think in these materialist terms.

FulBe survival depends of course just as much on the work of women as on that of men. All the Fulani give priority to the women's task of taking care of small children. Little girls begin to help their mothers, older sisters, or other relatives with child care when they are as young as five years old, and by the age of seven or eight they may have considerable responsibility for a baby for long stretches of time. Women have complete charge of all children until they are five or six years old, at which point the father may or may not begin to intervene to direct certain aspects of the children's work or education, particularly but not only for his sons. Women are also in complete charge of feeding everyone in the household. In some families the man may dole out or specify how much grain is to be used per day, but most of the time it is the women who make those decisions, considering such factors as how many people are expected to be eating or how much grain is left in the stores. When guests arrive, however, unless the visitor is primarily a friend of the woman, it is the head of the household who will decide whether to slaughter a goat or some other animal in their honor. The women also have complete control of the milk of the cows entrusted to them. Except during transhumance, when there are no women in the migrating group, it is women who do all the milking. A married woman, or her daughter, milks any cows belonging to her and also those which have been entrusted to her by her husband or other people for milking. In principle, she can do whatever she wants with the milk; in practice she balances the gift of the milk to the family for food with its use for her own purposes, such as for making butter for sale, for gifts to friends and relatives, and for rubbing on her head and body. It is partly because butter is a good source of income for women that many of them like to go with the men to the remote bush camps in the rainy season; the cattle are numerous and well-nourished, so they give lots of milk from which the women can churn butter. A season in such a camp will enable a woman to put aside one or more large earthenware pots of it, in other words over five gallons.

Women have one other essential task for the survival of the

household, which is the building of houses and beds, and often the packing, transporting, and unpacking of household goods from one camp to another. Essentially, FulBe women are in charge of anything to do with straw and woven grass, for in those instances where the family lives in a mud brick house—certain prestigious Koranic scholars, or many people living in cities or towns—it is the men who are the architects and builders. FulBe, however, do not normally build such houses, and if they live in them they have them built by hired workers. In addition to house building, many women are expert in other arts using straw. They weave plain and colored straw for prayer and sleeping mats, bed-canopies, hut coverings, and hut doorways. They also coil finer grasses to make flat, circular covers for calabashes and bowls or large, circular winnowing fans. These objects (called *beDi*, sing. *mbeDu*) are also important as ceremonial gifts at naming ceremonies for FulBe babies. All the produce of these crafts is under the maker's control: many of the objects are used in the woman's house and in her daily work; others she can give as presents or sell, as she wishes. They are often strikingly beautiful, with their vegetable-dyed grasses and intricate designs of contrasting or swirling colors.

We shall examine further on in more detail the work of child care; here I would like to describe somewhat more fully what goes into preparing food. In fact, the preparation of food seems to be a never-ending task and goes on regardless of what other things a woman is doing, including caring for children. In addition to measuring out the grain, women draw the water and gather firewood for cooking. Both these items may at some times of the year be quite far from the camp. In Petaga it was sometimes necessary to walk a kilometer each way to get water, and in other villages I visited the distances were sometimes three or more kilometers. The basic preparation of millet foods is exactly the same for the FulBe and the RiimaayBe. The only difference is that in general the RiimaayBe make more elaborate sauces. In fact, FulBe women buy some ingredients that they do not make themselves from RiimaayBe women.

The preparation of a meal of *nyiiri* and *hoy* (cooked food and sauce) probably takes a minimum of four hours. Co-wives of the same husband rotate their cooking on a strict daily basis, so that the one with whom the husband will spend the night is the one who cooks the evening meal, and then the breakfast and midday meals the next day if there are any. Co-wives continue to pass responsibility for meals back and forth even in the absence of the husband. The person whose turn it is to cook may get help from her co-wife, from her children, or friends or relatives. Generally both FulBe and RiimaayBe women prefer to prepare food in company; FulBe often take their mortar and pestle to a neighbor's front doorway and pound their millet into flour along with others doing the same thing. The task is very difficult and tiring. It gives the women enormous calluses on their hands. Of course their small children go with them no matter where they go, and if the child is fussy the mother has to keep stopping her work to respond to the child. Notice how easy it was just now to speak of cooking as work and child care as something else. This Western way of regarding child care in relation to other activities is an ever present obstacle to our understanding how the Fulani live their lives. We shall try to surmount it as we proceed. FulBe women rarely prepare two hot meals a day, but the preparation of certain cold dishes is quite time-consuming too. It requires just as much pounding of millet, but simply does not need to be cooked.

In sum, we can see that FulBe women, like FulBe men, require assistance from time to time in carrying out their tasks. Just as a man could not all by himself both cultivate a field and manage a herd of cattle, so a woman would find it nearly impossible to do all her subsistence tasks and care for small children at the same time without people to hold and play with the baby at times, for example, while she races to reach the cows before the calves can get to them and suck them dry—quite a typical event.

How RiimaayBe Survive

The RiimaayBe economy is almost wholly based on the cultivation of millet as a subsistence crop. They also grow condiments such as okra, and they tend to grow a few cash crops that FulBe usually don't grow, such as cotton, peanuts, calabashes, melons, and squash. Not taking care of any cattle, RiimaayBe are not pulled in two directions by the differing demands of their husbandry. During the growing season they concentrate on weeding their millet and are usually able to grow larger crops than the FulBe do. Once the harvest is in, however, there is no one particular type of work that RiimaayBe men do. Whereas the FulBe are all occupied with the care of their cattle throughout the dry season, particularly as water and grass become scarce, RiimaayBe men take on a great variety of jobs. Some make bricks, some build houses, some invest in a wheelbarrow or a cart and use it to move things for people, some do carpentry, some leave the area to work elsewhere, and so on. In some parts of Burkina Faso the emigration of workers at that time of year is enormous, but this is not the case in the Djibo area. All the same, sometimes people who leave for work at the end of the growing season decide not to come back, and others find a line of work that keeps them occupied pretty much year-round so that they do not have the time or inclination to cultivate their own fields. I think this fact largely explains why RiimaayBe women are beginning to plant and cultivate their own fields. RiimaayBe women have generally given some assistance to their husbands in weeding their crops, but we are also witnessing situations where a woman whose husband is either absent, unable to work, or engaged in some other work, will cultivate a field of millet that is her own from start to finish. In these cases, of course, the woman is the sole owner of the product as well.

In the town of Djibo, which has a daily market, nearly all the RiimaayBe women engaged in some commerce. Most of them prepared food for sale, either on a regular basis or occasionally. If they had millet of their own they would use that; if not, they would take some from their husband's granary, either with or without his permission. The most common food they made was *cobbal*, baseball-sized millet dumplings cooked in water. These take a long time to prepare, but people like them for the midday meal because once cooked they can be eaten hot or cold, in a variety of ways, (often they are mashed and mixed with soured milk and water), and are easily transported. A number of women specialize in preparing certain town foods which are hardly known in the bush. The main ones are lacciri, which can be eaten with milk like a breakfast cereal or reheated and served with sauce, and *maasa*, a millet pancake about six centimeters in diameter made from a dough that is allowed to sour overnight. People eat this as a breakfast or snack food. Though the market is closed in the evening, in many houses one can buy nyiiri and sauce, the staple food. These foods are all very time-consuming to prepare, and once they have been made somebody has to sell them. Normally it is the producer who does the selling. If a woman has a daughter old enough to take the responsibility (at least ten) she will often have the child do it. Sometimes when two friends selling the same thing are sitting next to each other in the market one can ask the other to sell for her while she takes a break to do something else. These small producers, as is the case with other craftspeople in the area, do not normally sell wholesale to traders or to persons who would sell their products on commission.

RiimaayBe women do not work in straw as FulBe women do. Most of them spin cotton, however, and then either sell their thread or pay a weaver to make it into cloth. A few of them have learned the art of weaving a strong and durable mat from strips of palm frond. These are appreciated because they are less prickly for sleeping than straw mats, they break less easily on rough surfaces, and they last longer.

If both the FulBe and the RiimaayBe are pretty much self-sufficient in their food production, what do they need money for? Probably the most important single factor inducing people to use money originally was the requirement to pay taxes. The FulBe generally have very little cash on hand at any time. Men and women sell cattle or other animals only when the need for money arises (tax payments, health expenses, clothing, travel—including for some the pilgrimage to Mecca). Any money that men have on hand tends to disappear quickly into direct gifts or gifts in the form of cola nuts to beautiful women and musicians at festive gatherings; women spend their money on gifts to friends and relatives, or jewelry, cosmetics, and clothing for themselves. Money is often used as a part of marriage payments, and to pay for services of various kinds, usually by non-FulBe, such as native healers and magicians, musicians, extra agricultural labor, or transportation by ass-drawn cart.

RiimaayBe are generally more involved in the money economy than FulBe are. While the latter use money only occasionally, the former, especially in larger towns, use money for many of their daily needs. Most of the RiimaayBe women I knew in Djibo, for example, bought small quantities of condiments, meat, or soured milk nearly every day. Some women, rather than draw water from the town wells themselves, bought water daily from vendors who sold it from barrels on ass-drawn carts at two buckets per *mbuudu* (pl. *buudi*, five CFA (Communauté Financière Africaine) francs, worth about two cents) and nearly all households used this service from time to time. In addition, most people had a small amount of loose change on them at all times. It was common for grownups to make a gift of the smallest coin (mbuudu) to a child present when they dropped in to visit the parents. Mothers often tried to calm fussy or whiny two- to four-year-olds by promising to give them a mbuudu. To distract four- to six-year-old children they would sometimes send them to the market or a nearby vendor's stand to buy a mbuudu's worth of sugar, salt, or cola, or else a treat for themselves, such as peanuts, dates, or candy. As we shall see when we study mother–child interaction more closely, money is used in these situations in a way that exactly parallels the use of food, which in turn seems to be a continuation of the way nursing mothers offer the breast to their babies when they are in any kind of discomfort.

The Importance of Relatives

We have seen that people depend on one another frequently in the conditions of life as lived in the Jelgoji. Women taking care of small children need assistance at many moments during the day if they are to accomplish their other tasks without neglecting their children. Among the FulBe the multiple and conflicting demands of cultivating fields and herding cattle almost necessitate the cooperation and pooling of the resources of two or more able-bodied men. The agricultural mode of subsistence of RiimaayBe families does not appear to require cooperation to the extent that the mixed mode of the FulBe does, yet the RiimaayBe practice many forms of mutual aid.

From a sociological perspective one might want to argue that the obvious benefit of cooperation for people's survival explains the fact that people live together and cooperate. Whether or not this view is valid, it would be a mistake to stop there in our attempt to understand Fulani life. Such a cost/benefit interpretation of the way people live is, in fact, a nearly exact opposite of how the Fulani see themselves. The Western interpretation presupposes the idea that the individual is the basic unit of society, and that what we are trying to explain is how society emerges, as it were, from a collection of individuals. From the Fulani point of view, however, there is no such thing as what we call "society." First of all, there is no word in their language that means the same thing; second, in their thinking the world is made up not of "societies," not of "cultures," but of "lines" or "houses" when viewed as social relationships, and of inhabited areas of several kinds as opposed to the wilds or bush, when viewed geographically. The notion of line (*lenyol*, *asli*, and so on) or house (*suudu*) applies both to divisions close to home among people who consider themselves distantly related through a common ancestor, and to the whole range of divisions at higher levels of abstraction, including those separating people of different societies or ethnic groups, as we would call them.

People who live together in a camp, village, or quarter of a town think of one another as relatives in a way that is both inclusive and highly differentiated in several ways. There is an underlying "we-ness" (a possible literal translation of *enDam*, the usual Fulfulde word for kinship or bond); there is the sense of other people as belonging to different kinship categories with respect to oneself, such as father's brother, mother's brother, sister, or child; and finally there are all the feelings and memories that each person has concerning all the others with whom he or she lives. These factors are in constant interaction, such that it would be incorrect to say that any one way of experiencing relationship is more or less important than the others at all times. The crucial point here is that society, for the Fulani, is simply the people one lives with, and the people elsewhere with whom one is related.

It is even more true for the Fulani than it is for us (today) that the family, as Robert Frost said of home, "is where, when you have to go there, they have to take you in." But the Fulani view of this fact is from the back side, as it were. Rather than emphasize the family as people to rely on in time of trouble, the Fulani see the creation and maintenance of a family as both the main goal of life and the expression of success. This would be so obvious as to go without saying for a Sicilian anthropologist, but for a middle-class American imbued with the ideal of individual achievement and independence, the point must be underlined. The implication of Frost's poignant aphorism is that our normal goal is to leave the family and stand on our own two feet, and we only return to it when we have failed somehow. While some Fulani do indeed act in a way that looks like "striking out for oneself," it would usually be a serious error to attribute to them motives like our own. Many times, for example, young men told me they would love to come with me to the United States, and I mistakenly thought that this was because they were genuinely interested in discovering a new country, or at least learning a bit more about me. Not in the least. They—like many of us, actually—wanted to go in order to come back. In further discussion with people about their expectations from such a trip it became clear that what they mainly hoped for was to gain renown and popularity upon their return.

It might be argued at this point that in fact many people who leave on such adventurous voyages never return. But this is in no way a proof that they "really" wanted to leave or were dissatisfied with life at home. On the contrary, one reason why people often stay away is precisely because they remain highly imbued with their family values: they believe that by those values they have failed, and they stay away out of sheer shame. On several occasions I offered rides back to their home villages to Fulani living in Ouagadougou, and was surprised when they declined. One friend revealed the key, I think, when he told me that he couldn't go back until he was laden with presents for everybody back home; he had to save enough money to buy all these gifts before he could make such a trip. The only way a person in this dilemma could visit home would be if a close relative died there and he went to participate in the mourning. Such a trip wouldn't "count" as a real homecoming. Thus where we Westerners might see a large family and many hangers-on claiming distant cousinship as an obstacle or weight hampering a person's individual achievement, for the Fulani (both FulBe and RiimaayBe) the presence of such an entourage is a goal to which everyone aspires. It is not wealth itself that proves success but rather the collection of dependents, which wealth enables one to support.

4

WHAT LIFE IS ALL ABOUT

In this chapter I will present my sense of how individuals in different circumstances, and at different stages of their lives, see the meaning of life for them. I will sketch out what their hopes and fears are, their ideas of what the good and bad things are that can befall one in life, and their ideas about how to gain the former and avoid the latter or, in the case of misfortune, how to face it or combat it. It is absolutely essential to try to put ourselves in the shoes of the Fulani. Only when we can see how things look to them can we understand the goals they are trying to achieve by their actions or the situations they are trying to correct.

One point made in the previous chapter is so important it bears repeating here. Most people feel, most of the time, that life is full and good when they are surrounded by other people. Other people, of course, means people who are significant for you and for whom you are an important, valuable person. In Fulani society, as we have seen, this means nearly always that these people are your relatives, and the sine qua non for having relatives throughout your life is to marry and have many children. Not only are there many material obstacles to mere survival for oneself and one's family, but also, getting along with one's relatives and keeping alive the feeling and the bonds of relatedness are tasks that preoccupy most people for the greater part of their lives. There is no one right or best way to accomplish this, and how people go about it varies enormously depending on their particular circumstances. In addition, part of maintaining one's relationships with people involves the very maintenance and transmission of a sense of the task's importance, which is not something that people just know automatically.

My information on how people perceive what their situation ought to be at different points in their lives is far from complete. What I will present here is not an outline of the typical life cycle so much as an image of the world from the individual's point of view at various stages in his or her life. I will begin my descriptions of these life plans with adolescence for two reasons. First, the question of whether one's life is going "according to plan" really arises first at the point when a person has the power to make independent choices and, particularly, can decide to follow one course of action rather than another. In earlier childhood, even if the individual has some sense of being on course or not, it is parents and other relatives who would be making the major decisions. These decisions range from that concerning the age to begin religious instruction (for both girls and boys, though few girls are given any outside the family) which ranges from about age five to ten, to male circumcision, which can take place as young as about seven and as old as eighteen, to major medico-religious treatments such as for serious illnesses, madness, or bed-wetting. The second reason for focusing here on the period from adolescence onward is that I will devote several subsequent chapters to detailed presentation of information on childhood, so it would be redundant to dwell on that now.

The Pullo Male Life Plan

The things that are on a boy's mind between the ages of fourteen and about twenty change a good deal as time passes. This is a period of great freedom and fun for most boys, so long as the region is not going through famine and their fathers have at least a small herd of cattle. At the beginning of this period few boys are thinking about sex. They often have to work for their fathers and uncles, but the work is sporadic and they have a lot of free time. They wander about in the bush a great deal with friends their own age; they gather fruits and berries in season; they try with various devices to trap birds, fish, and hares and cook and eat their catch out in the bush. They are too young and small to do the work of drawing up water for the cattle in the dry season, though they might have to do it if there is no one else in their family who can. They do have to pasture the sheep and goats from time to time, they have to help drive cows on occasion, and from fifteen or sixteen they might be considered big enough to accompany the herds on transhumance. The most arduous work they must do is usually the hoeing of weeds in the millet fields. Here they will work along with their fathers, uncles, and older brothers. They can also help in certain other collective work projects, such as enclosing a field with thorny branches to make a barrier to prevent cattle from getting into the growing millet, or serving in a sort of bucket brigade to carry away and dump the mud from a well that is being dug or deepened in the dry season.

So long as the boys have fathers, they don't have to worry about whether they will be able to get married or not, or how to amass the resources necessary to obtain a bride. The only exception to this would be the situation where a boy's father was acting selfishly or had suffered some kind of disaster. In that case a boy of fourteen to sixteen might very well just leave his father and go ally himself with another male relative, such as a father's brother or mother's brother who was well-disposed to him. In the case where the family could do without the boy's services—and if the boy had sufficient interest and self-discipline—he might go to study the Koran beyond the basic rudiments necessary for prayer. In most cases boys abandon such studies after a few years, but a few become ever more hungry for religious knowledge. However long his studies, a boy becomes like a son to his master and as long as he is with him both serves him and depends on him for everything. In fact, should he remain a scholar and choose the life of a *moodibbo*, it is his master, not his father, who will ensure that he gets married. His eventual wife is likely to be a woman "given" to the master as a religious offering by a particularly pious man.

By his middle or late teens, depending on his state of maturity, a boy might start to get interested in girls, but his goal would not be sexual pleasure so much as the esteem of both women and his peers. This is the age when boys often do rather crazy things, either just for the hell of it or to achieve notoriety. I doubt that any boys of that age want to get married yet. They prefer stealing other men's wives to worrying about who is stealing theirs, and they do not yet experience any anxiety about whether they will be successful in producing and raising children. On the other hand, it is during this period of their lives that they make certain decisions, not always consciously, that could have long-term effects on them. Depending on circumstances, they can decide to begin, continue, or stop serious religious studies. They can decide whether to be playboys or to begin seriously working for their fathers and ultimately for themselves in agriculture and in cattle care. They can decide whether to be basically an ordinary person or to seek renown in some form or other. In the latter case, though there are no longer opportunities for glory in war or cattle rustling, many men still put much effort into seeking magical means of gaining strength, protection, wealth, popularity, and women (not necessarily in that order).

What are the factors that affect their thinking at this juncture? Their physical qualities are profoundly important to them during these years: how big they are, how handsome or ugly, the color of their skin, their ability to wrestle, run, dance, and sing, and whatever ineffable qualities contribute to their popularity both with their comrades and with girls. On top of that, there is a subtle interplay, a bit like what happens in our society, between the "egalitarian" manner in which all boys of approximately the same age treat each other, and the effects of the person's wealth and family background. These factors are of minimal importance in adolescence, but they are decisive for the selection of a man's first wife, and as he begins to raise a family they take on more and more importance in his relations with his peers.

Boys of this age tease and insult each other a great deal. I personally saw very little of this; in fact, I had been in the village for a whole year before I learned that insulting bouts were common practice. My failure to learn about these earlier was due mainly to the fact that people did not want to offend us. I discovered only late in my fieldwork that the quiet, peaceful behavior of the young men gathered around my fire in the evenings was quite unlike how the same group of people would commonly behave if I were not there. Normally, as I learned in a lucky conversation one night, the young men sit around in the evenings insulting and teasing each other, testing to see how far they can go. But suspecting that my wife and I wouldn't like that, for the whole two years we were with them they refrained almost completely from this activity in our presence. These insults are both joking and serious at the same time. In a society where the person insulted may respond by killing his offender, to insult a person implies either that you have the power to dominate him or that his friendship and goodwill toward you can overcome any bad feelings stirred up by your words. Thus, to be insulted regularly by your friends is a sign of your being accepted by them as part of the gang, and yet the insults can indeed be genuinely painful—just as a friendly punch in the arm or thump on the back can be in our society.

People are constantly playing on the dangerous borderlines of these insults. One young man who had gone through a period of estrangement from his comrades after returning from long years of religious study elsewhere (Riesman 1977:78) unintentionally illustrated this point as he explained to me why it was so important for him to have married his father's brother's daughter. Marriage with this particular relative is the normal first marriage for a Pullo youth. If a young man has a marriageable paternal cousin and does not marry her, then the man who does marry her has the added pleasure of congratulating himself for having beaten out, as it were, the girl's rightful husband. In the case of Aamadu's wife, had someone else married her, not only would this have been a constant source of bitterness in itself, but it would have provided her husband with opportunities to insult him with impunity. Aamadu told me that when the girl bore a child, the father, whoever he was, would name him Aamadu, just to annoy Aamadu himself (*mettude kam*). Then, one day, when the child was close to Aamadu sitting among people, the father would call to the child, saying, "Hey, Aamadu!" Big Aamadu would look around, then realize that the father was calling his child, but it would be too late, for the father could then say, "*nyammu yaaye ma* (Your mother's vagina)" and get away with it. He would be insulting his son, which is perfectly normal for fathers, and there would be nothing Aamadu could do about it.

I witnessed what was probably a more typical kind of teasing during the transhumance trek I took with a group of five young cowherds in the middle of my second rainy season with the FulBe. Three of the men were in their early twenties, and two in their middle teens. One of the latter was not a relative, but had just

joined up his herd with that of the others, who were closely related, for companionship and safety. Umaru, the other teenager,
was constantly being teased by the older boys. As we were all
walking along in front of the moving herd, the others would start
to laugh and dance in front of Umaru, saying, "*A may-kural!*
(What a hyena you are!)" May-Kural was the name of a captive
hyena that had been put through its paces in small bush communities by a traveling Hausa showman the year before. Fulani consider the hyena an ugly, misshapen, good-for-nothing animal.
When I asked the boys why they called him that, they answered,
"Can't you tell by his looks?" Behind the teasing, however, was
some real criticism, for these men felt that Umaru was not doing
his fair share of helping with the cows during the trip. "Umaru
received these jibes with a sort of sickly smile," I wrote in my
notes at the time. "Even when alone with him," I continued, "I
have never been able to get a sense of his personality. It is almost as
if he didn't have one. What struck me most of all in him was a sort
of resignation. He seemed to have little desire to assert himself,
and at the same time he had a certain tenacious resistance to being
ordered around all the time. Yet he bore the others no ill will that I
could detect."

One of the rare times I did hear people insulting each other
around my fire occurred at a time when one young man was carrying out a very brazen love affair with the wife of a close relative
and friend, for which the whole community was criticizing him
(Riesman 1977:239–44). Looking back on the incident, I think
that context explains the tension that seemed to be in the air that
evening. We were passing the tea glass around. Eggori, the offender, told me to tell the other boys to put their finger up their ass
and then sniff it. "*Ittan goddi* (That'll satisfy your envy)." A little
later he actually said this to Ulo, a twelve-year-old boy. Ulo replied, "*Wattu honndu ma ley fuudo faa to wooDi, de mettu* (Stick your
finger up your ass as far as you can reach, then lick it)." Eggori
didn't reply, but that Ulo answered him at all was unusual, since it
is an extraordinary lack of respect for a younger person to answer
back, let alone insult, an older person in public. He could probably
get away with it that time because of everyone's disapproval of
Eggori.

The point of this discussion of insults has been to give some of
the flavor of peer relations among adolescent boys and youths, and

to show what an important role those relations play in boys' lives. While there is no way I can know for sure how Umaru felt about being teased, or how Eggori felt about being insulted by a twelve-year-old, I think the reader has enough information to sense the range of possible feelings and the inherent ambivalence any exchange of insults entails.

A very important quality of interpersonal relations among youths emerges from this discussion of insults, namely that everyone is, at one and the same time, a member of the judging audience and an individual in joking or serious competition with all other members of the group. We can see this same quality of personal relations clearly in another situation, namely that of games. One very popular pastime among FulBe and RiimaayBe youths is the game of *dilli*. This is played on a "board" scratched in the sand, six squares by five. Each player has ten counters (twigs or pebbles) and tries to align three in a row, somewhat as in tic-tac-toe. Each time he succeeds in achieving a line, he gets to remove any one of his opponent's counters.

One of the most striking things about the way people play this game is that it is hard to tell who the players are. It is a game that appears to be for two players, but in fact all the people present participate in it, and the actual moves may be made by any number of people. However, there is only one winner and one loser. Often the game never gets to the end. Sometimes they see fairly early who the winner is going to be. Then they stop and start over again. Sometimes the player who is losing disputes this and tries to get the others to stop taking pieces off the board, but he usually gives up. It is very hard for one player to make the moves he would like to make. In any given turn several pieces may be moved by different people, only to be put back by the actual player so that he can make his own move. I would find this situation very frustrating, but it seems to be the very essence of the game here. Would two people play this game by themselves? Perhaps not, since for one thing it is not that interesting a game by itself. It takes the presence of the others to liven it up, and to give the good player a chance to show off. For the good player can show off despite all the obstacles just mentioned. He simply has to be quick enough to move before the kibitzers can get their hands on the board.

This same undercurrent of competition is present even in the most normal and necessary activity of watering the cattle at the wells. For example, some of the wells are dangerous. One of the wells at Petaga was deep (ten meters), with sharp rocks at the bottom, and had a gaping opening about two and a half meters across. A few heavy poles and logs were laid across the opening to enable the drawers to stand directly over the water as they lowered and raised their buckets by hand. The logs were worn and slippery, and they were constantly splashed by water, so that standing on them to work was dangerous. Anyone watching the boys drawing up the water would think they were having a good time and felt no fear. But that is bravado, for when I asked them if it was scary to work at that well they freely admitted that it was. But no one would consider trying to make the situation safer, for that would be a sign of cowardice.

There is another important point about Fulani social life to be learned from the description of the game of dilli. Notice that there is only one winner and one loser, regardless of how much participation by other people took place in the game. This situation is, I think, an exact reflection of how people participate in action generally. If a family head sells a cow, or clears a new field, it doesn't matter what member of his household actually did these things; it is always the head who is said to have done it. In war, if a man's MaccuDo kills an opponent, it is the Pullo who will be said to have done it. We have many analogies to this sort of identification in Western society as well, as when we say "The President imposed import quotas" or "Boston defeated Chicago at Fenway Park." These analogies can help us understand the Fulani experience of life, but the experiences are not identical. The principal subjective difference, I think, is that the sense of being part of, or representative of, a significant group of people is a nearly constant feature of the Fulani world, while it is at best an episodic aspect of life for the middle classes in industrial and post-industrial society.

Despite what I have just said, it is also true that for many FulBe men life is a highly personal quest for success during the years of youth and early middle age. The competition that lurks in the relations between adolescents emerges more openly in young adulthood as men compete for women, wealth, and renown. It is quite common for young men to fight each other hand to hand or with clubs because of women. Men deliberately provoke each other by trying to seduce each other's wives; the women participate willingly in these intrigues partly because the fact of being sought after by other men gives them more power in relation to their husbands. And yet there is another social dimension even to this seemingly antisocial conduct. It is bad form to love one's wife (or to appear to) and it is bad form to be jealous. The ideal is to appear not to need one's wife, to be tolerant of her peccadillos, and to keep one's equanimity no matter what. Consider the following proverb: "If you see grown men chasing each other at midnight, you can be sure that the one in front is the offender." The man who runs after the seducer of his wife is considered perfectly justified, yet a little ridiculous. This person reveals two shameful weaknesses: he displays an inordinate need for his wife, and he fails to master his anger against her lover. Not only are such weaknesses ill-suited to a true man, but they are dangerous to men because they create dissension among them and undermine efforts to maintain a myth of male superiority. It seems, then, that the male quest for other women is not bad in itself but may even signify a good, as I suggested in my early article (Riesman 1971); the resulting imbroglios are just so many tests of male self-control and harmony. While people liked my own apparent tranquility and were probably just as glad that I didn't try to seduce their wives, they were puzzled at my attitude and seemed not fully satisfied by my excuse that bigamy was illegal by the laws of my country.

In the following section concerning the Diimaajo male life plan, I will discuss at length the search that many young men—both FulBe and RiimaayBe—undertake for magical means to assure success in different ventures. Here I will discuss briefly the religious path, which is taken by a minority of young men, predominantly FulBe.

Though most mature and old men and women consider their personal salvation important, it is unusual for a youth to do so. As in our society, to commit oneself to a life of learning is to enter a different world from that of most people. In theory it is a possibility open to people of all social backgrounds, but it is my impression that the majority of those who persevere are from moodibbo families. I asked Tijjani, a very respected scholar of Djibo, to tell me his life story. He was from a moodibbo family and began his studies at about age five, which is common in that milieu. He was his father's only son, but his father died while Tijjani was still in his teens. Tijjani quit his studies and began to go to parties and spend money on women and musicians. His father's sister was upset by his behavior and spoke to the chief of Djibo, begging him to help set Tijjani back on the path. The chief called him in and said he had a choice: he could go and study with So-and-so in Baadunoogo or with So-and-so in Borgende. Which of the two did he prefer? Tijjani replied that he didn't want to go either of those places (nearby towns) but instead to Doori (a more distant town where he had studied previously for several years). "Oh," said the chief. "Whom do you want to study with there?" "With Hamma Moodi," said Tijjani. The chief gave his accord, but sent a letter ahead asking the teacher to be sure and keep him informed of Tijjani's work, whether it was satisfactory or not.

From that time on, Tijjani never stopped studying. He listed many places that he went to study with scholars. He would go to one person and study dogma and law; with another he would study theology; with another logic; with another grammar and conjugation; with another mathematics, and so on. As he got older he would in turn teach the others what he knew. His whole life has been one of traveling to seek and share knowledge. "You won't have knowledge," he said, "unless you have six things: a good mind and a passion for knowledge, these two are the fire of it. Then you need perseverance. You have to be satisfied with your material level of life and not need to seek something better. You need to find a teacher who not only has knowledge but who is willing to reveal it to you. And lastly you have to have a long life so that you can pursue knowledge a long time. These are the things you need if you are to get knowledge."

In talking with this thoughtful, engaging person, I was in the presence of a true intellectual. At the same time, however, he insisted that the purpose of all this study was not knowledge for its own sake, but rather to understand the will of God. The most important parts of the studies were those having to do with the proper ways to pray, the different prayers for different times of day, different times of the year, how to know which was which, and so on. If we know these things, if we follow God's will, then we do not need laws and policemen to keep us from doing bad.

It is worth reflecting briefly on the intervention of the chief at a crucial moment in Tijjani's life. The young man had deviated from the path of his lineage, and appeared to be in danger of losing it entirely, of failing to "do what he found," his tawaangal. Why does the chief step in, though? What business is it of his whether a person strays or not? In particular, Tijjani was not doing anything regarded as absolutely bad; he was simply acting like the majority of boys his age. I do not know for sure the answer to my question; however, we can draw some tentative conclusions. Not only are members of a person's immediate family concerned with a person "doing what he finds," but so are outsiders. Had Tijjani irrevocably strayed from his family's path, that would have brought shame on the family, so that it is not just a matter of one individual's welfare. I suspect that it concerns the chief for two reasons. First, the chief upholds social order, and it is of vital concern to him that everybody follow the paths laid out by tradition. Second, he was asked. Though I don't know the reasons why Tijjani's aunt called on him, once he was appealed to it was probably a matter of honor for him to prove his ability to help.

For men in the prime of life, the three most important assets to have are health, children, and a certain level of wealth. In greetings and partings and on many formal occasions Fulani wish one another good health and many children. As a rule, however, people do not specifically wish wealth for one another. Instead they ask that God bless the person in a general way, or that He ensure his salvation. One friend of mine said, "People say that God gives to his friend and his enemy alike four things: physical beauty, bodily health, wealth, and children. But to his friend He gives four additional things: the ability to pray in the correct fashion, religious faith, patience, and generosity." Yet just prior to telling me that, my friend said that "everybody likes a rich person, because they think perhaps God likes him."

In conversations with me and often among themselves as well, men would talk about wealth and poverty, and how unpleasant it was to be poor. These matters were far from self-evident to me, because among the FulBe there were few visible signs of wealth displayed in everyday life. At first it seemed to me that everyone

was poor, for all lived very frugally and I was seldom aware of one
family eating better than others, or having better clothing, housing,
or more possessions. As my friend put it in the previously cited
conversation, "The thing I hate most of all is poverty (*wannde*). If a
person has nothing then he can't even feed himself, let alone his
father and mother. Not to mention somebody else. If a person has
at least something, then he can take care of his whole household,
very well too. He will work well for them, his work will be respectable. But the man who has no wealth will end up doing shady
kinds of work." A proverb states the harsh truth succinctly and
ironically: "Three things are never together in one house—a man,
a woman, and poverty." This refers to the fact that if a man and
woman are living together and the man is poor, either the woman
will leave to find a better man or the man will leave to seek wealth.

The following case is a good example of how poverty can affect
people in actual circumstances. In fact, this case offers glimpses of
several important aspects of Fulani life, but we won't try to examine them all at once. I learned of the situation through being
present at a judicial hearing before the sub-prefect of the district. It
was the only formal hearing I was permitted to be present at during my four years in the field, though I heard at least fragments of
numerous informal ones held in the villages of local chiefs. I think
the sub-prefect, who did not speak Fulfulde, let me observe because I knew the participants personally and because he wanted to
learn from me afterward how good his interpreter was.

The main actors in this story were Haamidi son of JaaYe, Bukkari son of Yerolde (a much older brother of Haamidi), and Bukkari's son Hammadum. Haamidi and Hammadum were young
men of about the same age; Bukkari, old enough to be Haamidi's
father, was actually his classificatory son, since Haamidi was his
own father's younger brother. Bukkari was bringing a complaint
against Haamidi on the following grounds. Some six years earlier
Haamidi had made a gift of a heifer to Bukkari's son Hammadum
in appreciation of three years of work Hammadum had done herding cattle for Haamidi. Bukkari had been very poor at the time,
owning only three cows. Bukkari claimed that he heard from
Haamidi's own lips what he was doing and why. He took the
heifer and added it to his own three cows and took them all to the
distant pasture where Hammadum was herding cattle for some

Dogon in Mali. But Bukkari soon learned that his mother was very ill, so he came back home leaving his son with their four cows and the Dogon cattle. On his return to Petaga, he was approached by Haamidi, who asked him if Hammadum was pasturing his cow in Mali. Bukkari said yes, but was suspicious of Haamidi's motives. He feared that Haamidi would go after his son and perhaps bring him some harm by fighting with him over the cow. He went to the local chief and asked his advice: should he go north to see if he could prevent the two young men from getting into a fight, or should he just wait to see what happened? The chief advised him to wait and see. As Bukkari tells it, what Haamidi did was to present himself to Hammadum as a messenger from his father Bukkari. He told Hammadum that Bukkari was very pleased with his good cow herding, but that he should now turn over all four cows to Haamidi to bring back to Petaga, as his father needed them right away. Haamidi then brought back the four cows, but put them in his own herd. Bukkari's three cows eventually got back to Bukkari, but Haamidi sold the heifer that he had previously given to Hammadum. Prior to its sale, however, it had had a calf. At the time of the complaint, six years later, that calf had had two calves of its own, and one of these had in turn borne a calf, so that there were now four cows from the original one. It never became clear why Bukkari was bringing this complaint now, rather than six years ago, but he was seeking the restitution of the four cattle which were now the fruit of the original cow that had been given to his son.

Haamidi's version of the story was very different. He denied that Hammadum had ever worked for him as a cowherd. On the contrary, what had happened was that Hammadum had come to him seeking his help as a wealthier relative, because his own father was so poor. He had asked Haamidi, who was in the generation of his grandfather, though of similar age, to take him in and feed him, clothe him, and obtain a wife for him. In exchange he would weed his millet for him and herd his cattle. Haamidi said that he would be glad to take Hammadum on under these conditions, and would give him a classificatory daughter for a wife. But before they formalized their agreement they would have to wait for the return of Bukkari, Hammadum's father, to make sure the arrangement would be all right with him. Bukkari came to Haamidi without being called, for he had heard that his son and Haamidi had talked. But Bukkari refused to let Hammadum work for Haamidi on such terms. Haamidi reported that Bukkari told him his son was no MaccuDo and could not be bought in exchange for a cow. That is why it seemed to Haamidi that the deal was off and that he had every right to take back his cow.

Bukkari of course denied to the court that he said what Haamidi had attributed to him. All he had done on going to Haamidi himself was to ask him if indeed he had given his son a cow. When Haamidi told him he had, he then simply thanked him by asking God to bless him.

The case is messy, and I was not able to come to a clear opinion of my own as to what had "really" happened or which of the parties was in the right. But the major themes of life which are at stake here do emerge fairly sharply. Poverty prevents a man from maintaining his independence and from successfully marrying. It is a shameful state for the impoverished person no matter what: if Hammadum stays home with his father he fails to get a good start as an adult, but if he works for his "grandfather" he is in some ways like a MaccuDo for that person. Either situation is hard to bear.

The difference between youth and maturity in FulBe men, in Jelgoji at any rate, is strongly marked. As men approach the age of forty or so they stop hanging around in gangs with the other young men, they stop going to music, dancing, and flirting parties, they spend more time with the older men of the area, and they spend much more time at the mosque. In many cases also they begin to wear not the homespun, hand-dyed tunic of the cowherds, but the machine-woven white cloth of the devout. What makes this transformation possible is that most men of that age, if things have gone more or less right in their lives to that point, will have sons who have reached adolescence about then. Since a son of that age is able to do nearly all the work of cattle care and agriculture needed for the FulBe way of life, a man can begin to leave many of the tasks he used to do to his son(s) and spend more time in politicking, religious study or contemplation, or some other activity. Two factors are important here. On the one hand, for a son not to assist his father in this way would be extremely shameful for the family. Such a state of affairs would indicate disrespect of the son for the father, and would greatly lower the latter in the eyes of his own peers. In some cases the father is actually a bad lot himself and people would say he had it coming to him because of the way he had been treating his son. However, this would not truly excuse the son's behavior. The proper way would still be to obey and assist his father at least until he had become a father himself. Many people, as we shall see in more detail futher on, would explain this sort of bad behavior as the emergence of qualities inherited from the mother.

Thus for a man much over forty to be doing hard work is not merely physically burdensome, but is a sign of some kind of failure. As for showing up at parties and so on, this is not appropriate for several reasons. First, it implies a lack of self-control on the man's part, an inability to restrain or at least decently disguise his sexual needs. Second, it means that the man will either be a wet blanket on the fun of the younger generation—for he is a "father" and uncle to most of them and thus decorous behavior is called for on the part of all—or, worse, he will suffer great embarrassment and further shame because of the failure of the younger people to inhibit their behavior in his presence, which exposes him to their indirect but likely well-aimed jibes.

Almost all men at around this age seriously consider taking additional wives, if they haven't already done so. If a man has no sons who are beginning to be useful, or especially if he has none at all, he will think of himself as being in a very precarious situation, perhaps a desperate one. The future looks grim for such a man because just at the time when he should be starting to be more self-sufficient through his offspring, he in fact must continue to stay in a more dependent relationship with other men, such as his father, uncle, or brother. The actual personalities of the people involved can make an enormous difference here. If people don't get along with each other well, a person in a dependent relationship can be quite miserable, while in other cases the situation is a lot more bearable. The reason for marrying more wives is not only simply to obtain a greater number of children, but also to ensure, for the man, a regular supply of adolescents throughout his life, so that there will always be a dependent or two who in fact do most of the work, and thus prevent the aging man from becoming overly dependent on other grown men.

Now, I have to admit that I haven't heard people talk this way about their reasons for marrying and having many children. What I have presented here are my inferences from the way things seem to work out in people's lives. While we were living in Petaga there was a man in the community, Haaruuna, who seemed to be adapting reasonably well to the predicament of having no children. I was never able to find out what the reasons for his childlessness were—or even what people thought they were. He was in his late thirties or early forties when I knew him, and had two wives. The first had never had any children, while the second was a widow who had borne two children to her late husband. He lived near the village chief, who was his good friend, and to whom he often acted as an advisor and assistant. For instance, this man was put in charge of conducting to the regional capital two men who had come to blows over the destruction of the crops of one by animals of the other. How did this man manage to keep two wives, even though he had not had children by either one? How did he manage to attain value and importance in his relationship with the chief when we might expect that a childless man would lack weight and not be taken seriously by most people?

I unfortunately did not think of asking these questions in the field, but there are some indications to be found in other information I have about the situation. There are three points that seem very important to me. First, Haaruuna and his own uncles and brothers (his father is dead) are relatively well-off in cattle. Haaruuna is the eldest son of his family, and is thus the nominal leader of his two younger brothers. The first of these is married but his children have been dying in infancy; the second brother is just old enough to marry but is quite a playboy and didn't appear at all interested in matrimony during the period I knew him. Second, Haaruuna is a cross-cousin of the chief, for his father's sister was the chief's mother. Cross-cousins are expected to feel comfortable with each other and can take things from each other and tease each other whenever they feel like it. Third, Haauruna is thoughtful, decent, loyal, and a good talker. Thus he serves well as a sounding board for the chief when he is trying to figure out how to handle a tricky human or legal problem. It is possible also that these personal qualities and his relative wealth are factors enabling him to stay married to two women. Finally, since Haaruuna is not a close agnate to the chief, but is connected to him through a female relative, he in no way poses a threat to his power. His childlessness may even be an asset in assuring the chief's confidence and trust in him, for Haaruuna would have no conflict of loyalty between gaining something for his children's benefit and helping the chief and his family. The chief does not rely on his own brothers in anything like the same way, though often quite a few of them share the same village with him. There is a definite relation of hierarchy between the brothers, of whom the chief is the eldest, which prohibits free and easy discussion of issues, or even just relaxed chitchat.

The life plan of FulBe men that I have been describing until now differs in many important ways, as we shall see shortly, from that of RiimaayBe men. In the period of old age, however, it is fair to say that the life plans of men in both groups converge. Therefore I will discuss the period of old age for both FulBe and RiimaayBe men together toward the end of the subsequent section concerning the Diimaajo male life plan, and also, in relation to both sexes, at the end of the chapter.

The Diimaajo Male Life Plan

My knowledge of the lives of RiimaayBe adolescents and youths is less rich than that concerning the FulBe. One reason for this is simply that during my second field trip, largely spent with the RiimaayBe, I was focusing my investigation on small children and their mothers and had less time to spend with other segments of the population. But perhaps a more important reason is the fact that I had children of my own with me during this field trip, and so I was no longer thought of by people as a youth. While living with the FulBe I had spent more time with adolescents and young men than with any other single group; while living with the RiimaayBe, apart from my regular visits to the mothers and children I was observing, I spent most of my time with mature men, the fathers and grandfathers of those children.

The world looks very different to a young Diimaajo than it looks to his Pullo counterpart. The most important difference can be identified as the tawaangal of each group. For the Pullo to "do what he found" is to follow a tradition that is noble, glorious at times, and prestigious; but the Diimaajo doesn't have a tradition of his own that amounts to anything. The very nature of his origin is ignominious, and it is particularly important that the very idea of family line does not exist. This means that a young Diimaajo becoming aware of who he is and what his possibilities are is not likely to be attracted by his tradition in the first place. During the period of slavery, which officially ended around the end of the First World War but some aspects of which have faded only gradually, a young man born into slavery would have no choice about "doing what he found." He would do what he was told or else suffer severe punishments. MaccuBe were classed as a form of wealth (*jawdi*) and were, as we saw above, often compared to cattle. As with cattle, ownership of a MaccuDo was determined by who owned the mother. RiimaayBe and FulBe alike have told me that in the old days FulBe would beat MaccuBe who failed to behave properly. One old Diimaajo told me of several cruel tortures that FulBe sometimes imposed. For instance, if a Pullo wanted to punish a servant girl (*korDo*) he would tell her to boil water and then would force her to put her arm in the pot, or carry it on her head. The man who told me this in 1975 was near eighty, and he had seen the disfigured people to whom this had been done.

The lack of traditions and reputations to uphold has enormously different implications under modern conditions than it did in the past. One of these is that, ironically, a Diimaajo youth today might feel in some ways freer than a Pullo in thinking about what he will be "when he grows up." That this is in fact the case seems clear from the observation that RiimaayBe youth today seek all kinds of training and work. Many of them try to get some schooling, and nearly all would jump at the chance to learn a trade or try their hand at a new line of work.

A good example of this thinking occurred in a conversation I had with a middle-aged man concerning a proposed new road through the town. The project would require the destruction of many people's homes, so I assumed that the man would be against it. Much to my surprise he said that he would like nothing better than to have his house destroyed. That would give him the chance to move out. He told me that in fact all but a few old people would like to move out of their houses, but people would not dare deliberately to abandon their ancestral homes.

We can see the same kind of thinking in the remarks of a young man explaining to me why he had returned to Djibo from a good job in Côte d'Ivoire. Muusa spent three years there going from job to job until he found good work on a cacao plantation. He worked there for six months, and was fed and housed by his boss. At the end of that time he went home with his final payment of 40,000 francs ($160) in his pocket, a very substantial sum, since in Djibo a person would have to work one to three years (depending on occupation) even to gross that much. I asked him how he had liked living in Abidjan. He said that it was better than Djibo: work is easier, food is better, climate is not as hot. "Well, why did you come back?" I asked. Muusa replied that his adoptive father had written him asking him to return. This old man, a prominent village leader, had adopted him because he had no children of his own and had taken care of him since his childhood. The old man had said he had no one to cultivate for him and, besides, that he had picked out a wife for him. So Muusa came back to Djibo. I asked him what would have happened had he refused to return. "Well," said Muusa, "my wife would have been given to someone else, but the old man would not have starved. He would have been able to survive. But it would have been bad to refuse, since he has been like my own father to me."

Muusa was willing to venture into another world, then, and might very well have stayed there had he not been asked to come back. But does his return weaken my contention that RiimaayBe feel freer to try other kinds of work than FulBe do? No, it does not, because the issue is not that of the kind of work to be done; rather it is one of fulfilling an obligation to his "father." Both FulBe and RiimaayBe, as we have already noted, sense very keenly the importance of maintaining kin ties, especially those with their parents. Now, it happens that a number of FulBe youths also take off for Abidjan and other places looking for work. This is seen as a tragedy, or at least highly dangerous, by the families of those concerned. Unlike the departure of RiimaayBe youths to seek work, that of FulBe youths is definitely perceived by others as a rejection of FulBe values.

RiimaayBe youths are at first no more eager to settle down in

married life than are FulBe. First marriages for them, as for the
latter, are arranged by the parents. Though the RiimaayBe don't
have lineages, issues of prestige and reputation are still highly important. In addition, within Djibo there are rivalries and alliances
between the different quarters of the town which affect people's
initial choices of spouse. Success or failure of these marriages,
however, unlike in the FulBe case, does not have wider political
repercussions. It was my impression that, though both FulBe and
RiimaayBe youths were equally interested in carrying on affairs
with other men's wives, in the case of the RiimaayBe the goal was
mainly to make life more interesting and did not include the sense
of rivalry and bravado that characterize adulterous relations among
the FulBe.

Let us look a little more closely now at people's aspirations.
RiimaayBe, like the FulBe, want to have as many children as possible. Before my wife and I had children, FulBe would sometimes
say, "May God give you children to beshit you." This was not a
joke, but rather was a delightfully compressed way of saying that
children are so valuable that you are glad to have them shit on you,
for at least you have them. In a conversation in the Djibo marketplace some men were philosophizing about the importance of
marriage and children. "Women can break up a family (*na hela
suudu baaba*), but if you don't marry you won't become respectable,
you won't become adult, you won't receive your due." One's
"due" (*ngeDu*) comes in three parts; your friends come and give
presents to the child, your wife's friends come and give presents to
the child, and the child and his friends insult each other. As one
man put it, "It's sweet to hear the words 'your dad's prick,' because
it means you have children."

We have seen how concerned the FulBe are about avoiding poverty. The RiimaayBe are perhaps even more concerned than the
FulBe; at least I heard them talk about it more. One possible reason for being more open and vocal about their concern is the fact
that the FulBe in fact do generally have more wealth than the
RiimaayBe. FulBe don't normally think of cattle as money, and
hate to sell a bull or a cow to deal with needs that arise. But at least
they have them. RiimaayBe, on the other hand, usually do not
have as much "capital." Not only that, but what money they do
gain usually comes from their own hard work, and they realize

that. FulBe see their "wealth" as reproducing itself. Though they work hard in taking care of their cattle, it would never occur to them that they were directly creating their own wealth. They see God and perhaps other supernatural forces as entirely responsible for that. As we have also seen, they live frugally, and would think it shameful to draw upon their capital to satisfy hunger, a desire for better food, better clothes, shelter, or other wants. Except for special occasions, the RiimaayBe live more lavishly than the FulBe. They generally live in permanent houses, they have more possessions, more comfortable beds, wear better clothes, and cook more and richer foods. As one crusty old Diimaajo put it to me, "MaccuBe are like vultures; we eat anything; we have no shame." He gave the example of a certain large lizard he was skinning. It is an ugly animal, but it tastes good, he said. FulBe are not supposed to eat it, but they occasionally do, in secret. Issa said that if a MaccuDo came upon a Pullo who was eating one of these lizards he could just take it from him if he wanted to. The Pullo would know that if he resisted the MaccuDo could bring great shame upon him by telling people that So-and-so eats lizard.

"It is better to be known as owning a suit than to be seen wearing one," goes a proverb. The person wearing a suit could have borrowed it from somebody else. In fact, however, people are constantly wearing one another's suits so as to give an impression of affluence. Another proverb goes, "If one grouse towers above another one it's that the first one is sitting on a termite hill." What this means is that people are essentially alike and that it is wealth that makes one seem better than another. These proverbs are known and said by FulBe and RiimaayBe alike, but the RiimaayBe talked to me more about their understandings of how human society works. The belief in the fundamental importance of wealth is firmly rooted in their thinking, and came out in many contexts.

I was surprised and shocked to hear people say, for instance, that the only people likely to get into heaven were the rich. It is not that the rich are morally better than the poor, but that they have more power, including especially the capacity to help others. A poor person hasn't much chance to get in no matter how good he is, because no one cares about him and he can help no one. This means that no one will come to him for help, and hence no one will ask God to bless him for what he does. When a poor person is sick, people asked me, who is going to come and wish him well? Who is going to pray to God to help make him get well? No one, for what good has he done anybody? Yet another proverb expresses this idea with stark humor: "Dad came home, we went to bed without any dinner; Dad left, we went to bed without any dinner. When he dies people will cry out of pity and familiarity only; there's no use in him." The force of this proverb is all the greater when we realize that it is a man's ability to take care of the needs of his family (and other dependents) that justifies his dominance over them in the first place. Several people told me that "There are two who do not know 'I don't have any'—your wife and child. They will just say you refused." "A man's strength is wealth," said one man. Another one told me he thought that the principal difference between a Pullo and a MaccuDo was that the Pullo has wealth while the MaccuDo does not. Thus a man of Pullo stock who lacks wealth is like a MaccuDo, while a rich MaccuDo is a "noble" (the person used the French word *noble* here).

But where does this all-important stuff, wealth, come from? Theories abounded, but most people felt the true sources were very mysterious. While they recognized the importance of work for basic survival, as I've mentioned, neither FulBe nor RiimaayBe believe that a person can get rich through hard work. Toward the end of my stay I happened upon a fascinating debate among half a dozen or so mature men on the subject of raising millet. One side was saying that growing food is the basis of everything else because without your own food you are completely stuck. The other side held that cultivating your own food was useless because by the time the next year comes around you've eaten it all and you are back where you started. What's the good of that? In addition, people felt that trying to save a surplus over more than a year was unwise because there were such serious losses in long-term storage.

Some of the group argued that hoeing millet caused you shame, because you had to bend over in an unseemly posture. "Have you ever seen a merchant or a scholar, or any person who has other work, hoe a field?" asked one. "Why say agriculture is so important," he continued, "if everyone who possibly can do something else does so and stops raising millet?" "The Europeans lied to us," said another, "when they told us agriculture was honorable, for who ever sees them doing it? Anybody who hoes stays at the bottom. If you want to get ahead in the world the first thing you must do is abandon agriculture."

The main response to this, upheld by only a minority of the men, was that cultivating your own field assured your survival and that of your family, and put you on an equal footing with other people; that way you would not be dependent on anyone. Most of the others present accepted this argument up to a point, but they felt that being equal didn't amount to much these days. One person said that only when you hoed your own field did you really own the crop. This meant that when you gave alms (*sadaka*) of millet or nyiiri it was truly your gift, for it was your own labor that had produced the grain. People who don't own their own millet by right (*halal*) cannot get the religious benefits (*baraaji*, blessings) from giving alms or from offering hospitality to strangers.

At this point I joined in the discussion and said that by his logic we Americans didn't own any food "by right." The man appeared then to back down from his position, for he said that we really did own our food "by right" because we worked for the money that paid for it. Another point I tried to make was that *somebody* had to raise crops because otherwise there would be nothing for people to eat. No one in the group took this seriously. They assured me that there would always be millet and that they would simply rather buy it than hoe it.

While it seems agreed, then, that a man can survive through his own work, survival is hardly living. Wealth is mysterious because in a sense it ultimately comes from God. Cattle, the major form of wealth in Jelgoji, just multiply by God's will, and it is up to God, people say, whether a given person's cattle will sicken and die or whether they will become numerous. Now, people do not have the power to make wealth grow, but *some* people have *power*. In some situations power is like wealth, while in others power enables one to obtain it. There was an old man who used to sit in the same spot day after day. He would sit in a chair under an awning set up beside a house that faced the Djibo market and was located near the crossroad of the main thoroughfares coming into town. Half a dozen or so other men were often gathered there watching people go by, playing the board game *wari* or chatting. All of them were habitués of this spot, but the most regular person there was the old man. He was a prince of the town; his father had been chief of the region, and then power passed to his father's brother, who was the grandfather of the current chief. Thus Nuhu was a kind of uncle of the latter. One day I asked him why he always came to this particular spot (which was fairly distant from his house).

He took the question to mean why did he sit all day long doing nothing, and replied that the reason was that he had no needs and he had no work. He said that he had never worked in his life; he never herded cattle, never hoed a field. He also said that he owned no wealth himself—not even one cow—so that he had no worries about his possessions. For instance, he didn't have to go wandering out in the bush looking for lost animals. "Well, how do you live, then?" I asked. "The whole country makes me live," replied Nuhu. When I asked him what he meant by that, he said that in the past all the MaccuBe of the region had belonged to his father, and therefore he could now go to each one of them and ask for and receive a bundle of millet whenever he needed it. He would either go to them and ask for it, or he could ask that it be sent to him. If he needed cash, all he had to do was pay a visit to some subordinate chief and he would receive a present of a cow, sheep, or goat. In a word, it is *laamu* (rulership) that allows him to live.

These observations were part of a much longer conversation that touched on many subjects. During it, however, I became more and more uncomfortable. I hadn't known Nuhu very well before the conversation, but because of his pleasant face and his soft voice I had formed the impression that he was a friendly, gentle person. As we talked he began to appear to me in a very different light. Not only was what he was saying anathema to my own values, but also the way he spoke, it became clear, was the way of a person who was quite unaccustomed to disagreement. In fact he said at one point in our talk that people listen to the powerful and treat what they say as truth. Here I am, I thought, a humble seeker after truth, and before me is a man who doesn't give a damn about truth, who believes that his authority suffices to determine what will be truth. So that's what it's like to be an underling. "The head-pad had a fit but the water pot didn't notice (*tekkere Berni loonde maataay*)."

I mention my reactions here because I was surprised by their violence. I have always been an anti-authoritarian person, but I think something even more profound is at stake. It is absolutely essential for my moral sense that truth be the opposite of dogma. Truth must remain beyond humanity and ever to be discovered, not to be decreed. And the reason for this is as much personal as philosophical, for I am willing to submit to truth so long as it is I who discover it for myself. That is the key; to me it is both irrational and degrading to submit to another person "merely" because he is stronger. For the Fulani, on the other hand, it is exactly in such submission that reason consists, for to try otherwise would be folly. That is why people submit to God, to their chief, to fathers, and to elder brothers.

Nuhu represented one very widespread idea of the successful man. Even if individuals hated what he did to them, they admired him for being able to do it. Several RiimaayBe of Djibo told me about about a famous slave owned by the chief of Djibo in the nineteenth century. This man had a pistol and he would go out into the bush every now and then hunting for humans. He would simply seize people on the paths at gunpoint and bring them back as presents for the chief. His captives are the ancestors of a whole quarter of the present-day town. "Now, there's a real man for you," is the implication of these stories. But another implication is that the qualities of a man like that, and powers such as he had, are useful and worth striving for today.

Many people, genuinely concerned about me I think, urged me to seek magical protection and powers. As far as I could tell, every adult had at least some protection of this kind, and some people sought a great deal of it. The most common sort was a preparation against metal. It was supposed to defend you against any metal object, such as knife, spear, or bullet. If someone tries to stab you, his knife will break. If someone tries to shoot you, either his gun won't fire, or he will miss, or the bullets will turn into water and run out the barrel of the gun. There also exist preparations to make you invisible, so that you can go anywhere and do anything without being seen. Such preparations are only the work of great Koranic scholars and are very costly (10,000 to 25,000 CFA francs or $40–$100). Before paying for magic like this you would give it a trial run, perhaps by going to the marketplace and trying to steal something without being seen.

I told Erku, a person who often talked to me about such matters, that it was hard for me to believe these things were possible, because we simply didn't have them in our country. Erku, in turn, could not believe me. "But you must have brave men among you?" he said. I said that we certainly did, but that I had never heard of them having protection of the kind he described. "But they must," said Erku; "otherwise how could they dare to do dangerous things?"

"Well," I said, "there are some people who do dangerous things expecting to die or even wishing to die."

"No," said Erku. "That's not possible. No one seeks death of his own free will; you only do that if your chief requires you to do it, or if you're in the army. It is only when you have *dabare* (magic) that you can be courageous. Bravery is not just a matter of will (*Bernde,* lit. "heart"). After all, when a man dies that's it for him, isn't it?"

Later in the year we had an almost identical conversation. Erku was trying to persuade me to solicit magical protection from a famous Koranic scholar who was visiting the town. This man could make me a magic shirt that would protect me against any attack by metal. If a crazy person were standing at the door of city hall and shooting people with a gun, and if I had that protection, I could walk right up to him and take the gun away from him; he would not be able to hit me even if he tried. I said that people in our country did not know about such things, and that for us bravery was not being afraid to die. Erku said no, that's not at all what bravery is; bravery is having magical protection. That is what allows you to do great deeds. "Because if you did something because you weren't afraid of death and then got killed, who would remember you? You would have accomplished nothing and would be considered merely stupid for having been daring with no good reason for it. It is the people who do great deeds and survive who are remembered, who get a name for themselves."

We have seen that to acquire such magical powers is very costly. All the procedures for getting them are highly secret, and those who have the secrets reveal them only on their deathbeds and to one other person, usually a favorite son. My original supposition in the field was that magical potency was somehow diminished by telling, such that the more people who knew a secret the less power would it have for any one person. Erku, however, saw the situation radically differently. For him the problem was that if everybody had some powerful secret, such as the ability to stop metal, then everybody would be equal and it would be impossible to have a fight.

"But wait," I said; "isn't peace better than fighting?"

"No," said Erku, "that is not our custom. It is not good to have everyone equal. Can a village have three chiefs? No, there can only be one. If everyone is equal, then no one can win." He went on to say that this is why people give their secrets only to one other person, and even then only on their deathbeds. For if he told the secrets while he was still in good health, the beneficiary, his son for instance, could simply take his place. Then where would he be? This is why religious scholars will never teach their most esoteric knowledge to people from their area. They will only teach it to students who come from far away. Hence students who want deep knowledge must always go far from home to get it.

Though I was greatly curious about these magical practices, and though a part of me half wanted to believe that they really could work, I never dared to pursue such knowledge with any determination. There was a bit of sheer cowardice in my attitude, for I would have been frightened to discover such a serious threat to my usual way of seeing things. Another factor holding me back was that I saw the possession of such knowledge, assuming it to have real value, as somehow unfair. It went against my whole sense of how people should relate to one another morally. Just as I resented what struck me as an "arrogance of power" in Nuhu, the prince of Djibo, so I felt that for myself I just wanted to relate to others as a plain human being. In fact, I couldn't see any good reasons why I should seek invulnerability to metal or invisibility. What would I be doing in life where I would ever need those qualities? It is very significant that Erku just couldn't believe people in my country didn't use magic, and that I just couldn't believe in magic myself. It suggests to me that there is a psychological equivalence between magic in Jelgoji and whatever it is that enables me and most middle-class Westerners to have confidence, to try daring things.

Reflecting on this now, I think the equivalent factor in my life is, as Malinowski (1948) suggested in his classic essay, science. For Malinowski, the reason why science gives us Westerners confidence is that it gives a truer picture of reality than anything else does, and it gives us more control over the world. I would argue, however, that the reasons why science inspires confidence lie deeper, and are more akin to those that give magic its force. The social world in which science is embedded is one whose regularities are by and large created by human laws such as constitutions and other codes of law. The very procedures of science, too, are established as codes that must not be infringed on pain of sanctions. What protects us in our world is thus not magic, but rather the power of society itself to maintain order, and the order in turn allows us to act with confidence because we can have reasonable assurance that our actions will get us the results we expect. In the Fulani world the very order of society is experienced as being maintained by people's wills, hence by the powers that individuals are willing to commit to that maintenance (cf. Riesman 1977: 175). As we have seen on several occasions, the only kind of order that is thinkable is hierarchy. If this analysis is correct, it makes sense, then, that to achieve a life better than one of mere survival people would seek to gain powers beyond those of the ordinary person.

But are not we in the West also always striving for powers beyond those of the ordinary person, such as greater intelligence, greater knowledge, or greater originality? What is the difference between such powers and magical ones? The difference is that the powers we seek in the West presuppose the order of society and of the natural world, and we strive to get ahead by working within those orders; the magical powers, on the other hand, are a response to the very disorder of the world, and are ways that individuals have of trying to establish at least a local order in which their acts can be effective. Thus in our world people can get the same sense of protection the Fulani seek magically by making sure that their actions are in accordance with the rules of society and, in science, with the rules of inquiry. For me to think that I was "just a plain person," then, was quite illusory. I had magical powers but was not conscious of them at the time because I didn't think of them as mine or even as created by my society. They were the powers, diffuse in the Western states and far beyond their borders in the underdeveloped world, to maintain order and command resources. For the Fulani I was acting much of the time like a person who feels guarded by the most powerful charms. No wonder Erku and many other friends of mine were incredulous when I told them I had no magical protection.

The goals and prospects of FulBe and RiimaayBe men in old age are similar in that for both groups, well-being depends on having been successful in raising children, especially sons. We have seen that FulBe men, however, try to stop doing physical labor as soon as they have sons who are old enough to do it for them. So long as they have adolescent or young adult sons working for them, they remain masters of the household no matter what their age in years. They retain control over the cattle belonging to those young men until the time when the latter have had a few children of their own and are taking on more adult responsibilities. I knew quite well three men who were between seventy and eighty years of age. All of them had a number of sons, but only one still had adolescent children. This man had a son of about eighteen and another of about fourteen during my first field trip. These boys cultivated his field and took care of the cattle owned by him and by themselves in a common herd. The other men of the same age were well taken care of by their children, but their status was different because they no longer ran independent households. They were deferred to in public, of course, and were occasionally asked for advice, but they had no important decisions to make in daily life; they were essentially under the care of their adult children.

While I knew many FulBe men over forty who did very little physical labor, I did not know any RiimaayBe who had stopped working before their physical condition had forced them to. In any case, for both FulBe and RiimaayBe men there comes a time when they cease making a valuable contribution to their families, either in work or resources. FulBe men continue to be more concerned than the RiimaayBe by issues of honor and shame, and as a result old men probably have less choice than do the RiimaayBe about whom they can pass their time with during the day. Old FulBe men pretty much have to stay with people of their own generation, while RiimaayBe men can sit and chat with family and friends of different generations in a comfortable, relaxed way.

What do the men do once they stop doing productive work? More frequently than anything else, they will be found chatting with each other at the mosque or while overseeing the youths at work drawing water or hoeing the fields. Much of this conversation resembles what you would hear men talking about in informal gatherings in this country: personal experiences, mildly dirty jokes, health problems and various remedies tried, events of the past and near future, telling of legends, tall tales, history, women, and so on. But in addition (at least among the FulBe) these men are a kind of informal law court and may act as such at any time. It is not a matter of their being legally empowered to do this by the state, but that these communities value their autonomy and thus try to settle their problems with as little interference from higher authorities as possible. Another thing that nearly all these older men do when they stop or reduce their work is to become more religious. Though I knew some men who clearly had little feeling for or interest in religion, I was often struck by the powerful desires some men had to deepen their religious knowledge and to attend properly to the word of God. Many women had such desires as well, but all but a few had to resign themselves to the impossibility of fulfilling them.

The Life Plans of FulBe and RiimaayBe Women

Among the FulBe the sexes remain apart during the daylight hours. This sexual segregation, I found, is not due to a rule that people are obeying, but rather follows from the concern to avoid shame (cf. Riesman 1977:53–56). One source of shame is to be seen in a state of need, or in the act of fulfilling a need, by a member of the opposite sex; another source of shame is the implication of dependence or sexual need when any person seeks out someone of the opposite sex. For instance, people interpret a man's hanging around his wife to mean either that he needs her or that he is jealous—which itself implies an inordinate dependence on her. These remarks hold also for the RiimaayBe, except that among them the segregation is less rigorous and the sense of shame much less acute.

Thus my own visits to women for my research did not mean bending or breaking a "rule," though of course people wondered about what I was up to. But once they felt they could trust me it became possible for me to talk with most women in the communities I studied in a sort of brother–sister relationship. Besides, the notion of Platonic friendship between a man and a woman exists, and people find it perfectly normal that men who are friends with each other could visit each other's wives without it being assumed they are having sexual relations. Which isn't to deny that sexual temptation still exists. The following story, told to me by a Diimaajo woman, illustrates the subtleties of these attitudes well.

There were once two friends who were inseparable. They were always together and they often traveled together. They lived in villages a few kilometers apart. One day one of the men planned a journey and asked his friend to accompany him. The next day the friend mounted his horse and went to the house of the other to accompany him on his trip. The mistress of the house was sitting outside the front door on a mat, spinning cotton, and while engaged in this she inadvertently disarranged her dress, revealing her thigh. The man on horseback, waiting for his friend to come out, was immediately aroused to desire for the woman. When the two friends finally set out, the first one could not forget about the woman. He told his friend that he had to go back for something he had forgotten. "You go on, and I'll catch up later," he said.

He returned along their path and arrived at his friend's house in the middle of the night. He attached his horse to his friend's horse-picket, he hung up the saddle where his friend usually hung up his. Then he came into the house and got up on the bed. But he just couldn't bring himself to touch the woman. His desire left him, and he turned his back to her and went to sleep on the edge of the bed. The wife, however, assumed all along that it was her husband who had come back. Early in the morning, the friend slipped out of the house, saddled the horse, and caught up to his friend. The two men were away together for four days.

When they returned, they found that the woman had left. She had gone home in a huff (o suutike). The husband and his friend went together to appease her (surude). When they asked her why she had run off, she replied, "Well, didn't you divorce me?"

"I divorce you?" said the husband. "Certainly not. What could I have ever done that would make you think that?"

"Well, you remember when you set out four days ago with your friend? You came back in the middle of the night and got into bed. You didn't say a word to me and you spent the whole night with your back to me without even touching me. So I thought you were divorcing me and went home to my father."

The two men broke out laughing and clapped each other's hands. For it turned out that the husband knew all about what had happened. After the two men had left the husband's hut on the morning when the friend had been seized by desire for the woman, the husband noticed that his friend seemed awfully quiet and gloomy. The poor man just couldn't take his mind off the woman. When the husband would ask him what the matter was, his friend would just mumble that it was nothing.

But something was bothering him, and the husband finally asked him, for God's sake, to tell him what was troubling him so. At length the friend told him about his desire for his wife.

"Oh, if that's all it is, why don't you go back and sleep with her," said the husband. And that is how the friend came to return in the middle of the night to sleep with his friend's wife.

Throughout their lives FulBe and RiimaayBe women work more steadily than men do. But, as we shall see in more detail below, work for women is almost always sociable. Or, to look at it another way, while work takes men away from the village and often separates them from each other, particularly by generation, work brings women together and places them at the vital center of social life. Adolescence for most girls may be the freest and most pleasant period of their lives. While they are still with their own families they are with the people who love them most and the demands placed on them are usually reasonable. That is, their help is needed, but at the same time they are free much of the time to go visiting or to participate in ceremonies and festivities that are occurring in the region. The work they have to do is at times undeniably hard, particularly the daily pounding of millet into flour. On the other hand, it is always possible for the girls to do these tasks together with their friends and/or with their mothers. Such work groups are always talking and laughing and give a visitor the impression of people having a good time. Adolescent girls, and younger ones too, will often sing while they work, and women of all ages up to forty or so will occasionally play clapping and rhythm games while pounding grain. Care of babies, often relegated to girls between about six and fifteen, is a job the latter seem to find endlessly fascinating and entertaining. Here is a brief description of the work a twelve-year-old girl was doing one day. I wrote as I did because I was so impressed by the sheer joie de vivre that flowed out from her even when she thought she was alone.

> I heard Asiyatu singing yesterday while I was out in the bush getting leaves to feed my sheep. Asiyatu was picking up *peDal* (fruit of the *BulBi*) for her goats, gathering the pods from the ground and putting them in a fold of her skirt. And she was singing. She was alone, and as far as I knew had no idea I was nearby. She was just singing to herself and she picked up the small, stringbean-like pods with a graceful, swooping motion—the same graceful motion with which she would pick up little Hamma (a baby she often cared for), lift him high above her head squealing with delight, kiss him on the navel or the genitals and then let him down again or swing him around onto her hip for carrying.

I have no idea what goes on in the heads of adolescent girls. Women over twenty (for the most part), and girls under twelve, were possible people to talk to. Adolescent girls, however, were giggly, scatterbrained, and a total loss as far as I was concerned.

One recurring event that would throw them into complete consternation was the occasional passage through the hamlet of this or that handsome young man of the region. As the man strolled or swaggered along (according to circumstances), the girls, often gathered in the hut of one of them or in our hut, would cluster breathless at the doorway, trying to peek out without being seen and jostling each other to get a better view.

What distinguishes this scene from what one might witness in an American high school as a local sports hero walked by is not so much the physical setting as the fact that all the FulBe girls are likely to be already either married or betrothed (the same would be the case for RiimaayBe girls of that age). Many boys and girls are betrothed at birth. We saw above that the expected—and the most common—first marriage for FulBe is with the child of the father's brother. Whether the girl has been betrothed since birth or not, there is a religious ceremony, described in detail below, that has to take place prior to bringing the bride to her husband's village. This ceremony can occur when the bride is as young as twelve, and most commonly when she is a few years older. As girls commonly get married between the ages of fourteen and eighteen, it is easy to see why an "unattached" adolescent girl would be quite rare. I did not inquire systematically concerning the age of first menstruation in the area; on the other hand, I met no woman, FulBe or RiimaayBe, who was younger than eighteen when she had her first child, and I estimate that the age of women when they gave birth for the first time ranged from eighteen to about twenty-three.

The meanings and implications of marriage and childbirth for women are different in important ways from what they are for men. The differences are to be found both in practical considerations and in ritual expression. In both FulBe and RiimaayBe marriage a major transition occurs for the women that does not for the men, namely the move from the family where one is native to another where one is a stranger. Thus the women are immediately subject to pressures that do not weigh on their husbands. They are the representatives of their families of origin and must therefore be on their best behavior for a considerable period of time. They must also help their mothers-in-law with heavier tasks and must work more assiduously than they would have been expected to do at home. Even when the move is to the hut next door, as it often is in cousin marriages, there is a change of attitude on the part of the older generation. I saw a good example of this when stopping by a household where some boys had recently been circumcised, a situation requiring some extra work in food preparation because of the boys' special requirements. The youngish mother of one of the boys was pounding grain together with a slightly older woman who was a sister of the boy's father. The mother was venting her anger at the behavior of a woman who was absent, the young wife of another man of the household, for she should have been helping her pound the millet but instead had gone off on some vague errand and not yet come back. "Calm down, forget it," said the older woman. "I will not forget it," said the mother. "My children have gone without food today because that good-for-nothing girl hasn't done her work." Perhaps I looked shocked at her vehemence, for she explained to me that since the girl had become one of them by marriage, it was normal for them to bawl her out and put her to work (*miDon kita o, miDon gollina o*).

The rites of marriage and of birth are the two most important non-Islamic rites of Fulani society (though they both have significant Islamic moments), and in each case women are the central actors. I have discussed both these rituals elsewhere, particularly the naming ceremony (cf. Riesman 1977: 58–63). Here I will present the marriage rites at greater length and analyze them from another point of view. In the first place, marriage rites are important because they bring about, or at least begin, the transition from girlhood to womanhood, and at the same time express the meanings of that transition for the larger society. In the second place, the wedding rites of FulBe and RiimaayBe differ in very significant ways. We can see in these rites a reflection of the status difference between noble and commoner or slave, and how this difference affects the nature of the marriage bond itself, as understood by the people concerned. Grasping this subjective understanding will be crucial for the subsequent argument of this book.

FulBe and RiimaayBe Weddings Compared

In Fulfulde it is impossible to say that a woman marries a man; a man can marry a woman, but if the woman is the subject of the sentence the verb must be in the passive voice. In English and French the words "marry" and "marriage" have the connotation of blending, of forming a harmonious unit. In French, the verb *se marier* is often used in this sense to speak of how different ingredients in a sauce go together to create a special taste all their own. There is no such idea in the Fulfulde terms. There are two verbs meaning "to marry," *hoowude* and *BaNude*. The first has the primary meaning of "to copulate" (from the man's point of view, i.e. to fuck), while the second means to bring the bride to the husband's village. These verbs have noun forms as well, which we could translate as "marriage" (in the sense of husband-wife relationship) and "wedding" (*koowgal* and *BaNgal* respectively). There is a third noun commonly used to refer to the husband–wife relationship, *dewgal*, which derives from the verb *rewude*, "to follow." The word for woman, *debbo*, derives from the same root, and both forms express a very fundamental aspect of the male–female relationship generally as understood in Fulani thought.

The wedding rites in Fulani society punctuate (in the sense of Gregory Bateson 1972:298) the process of beginning a marriage very differently from how this happens in the West. There are no ceremonies that correspond either to those we have for betrothal or the wedding itself, though Fulani ceremonies include those elements and others that are not normally part of the Western rituals. The first marriage for both the man and the woman is normally not their affair at all, but is entirely arranged by the parents, particularly the fathers, of the two young people. In some cases, as we have just seen, the children will have been promised to each other since birth, but in all cases there is a relatively long period called "asking" (*Yamgal*), when a stream of presents is sent to the girl's parents as a sign that the young man is asking for the girl. This goes on for months, and may go on for several years. When both families have agreed that it is time for the couple to get married, and when they have agreed on what the final gifts will be (these are quite different for FulBe and RiimaayBe, as we shall see, and their total value varies according to circumstances), there is a public ceremony called "the hitching" (*kaBBal*, from *haBBude*, to tie, to hitch). It is equivalent in its effect to the exchange of marriage vows in the West, for once the hitching has been performed the couple are considered husband and wife. Yet neither the man nor the woman normally participate in or are even present at the hitching. It is a ceremony that requires a representative from each family, three witnesses, and a moodibbo.

The next ritual is the one that most resembles what Westerners would call a wedding, for it is a joyous celebration that takes place at the man's village when the bride is brought. Yet it is also unlike a wedding in two ways: the couple is already officially married, and the husband is usually not there. Friends and relatives of both families come, and there is music and dancing all night—sometimes running on for two or three days and nights. This is the BaNgal ceremony. Now let us look at these rites in more detail so as to bring out the similarities and differences between the FulBe and RiimaayBe variants.

These rites are called by the same name among both groups, but occur in a different manner. There is one striking RiimaayBe rite, however, which has no counterpart among the FulBe. This rite, called *kuluujaa*, derives from the heritage of one of the tribes of origin of people enslaved by the FulBe, namely the Songhay. It is the only rite I ever saw which used a water drum, which is an overturned calabash floating on the water in a larger calabash and beaten with a stick or a small gourd. The instrument has a very deep, penetrating sound something like a large bongo drum. In addition, the word kuluujaa itself is not of Fulani origin, but is a Songhay word meaning "thanks." The ceremony it designates is one of farewell and thanks to the girl who is about to be married. Performed shortly before the wedding, it is organized by the mother and other older women in the bride's compound and is usually repeated on several nights. The bride-to-be is seized by surprise and made to lie on a mat while completely covered by a gauzy cloth. At her head and feet sit a number of older women on overturned mortars, while the drummers and singers sit on one side of her and the space at the other side is used for dancing. The girl lies completely immobile and undergoes this ceremony almost as she undergoes the wedding itself, as we shall see shortly. The younger women drum and sing songs, while the older women, apparently spontaneously and without regard to the words and music of the songs, lean out over the prostrate girl from time to time, fan her with a piece of cloth, and chant phrases like these:

> Kuluujaa to you, darling
> you are a beautiful laundress
> Kuluujaa to you, darling child
> you are a beautiful cook

> Kuluujaa to you, darling child
>> ever since you began to fetch water I never had to do it
>
> Kuluujaa to you, darling
>> you are a beautiful sweeper
>
> Kuluujaa to you, darling child
>> may God protect you . . .

The feeling this rite gives is one of sadness and joy at the same time. On the one hand the women are expressing their pride and their gratitude for the girl's help and helpfulness, but they are also indicating that she is about to go through an irrevocable change, and will never be in the same relationship to them again. The implication is that these good qualities of the girl will henceforth help to sustain another household than theirs. In addition, I was told that the girl really has to have these qualities for the ceremony to be held. The mother of an unhelpful or wayward child can refuse to have the ceremony, or if she wants to hold it anyway she will have to pay the other women to participate and they will mention in their songs that they are being paid to do it.

Since cattle are the wealth par excellence of the FulBe, while the RiimaayBe lack cattle, the ways in which the two groups use wealth at marriage differ significantly. It would be logical to assume that where the FulBe give the bride's family cattle in exchange for a woman, the RiimaayBe give goods of some other sort. In fact, things do not happen quite that way. In the case of the RiimaayBe, substantial gifts are given to the bride's family during courtship, but in the days following the BaNgal ceremony the bride's family in turn makes large gifts to the groom and his family, and they also supply the bridal bed and trousseau. These gifts are all displayed when they are brought. I suspect, but cannot actually verify it now, that the monetary value of the gifts in each direction is close to equal. In the case of the FulBe, on the other hand, the courtship payments are often not very great, especially when the two families are closely related, and the gifts in any case are not displayed during the course of the celebration of the marriage. It is an absolute necessity that cattle be transferred in order for a FulBe marriage to be legitimate. These cattle (called *koowruDi*, lit. "cattle to marry with") belong not to the bride's family but to the bride herself. They are given, however, to the bride's father and he keeps them in trust for his daughter. It is only years later, when the marriage seems to be on a sure footing, with perhaps several children born, that the bride will bring her koowruDi to be cared for along with her husband's herd. The point here is that the exchange of koowruDi for a woman is not actually a once and for all trade, whereas the gifts the RiimaayBe make to each other do seem to have this quality of permanence. Rather, the keeping of the bride's koowruDi in her family of origin is a part of the process by which relations are kept up between that family and the one she has recently joined. As we shall see below, the maintenance of these relations is also symbolized and furthered by other features of the FulBe marriage ceremonies.

The most striking difference between FulBe and RiimaayBe marriage practices, and the one that seems most puzzling at first, is the speed with which events occur. As I describe this aspect, other differences will also become apparent. With the RiimaayBe, the kaBBal takes place at night with many members of both families present. Men, usually classificatory fathers of the young people, carry out the negotiations, but the women as well as the men of the bride's family must assent to the transaction. In the particular kaBBal I witnessed the men handed over money in the place of goods, saying "Here are the four sheep, here are the twenty sheaves of millet," and so on. At this point arguments often occur as to whether enough has been paid; people are prepared for this and appease the bride's family by paying a little extra. Once everyone is satisfied, the moodibbo pronounces the couple husband and wife and all join him in asking God's blessings on the marriage.

From this point on the wedding (BaNgal) seems to be entirely a women's affair. True, one or more men are required to furnish music for the procession, but that is because men happen to be the flute players and drummers of the society. After the kaBBal has been completed, the negotiators return from the bride's compound, where the ceremony was held, to the groom's. The women there are informed of what happened and then they immediately make ready to go and fetch the bride. They get together a woven straw mat of the type used as bedding, a pair of sandals, a wraparound cloth of the kind women normally use for their skirts, and a long, narrow white cloth to wrap around the bride's head as a veil. Messengers are sent to inform female relatives that they are to come so as to help get the bride. People gather in the groom's compound, and the latter's father's sister heads the group. Women with small children have them on their backs, while many children over age seven join in the ceremony. In the BaNgal I witnessed, the kaBBal was over at about 11:00 P.M., and we set out to get the bride at midnight, stopping on the way to call upon the drummer and ask him to come. The bride's compound was in the same town, about a quarter of a mile from that of the groom.

In the bride's compound the group found many people, men and women, asleep outdoors on mats in the moonlight. It was the hottest season of the year, when most people sleep outdoors to escape the heat stored up in the mud brick houses during the broiling day. Someone announced why we had come and asked that the woman be brought so that she could be carried back. Altogether our group waited for an hour, and repeated its message several times before anything happened. Suddenly a faint sobbing sound could be heard, really more like a crying moan, at one end of the open space we were sitting in. The bride was not dressed in finery, but was wearing only a wraparound skirt and no jewelry. She stood in the doorway of a courtyard, her arm flung up across her face, and moaned. The women laid the straw mat on the ground in front of her, and placed the cloth on top of it (the cloth is about 1 yard x 2 yards); then they pushed the girl until she was standing in the middle of the cloth-covered mat, still moaning with her arm across her face. She was about fourteen or fifteen years old, but big for her age, and moved and stood as if in a stupor. Suddenly three or four of the women grabbed her and began to wrestle her to the ground. The girl came to life, and fought back kicking and screaming, but was soon overpowered. The women holding her down called for the veil, but were not able to hold her still enough to wrap it like a turban around her head. Then the woman who was to carry her on her back approached; she was the groom's cousin, daughter of the aunt who was leader of the group fetching the bride. The women holding the girl lifted her up to put her on the cousin's back, but the bride struggled and fought and partly tore the cousin's dress. Finally they succeeded in placing the bride on the woman's back, and then she held on like a baby with her arms and legs. At this point the women were able to wrap the veil around the bride's head and then drape her whole body with the cloth she had been standing on. Once the bride was settled on the woman's back she began to moan again, and kept it up for the whole trip back. Someone picked up the mat from the ground, and the procession set off.

The procession consisted of a rather tight mass of women, twenty or thirty perhaps, surrounding the bride and her bearer. The women began to sing marriage songs almost immediately, and though they never sang very loudly, they generally drowned out the crying of the bride. Soon after the singing began, the drummer who had been sent for arrived. He took a position near the head of the procession; sometimes he would face forward, other times backward, leaving a little space between him and the main body of the procession so that a few women could have a place to dance to the drumming and singing. Another ten or twenty feet ahead of the drummer, ten- to thirteen-year-old girls did their own dancing separately from the rest. The procession moved so slowly that, though it took no detours, it didn't arrive at its destination for over three hours. Several women took turns carrying the bride. Sometimes the group would halt its forward movement—not for rest, but to allow a more frenzied spurt of dancing. When they came to the mosque that lay along the route, everybody was silent as they walked past, for it was considered sacrilegious to be making secular music in this holy area.

The groom, who of course was not around at this time, had built his new house in his father's compound, right near his mother. But when the procession arrived at the compound about an hour before dawn it did not go right to that house; instead it went into a nearby uncle's courtyard. There the women unrolled the mat and sat the bride down upon it, and then covered her with the cloth. They continued to sing around her until dawn. The bride went into her new husband's house and fell asleep in the back. Two of her friends stayed with her. She was to stay there for seven days before coming out and acting like a participant in her new family.

The points I want to underline about these ceremonies are: first, once the men have completed the actual declaration and blessing of the marriage, the proceedings for fetching the bride are begun immediately. Second, not only is the long procession entirely a women's affair, but also in the course of it the bride seems to be thought of as going through a transition. Perhaps this is why the pace is so slow, because she is thought to have to work through her grief at the abrupt abandonment of her family and her girlish life-style. People told me that the crying was obligatory on the part of the bride; they jokingly—or so I thought—said that if a girl did not cry while she was being carried they would hit her and make her cry. And the mode of carrying, and the word for it, are those used of mothers carrying babies. This word, *bambude,* also means in a figurative sense to support someone, be the person's mainstay. The marriage songs express great joy at the marriage. They describe the pride each family has in having many relatives and much wealth, they describe the good fortune of both the man and the woman in obtaining the one they love, and they describe the qualities of each in glowing terms. The songs do not express sorrow at leaving the family of origin and the pleasures of youth, though one of them does take note of the bride's crying. Here are a few brief samples; the songs consist of a few formulas each, to which the singers add stock names for girls and boys and thus go on singing almost indefinitely.

(1)

Now Beauty is making her way
Now Jackie is making her way
Jackie the wealthy is making her way
Jackie child of the compound is making her way
Jackie child of strength is making her way
Jackie child of force is making her way
Great Jackie the wealthy is making her way
Tomorrow the blankets will be spread on the ground
Tomorrow the tapestries will be hung on the walls
Jackie child of the compound is making her way
Jackie the famous is making her way
Jackie cried but didn't run away and is making her way
Jackie cried but is blissful and is making her way
Jackie cried but hid not and is making her way

(2)

The sharp axe has been sharpened again; the head gets the praise
The sharp knife has been sharpened again; the family's child gets the praise
The axe sure is sharp; the family's child gets the praise
Hey son, hey son, son shining with gold, my son has succeeded

Hey son, hey son, son shining with silver, hey my lucky son
Oh lucky son, son shining with gold, my son has been blessed
Hey daughter, hey daughter, daughter shining with gold, my daughter has
     succeeded
Oh, lucky first girl of the compound, daughter of the wealthy compound, she
     has been crowned with success

(3)

Joy had sent for me to come, Honey had sent for me to come
     So tonight it is that Beauty will be married to her lover
Joy had sent for me to come, Honey had sent for me to come
     So when night has come Beauty will be united with her lover
Joy had sent for me to come, Honey had sent for me to come
     So tonight it is that First Daughter will be united with her lover
Joy had sent for me to come, Honey had sent for me to come
     So tonight it is that First Son will be united with his lover

The FulBe marriage ceremonies have the same names as those of the RiimaayBe, but they are different both in their specific components and in the rhythm with which they occur. Though in both cases after the kaBBal the couple are considered man and wife, among the FulBe several months and sometimes up to several years will go by before the next ceremony, the BaNgal (fetching the bride), occurs. At a FulBe kaBBal, unlike that of the RiimaayBe, only a few people show up, and the gifts presented at that time seem to be just tokens. They are called "mother's supper," as is the case with the RiimaayBe, but they consist normally of a single outfit of clothing for the bride herself: one or two wraparound cloths, sandals, and perhaps a kerchief or a blouse. Among the FulBe, the bride is fetched not by the groom's female relatives, but by his male ones. During the day and early evening the women of the village are preparing an enormous meal, while the men go off to get the bride. But she, with the help of her girlfriends, goes into hiding, and the men have to look all over for her before they find her. Once they do, they bring her back rapidly, usually on horseback, or nowadays sometimes by bicycle or automobile. While in the RiimaayBe wedding procession the arrival at the groom's house is at dawn, the FulBe bring the bride, without music or fanfare, at nightfall or soon thereafter, accompanied by many of her girlfriends. Another difference from the RiimaayBe wedding is that no house will have been built for her by the time she arrives. Among the FulBe, as we have seen, it is the women who build and own houses anyway, and a new bride will live in her husband's village for several months to a year before her mother-in-law will construct a separate house for her. So when the bride arrives she is taken to the hut of her mother-in-law or the person acting as such for the occasion. Before she enters the hut, which has been temporarily vacated, she passes between two rows of village women. They have filled their mouths with milk and blow milk onto her as she goes by. Then she and her girlfriends go into the hut and the door is shut behind them. Outside stand the women of the village singing a song of welcome, the same one that the RiimaayBe sing when the bride has reached her husband's compound.

In the meantime, the young men have gone off to a convenient spot at some distance from the village, anywhere from a quarter-mile to a mile away, and have begun to make music. Gradually the girls of the village as well as those who accompanied the bride drift into the party, and the music goes on all night long. Once the women of the village have stopped singing the welcoming song and gone off, not only do the bride's friends go to the party, but the bride pulls apart the straw at the back of the hut and runs away home again. The husband has made himself scarce throughout the whole proceeding and shows up at dawn, if then, as if nothing had happened. Once or twice more the bride will have to be sought after at her family's village before she will stay in that of her husband, but these comings and goings are not occasions for further ceremonies or festivities.

These accounts of the rituals offer considerable food for thought. We can see that in the marriage ceremonies of both groups the bringing of the bride to the husband's village is a rite of transition for the girl. In the case of the RiimaayBe she symbolically becomes an infant, to be cared for now not by her own family but by that of her husband, whose women carry her on their backs until dawn. Once she is in their power, however, all she can do is cry, and her cries are drowned out by the songs of joy which seem to override the bride's feelings and insist on the positive meanings of the transition she is going through. For the Pullo bride, on the other hand, the transition to womanhood seems incomplete at the conclusion of the wedding. FulBe could not tell me what the meaning of blowing milk onto the girl was, but I think it must be a kind of blessing, an expression of people's hopes for a rich life and many children for the bride. But the fact that the bride escapes and goes back home suggests that the transition for her is not a once and for all event, as it seems to be in the RiimaayBe ritual. When the groom's friends and relatives go to get her on subsequent occasions, she has to be coaxed to come, and incertitude as to whether or not she will stay persists for a long time, as is symbolized by the delay in building her house. Finally, at some time after the house is built by the women of the groom's village, the nuptial bed is built by the women of the bride's family. Thus it could be said that for the Pullo bride, though her journey to her new husband's village is rapid, the transition from girl to married woman is coaxed and drawn out, rather than forced and abrupt. Rather than being a handing over of the girl from the control of one family to that of another, the very rituals require considerable coming and going between the two families involved. These observations suggest that the marriage both symbolizes and maintains a tie between these two families, while the woman who embodies this tie is conceived of as being under the full control of neither. Thus her coming and going between her husband's village and her own express two meanings at the same time: the existence of the link between the families that she joins, and the fact of her own freedom and integrity.

The FulBe's own explanation of this slowness with which the marriage bond is established is a little different from the one I have just given, but is not incompatible with it. FulBe and RiimaayBe alike are quite aware of these differences in their ceremonies and comment on them frequently, just as they comment on other differences between the two groups. For the FulBe, the fact that they don't fetch the bride right away after the kaBBal, the fact that they don't have a house for the newly married couple when the bride arrives, and the fact that the husband generally avoids his bride for a long time after she does arrive—until well after her hut has been built is common—are all indications of respect, proof of the respect that the man has for his wife. In RiimaayBe customs there is nothing like this. In theory, the man should consummate his marriage the night following the dawn that his wife was brought. In practice, many FulBe men do not wait the months or years between the kaBBal and the building of their wives' huts before they sleep with their wives. If they do sleep with them, though, they do so surreptitiously and are considered to be "stealing" their wives (for a different analysis of these points, see Riesman 1977: 109–15).

The notion of respect, and the concomitant ideas of honor and shame, dignity and embarrassment, are central to the FulBe sense of identity. Both FulBe and RiimaayBe insist that having a powerful sense of shame is one of the most important of the traits that distinguish them from each other. While we have seen that certain aspects of the FulBe wedding ceremonies can be understood as expressing a high sense of shame and self-respect, it would be fruitless to look for the exact opposite among the RiimaayBe. Their weddings cannot be said to express shamelessness and degradation. There is another way, however, in which the ceremonies of the two groups could be said to express contrasting sentiments. While the RiimaayBe manifest much concern with, and pride in, wealth, opulence, and splendor, the FulBe emphasis on respect and shame is tantamount to pride in one's family and that family's place in society. The very gradual development of the marital bond brings out this connection. The man holds back from consummating his marriage both because to give in to sexual passion, or to anything else, betrays a weakness that would be a shame for the family he represents, and because his wife is by no means his chattel, but, like him, is representing a family.

But don't RiimaayBe spouses represent their families too? Certainly they do, and young wives will go home from time to time to visit their parents, brothers, and sisters. What is significant is that the family is not the source of pride that it is for the FulBe. Rather, it is their work, their products, and their possessions in which RiimaayBe take pride. The reason for this is that slaves do not have lineages, and the descendants of slaves have not been free long enough to create a lineage ideology. Not only that, but the FulBe are still the rulers of the region, though with far less power than they formerly had. It is the fact that they are rulers that is the ultimate source both of the importance of family and of pride in family for the FulBe.

The point is not so much that the FulBe are ruling others as that there are no others ruling them. FulBe political organization is based on lineages, on the principles of patrilineal descent and seniority both in generation and age. This means that all relations between relatives are political. These relations *are* the very political structure of the society. What this means in practical terms is that a person's land rights, water rights, pasture rights, ownership of cattle, and protection from theft and oppression all depend on the effectiveness of the lineage he or she is born into, and this effectiveness in turn depends on the number of members the lineage has and the ability those people have to maintain proper relations with one another. Now, both of these factors are directly affected by marriage. The fertility of the women married into a lineage is an important factor in determining the number of members it has. In addition, however, we have just seen how a marriage symbolically and actually creates and maintains relations between the families represented by the boy and the girl. We can now see why this is so, for the families thus linked are political forces in the society, and marriages are a part of the political process. The importance of FulBe lineages is easier to understand in the light of the contrast with RiimaayBe marriages, for in the latter case there is no symbolic expression of the woman's role as link or mediator between families. Rather, an emphasis is placed on her transition from girlhood to adulthood, and on the transfer of her services from her family of origin to that of her husband. The reason why the linking of the families is barely expressed symbolically is that RiimaayBe families are not political forces and play no part in the maintenance of political structure. This is so because under slavery each person's political allegiance was to his or her master, while today no new political system has yet evolved to replace the old, which has not entirely crumbled.

The Adult Life of Women

In the next two chapters I will be describing in detail the work of mothers as they take care of children; hence I will focus here on other aspects of women's lives. The bulk of the work done by FulBe and RiimaayBe women is the same, namely child care and cooking. In addition, relations with husbands and lovers are very similar, as are those with co-wives. There is some difference, as we have seen, in the particular crafts practiced by women of the two groups, but the most important differences lie, I believe, not in what the women are doing, but in their sense of themselves as they go through life.

In the sections describing the life plans of men I focused a lot on their possibilities of choice, and on their quest for success of various kinds. It is very significant that the same focus does not make sense when talking about women's life plans in Fulani society. As it is the man's responsibility to feed and clothe the women who are his dependents—and that is how they are thought of—women do not perceive the work they do in the family as creating dependency or obligation in its turn. At best, perhaps, it is a discharge of their obligation to their fathers and husbands whom they see as protecting and feeding them. This would explain why women resent it extremely if the protection and food are deficient. And yet women, too, build up a kind of dependency in their children. This is symbolized by the notion of milk. As we shall see in detail in the next chapter, the quality of the mother–child relationship in nursing carries over into subsequent stages with the other foods the mother gives her children. But the bond that these gifts establish is a bond of oneness, of love, and compassion; these are all connotations of the word enDam, (kinship), which derives from the word for "breast" (endu) and whose basic meaning is "mother's milk." Thus while it is undeniable that care of children and preparing food take great effort, the gift of that work has a very different effect on the receiver from the gift of the basic foodstuff itself—and this is so whether the giver of the food had to work hard or had to do no work himself to procure it. Looking at this situation another way, we can see that the very food that a man supplies to his wife and children cannot get to them except through the work that the woman does in giving her milk to infants and in preparing other food for the whole family. This point emphasizes once again the way in which women are socially perceived as the true channels through which relationship is created and maintained, and this fact profoundly affects how women perceive themselves as well.

For women, success is not something sought in the world, but rather is closely tied to their own being. The main elements of success for them are getting and staying married to a successful man, and having many children; both of these kinds of success depend on the woman's own qualities, such as her beauty and her fertility. It is interesting that we would call these "endowments," while the

Fulani would call them God's gifts—which amounts to the same thing. But just as men can seek wealth by means of magic, women too can use magic to enhance their charms, to protect themselves against the spells of others, to get rid of rivals, and to ensure the survival of their children. As in our own society, both men and women vary greatly in their levels of ambition and their desire for power. I was personally impressed by the philosophical resignation of many women, and this attitude is in fact one of the ideals of womanhood; I say *one* of the ideals because people also admire a tough, assertive woman who thinks a lot of herself, so long as she is worth her self-esteem and so long as she doesn't outrageously infringe rules of propriety. Here are some examples of both types.

One of my best FulBe women friends, Raynata, was an extraordinary person in my eyes. She exuded an inner strength and serenity that are rare anywhere. She was a wife of one of my best male friends and had four children whose ages ranged from early adolescence down to about five. She had a delightful, ironic sense of humor and seemed to float through life like a bark on the waves, rather than striving and struggling to fulfill ambitions. I kept her company sometimes during a serious illness she suffered and had long, fascinating conversations with her on those occasions. Once, after telling me about some events that had happened a decade previously, she said that at that same time her husband had met a beautiful *Jaljallo* (a FulBe clan) woman in Mali and wanted to marry her. The Jaljallo said she would not marry him, however, unless he divorced his present wife. "Good for you, then," I said, meaning that since she was still married to him her husband had chosen her over the other woman. But in Fulfulde my sentence was phonetically very close to "Good for him," which is what Raynata took me to have said.

"What do you mean, good for him?" she asked. "Bad for him, since he didn't get the beautiful woman."

"But good for you, since you didn't get divorced," I said.

Raynata said that divorce wouldn't have been so bad; she would just have gone back to her family. She added that in any case she would have had no say in the matter. Now, I think Raynata loved her husband very much, and admired him too, for the same reasons I did: his fine character, his decency, his liveliness. The attitude she expressed here included resignation, but it was more

1   RiimaayBe girls and boys, age one to twelve years, and a young woman posing for Paul in the courtyard in Djibo. Courtyards are walled in by mud brick walls. Cows are allowed to come in to be milked in the early morning and at night.

2   Community dignitary and leader of Djibo with his
daughter (left) and his two sons. His house is decorated with a
cloth woven by a local caste of weavers. The cloth is used as
a blanket by people who live in the rural parts of the country
and often as decoration by people who live in towns and
cities. As men grow older and have older sons and nephews,
they can pass on their work and feel freer to spend more time
with their young children.

3   RiimaayBe girls of Djibo making clay figures with a
little boy standing in the background. Ewes nurse their lambs
in the courtyard. The children sit on a small platform with a
woven mat on top providing shade from the sun. The girls all
wear pierced earrings and blouses or dresses.

4 (*overleaf*)   FulBe woman bathing her child, with her
husband at the door of their hut made of sticks and grasses
in Petaga, a small village in the bush. An old wooden bowl
contains plain water and an old calabash contains homemade
soap.

5   RiimaayBe mother giving her child *basi*, an herbal
drink. The herbal drink and this way of holding children are
used by both RiimaayBe and FulBe women.

6   In a Djibo courtyard, a young girl sifts flour while older women are standing up and holding a baby.

7 (*overleaf*)   A group of RiimaayBe women and children are getting ready to pound millet for the evening meal in a Djibo courtyard. Town people usually wear more clothes than country people.

8   RiimaayBe children and young women on a patio cutting up okra in Djibo. Okra is a delicacy added to sauces by town and city women, and sometimes by country women if they have enough money to buy it.

9   Paul Riesman with his children, Amanda and Ben, and a visitor, making afternoon tea Arabic style in the courtyard of the home they were given by the chief of Djibo.

10 (*overleaf*)   A RiimaayBe man carves a post for a patio platform with an axe. Most people in both town and countryside do not wear shoes. Work is often done outdoors with both children and adults milling around.

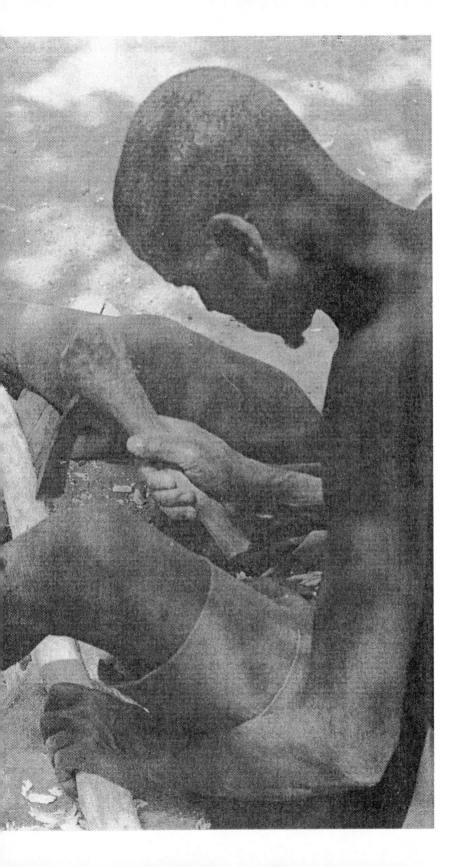

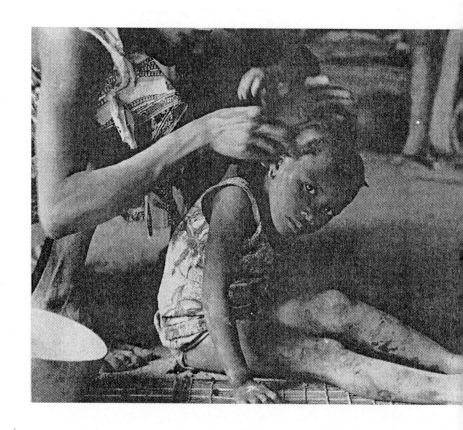

11   A RiimaayBe mother braids her daughter's hair in
Djibo. Houses and courtyards with dirt floors and bare
ground, exposed to the winds in the shrub brush region of
West Africa, make it hard to keep children clean. Thus, the
little girl's legs and arms appear dirty after a morning of play
and helping her mother.

12 A mother bathes her child in Fetagoba, a small RiimaayBe village in the countryside.

13   RiimaayBe girl of about seven carries her sister. Older sisters and brothers are taught how to care for their younger siblings and are given responsibility for them at a young age.

positive than that. I think it was a definite avoidance of trying to influence her husband unduly, and thus manifested both self-respect and respect for him. On the one hand, if her husband were the kind of person who could be influenced by wheedling, threats, or even magic, then he would not be the strong personality he seems to be; on the other, if Raynata were the kind of person who stooped to surreptitious methods, then she would not be worthy of him.

Numerous women at one time or another expressed their sense of power to me by saying that at any time they could leave their present marriage and get married to other men they wanted. Still others obviously enjoyed having other kinds of influence over people, or at least the reputation of having influence. As an example of this I will briefly describe the "fight" that my friend Kajjata, a Diimaajo woman, had with her relatives. I am sure that there is a lot more to this story than I was able to learn myself, but it is worth telling in its incomplete state both to give a sense for the kind of information I have, and to indicate the feelings Kajjata has about the situation. My account is based primarily on Kajjata's version of the facts, together with an encounter that I witnessed at the chief's court.

Kajjata's daughter Hawwa, aged fourteen, had been married during the previous twelve months to a cross-cousin of Kajjata's, the son of her father's sister, who lived in a village about thirty kilometers distant. The first sign that something was amiss occurred soon after, for Hawwa was sent back to her mother. At first the excuse was that the in-laws felt she would want to celebrate the end of Ramadan, which was approaching, back home with her mother. Kajjata found this odd, because her daughter's home was now with her husband, and it is appropriate to pray on this day at home, not on a visit to relatives. The next excuse was that Kajjata was very pregnant and close to giving birth, so Hawwa's in-laws felt that she should go home and see how her mother was getting on. Kajjata was not impressed by that reason either, since she had plenty of help and felt quite proud of her ability to manage, but she let matters rest. After the festival closing Ramadan (called *juul-daandu*), Kajjata sent her daughter, accompanied by her friend Binta, back to her husband. She told Hawwa not to come back again, but to be sure and stay with her husband. She also told her not to send Binta back right away, but have her stay as long as she liked to help Hawwa get started in her new household. But Binta came back only a few days later and the people who brought her back said that she had gotten tired of being away—it wasn't that they were sending her back. But then a few days after that, Hawwa herself came back, bringing most of her things, including a chicken that she had taken there on her previous trip. Kajjata was astonished, for coming back with all one's things is what happens when you are divorced.

According to Hawwa, it had been her mother-in-law (Kajjata's father's sister) who had told her to return. She had given Hawwa no explanation, but just told her to get ready to go to Djibo. Hawwa said that she merely did what she was told, since it is not good manners to disobey one's mother-in-law. Her clothes, her cooking utensils, her chicken, and some millet were all gotten together for her trip, and she was told to set out.

The same day that Hawwa came back to her mother, an older brother of Alu, Hawwa's husband, arrived at Kajjata's house on his bicycle. He left his bike outside and came in and sat down on the bare floor. "What's this?" exclaimed Kajjata. "Sit on a mat, not on the floor, and bring your bike inside; don't leave it out where someone might take it." The young man obeyed, but was very hesitant and roundabout in delivering his message. What he tried to say was that all the people in his family had gone mad; they felt that Kajjata had made them insane, and now they were coming to her to get help in finding a remedy for their condition. Kajjata then went with the young man to a Koranic scholar who prepared a spell for the family. He wrote it in ink on a wooden writing tablet, washed off the ink and bottled the water for the family to drink. This apparently helped the afflicted people. But Kajjata was still incensed that her relatives had accused her of "working" them and that they had sent back her daughter.

So, Hawwa spent several months with her mother and nothing seemed to be happening as far as her husband and in-laws were concerned. They neither said they were divorcing her nor did they come to get her and bring her back to her husband. Kajjata finally decided to ask the chief to summon Alu to court to find out what he wanted to do.

Present for the confrontation at the chief's palace were Alu, the chief, several councillors, myself, and Kajjata. Alu was a frail young man, perhaps twenty years old. He was dressed in a local-style white tunic, but underneath he wore tight pants with a small, plaid pattern. Wrapped around his neck was a red and white checkered woolen scarf such as might be seen at an Ivy League football game. His eyes were covered by dark glasses, and on his head he wore a cowboy hat with the brim rolled inward at the sides, and a leather thong under his chin.

After Kajjata had presented her story, in more detail of course than in my recounting, the chief turned to Alu, who seemed very ill at ease, almost cringing in his demeanor. He spoke in hardly more than a whisper, and his answers were extremely vague. When asked why he had sent Hawwa back, he said that he hadn't sent her back; she had returned of her own free will so as to be with her mother who was about to give birth to another baby. It was true that Kajjata gave birth to a child shortly after Hawwa had returned. But if that was why she came back, why, people asked, hadn't Alu's people come to retrieve her later on, when it was high time that she rejoin her husband? Besides, Hawwa had not ever mentioned the birth of the baby as the reason why she came to her mother. And finally, why bring the chicken, of all things? Alu replied to this that many chickens in his village were sick with a common ailment that kills off chickens. Kajjata then said that the chicken was theirs, not hers, and that it should die in their village, if that was to be its fate. It certainly should not have been brought back to Djibo. And if it was true that Hawwa had returned to her mother of her own free choice, Alu had no answer to the question of why he hadn't come to fetch her back to her new home. All he could say was, "No reason . . ."

"Well," said the chief to Alu, "what do you say now? Are you going to 'soothe' your wife to come back, or what?"

"I will 'soothe' her," said Alu in a dead voice.

The noon gong sounded in the distance at the offices of the state administration, and the chief said he was going to have lunch. He told Alu that it was now up to him to talk to Kajjata and Hawwa to 'soothe' Hawwa to come back, and with that the session ended.

As I was returning to my own house I ran into Kajjata who

also was heading home. It was unclear to me what the upshot of the audience with the chief really amounted to, so I asked her, "Who won?"

"Didn't you see that Alu had nothing to say?" Kajjata asked me, in turn.

"Well, are you going to accept his 'soothing'?" I asked.

"Never!" said Kajjata.

"Oh, so the case is not over yet."

"It's not even near that. It's going to go on a long, long time."

Fascinating as this material is, what was really going on in this case remains a mystery to me. But Kajjata seemed jubilant. She enjoyed every minute of this situation, and she reveled in the idea that people saw her as having driven her relatives mad even while protesting that it was not true. She clearly loved being known as the kind of person you don't mess around with.

Childlessness for women, as in the case of men, is generally thought of as the worst thing that can happen to one. Yet at any given moment other things can be worse, and there are often mitigating circumstances. I knew many more childless women during my first field trip than during my second, perhaps because I was studying community life in a holistic manner and therefore did not select specific people to whom I would pay attention. In my second study my focus was on the early years of childhood, and so nearly all the women I got to know well were mothers of small children. Having just looked at several successful women, let us now consider a few unsuccessful ones, as evaluated in Fulani terms.

Kajjilde disturbed me. Most of the time that I knew her she got on my nerves, because she was often whining and asking for things, and thereby seemed to contravene FulBe ideals as I understood them. Most other people didn't like her either, I think, but looking back on the situation now, I suspect that my irritation was partly due to my sensing, without fully being aware of it, that she was a casualty of the FulBe way of life. Here is a description, abbreviated and somewhat revised, that I wrote in the field as a way of trying to understand her better through empathy.

> Kajjilde sits in the dust on the fringe of the market. Only the locals would realize, because they don't know her, that she is a stranger, for nothing distinguishes her from the other women selling their millet, couscous, or dumplings nearby. She is perhaps a little more shabbily dressed than most,

but that is to be expected in an old woman. Who is going to buy an old woman clothes, when there are so many beautiful young women around? But Kajjilde is not yet an old woman; she just looks that way because she is miserable and half-dead with fatigue and the heat.

All her clothes have worn out; they are in such bad shape that she doesn't dare go anywhere in them. She was too ashamed of her poverty to show up for the smallpox vaccination, for all the other women were wearing their finery to it; she is here at the market, thirty kilometers from home, only because she has been able to borrow someone else's old clothes for the trip. Even now she doesn't really want to be seen, and she huddles under her tattered red shawl as if it were cold. In fact, she is a robust, good-looking woman in FulBe eyes. Her body is large, her face is broad, almost square in shape, and her big breasts don't sag very much yet. Her flesh is still fairly firm, and her skin is smooth and of pale brown, almost tawny, color—a shade that people highly appreciate here. Yet when she speaks the whine in her voice tells you instantly that she has a sad story to tell, if anyone would listen. Perhaps two days out of three she has a headache. Two days ago, while walking from home to the market here, her headache got so bad that she had to stop for nearly twenty-four hours in a village on the way, where she slept until she felt better. She is ashamed to ask for aspirin, yet her sense of shame is not strong enough to prevent her from asking anyway. Perhaps that is what the whine means; it is a combination of shame and pain. Proper FulBe don't reveal their pain. She feels degraded.

If only she had children. . . . After seven years of childless marriage she got divorced; she lives now with her widowed mother and her sister and the latter's daughter. She would so like to have someone she could depend on, but she has no husband now and no male relatives, so her whole household depends essentially on the charity of the village chief and others who help out from time to time. Young men of the village come to "play" with her at night sometimes, but they mock her behind her back.

She has brought home-made soap to the market so as to try to get money for a new wraparound. This will give her something to wear so that she can return to the market later on with her beautiful woven mats to sell. For two whole days she has sat in the market, her calabash of soap before her, waiting for buyers. She has not yet sold half the soap she came with. She has over a hundred small balls of soap that she shaped herself, each one selling for a five-franc piece. If she sells them all she will be able to get the cloth she wants, but it seems that people are complaining that her soap-balls are too small. Maybe she has the patience to hold out, but what is likely to happen is that some sharp person who knows the score will buy them from her for a low lump sum and then retail them himself. The sun beats down on the noise of the market, and wind whirling with dust spreads a film of dirt everywhere in its wake. In her hopes for just a little extra has she tried to make her soap go a little farther than she should have?

In calling Kajjilde a casualty of the FulBe way of life I mean that she exemplifies—and suffers—the perhaps necessary negative side of the high value placed on having children and of the patriarchal ideal of men providing the food for their families. As we have seen, the crucial role women play in FulBe social structure is that of a link between two families, but the link is only forged, as it were, when the bride becomes a mother of children. Only then can she acquire a solid identity as an adult. Thus women without children inevitably feel like incomplete people at best, and at worst may have little or no security and no sense of truly belonging in a community. Kajjilde was additionally unfortunate in her marriage because her husband's children by another marriage and her co-wife were all rather thorny people. Had she had children in that marriage she could have held her own against their teasing and their troublesomeness. As it was, she left the marriage by her own choice because she couldn't take the situation any longer.

Lobbel is a luckier person. She has given birth to children—whereas Kajjilde never did—but they died before living a year. After that she was married to another man, her present husband, and has had no children by him. In her case, several factors mitigate the unhappiness of her childlessness. First, in her youth she was one of the great beauties of the area, and she is still a beautiful woman with radiant smile and loving disposition. Second, she gets along well with her co-wife, who has four children, and the children all seem to treat Lobbel with much respect and like a second mother. Third, her husband is a local village chief, highly respected in the area, and while he probably loves Lobbel more, he is very correct in treating his two wives in an egalitarian manner. Fourth, Lobbel has several close male relatives in the area, in contrast to Kajjilde who has none, and she and they often help one another in various ways; this engages her more actively in ongoing family life than is the case with Kajjilde.

Finally, Lobbel's husband has given her a child to take care of, a daughter of his deceased sister. While adoption of the type we practice in the West is unknown in this society, it is very common for children to be kept for various lengths of time by people other than their parents. Both FulBe and RiimaayBe commonly let old women and childless women, or even women who need temporary assistance, such as new mothers, keep girl children for periods ranging from months to years, often until the girls get married. Boy children, however, are almost never sent to other households in similar arrangements. The one significant exception to this is the situation, which we have already discussed, of boys pursuing religious studies away from home. This difference between treatment of boys and girls (and men and women) makes perfect sense in the light of Fulani values and social structure. The purpose of the arrangement in the first place is to help the woman in her need both for companionship and assistance in household tasks. But while mature women spend most of their day with other women of all ages and with children, mature men are usually only with other mature men, and a boy who was sent to a mature man would actually spend all his time only with other boys his age. Even a mature man with children of his own could not spend much time with them without its being considered a shame for him. In addition, girls are useful to older women from about the age of six until adolescence; boys, on the other hand, cannot begin to do many useful sex-appropriate tasks until about age twelve or thirteen, at which age they start to get rambunctious and probably would not hoe another person's field or take care of his cattle unless there were something in it for him—which is the case when the field and cattle are in part his own, or when he is receiving instruction from a religious scholar. It may also be significant that I knew of only one case where a boy (other than an orphan) was given to another man to take care of; this occurred among the RiimaayBe, where there is no issue of maintaining family lines and herds of cattle.

The third person whose situation I would like to describe is also childless, but it is too early to say whether she will remain so, since she has only been married about a year to her present husband, and has had a miscarriage during the year. Ummu's case exemplifies the misery of being an unloved wife. It also exemplifies, however, that in human relations the better you know the people the less you may understand about what they are doing or why they are acting as they are. Her husband, Hammadum, had been married for several years to Hawwa, one of the most beautiful women in the region. He was so desperately in love with her that he was bringing shame on his family by constantly following her around. Hawwa was quite conscious of her beauty and her power, and often went home or on visits, perhaps just to torment Hammadum. He would follow her tracks or go to where he thought she was, and lie in wait, to satisfy himself that she wasn't meeting another man. But whether she was actually meeting another man or not, she had many admirers who tried to meet her. Hammadum sometimes came to blows with these other men. I think that Hawwa got sick of being watched all the time by her husband, and she went home for a long visit. It was unclear whether she would ever come back.

It was at this point that Hammadum married Ummu. Ummu is a beautiful woman too, but she has a frail, wispy quality, not the glowing, warm beauty of Hawwa, who is nicknamed "shining metal." Ummu had been married previously to an older man she had not liked. She kept running away from him and had just recently obtained her divorce from him. Many people sought her hand, but her family, and perhaps she herself, wanted this marriage because they wanted to ally themselves with Hammadum's family.

Right from the start things went badly. Hammadum did not stop hanging around Hawwa, wherever she was. In addition, for reasons that are not clear to me, Ummu never got along with other members of the family. For one thing, this family had grudges and prejudices against Ummu's family; some, for instance, disliked her brother and believed he was a witch. In addition, people found her voice to have a grating, whining sound, and they didn't like the fact that she was always complaining about her husband—even if they were mad at him themselves for his shameless behavior. For months the relationship within this triangle was the talk of the village. Hawwa eventually came back to Hammadum, and so the loved wife and the one married on the rebound were living side by side. But Hawwa kept going off home or on visits, and Hammadum would often follow after, which drove poor Ummu to despair. She too went home. She complained that her husband hardly ever spent the night with her, because when it was her turn he would often be off spying on Hawwa.

It may have been at a time when Ummu's sense of isolation from both her husband and the whole community she was living in was at its greatest, that a horrible djinn appeared to her and drove her mad for a brief time. People came to her aid and calmed her, eventually bringing her back to her senses. For a considerable time after that she always had someone with her when she went into the bush to relieve herself, or even when she went outside at night to urinate. Her brother gave her a charm to recite whenever she sensed the djinn trying to get to her, and it was effective. She said that the last time she sensed the djinn's presence was when it told her the charm was killing off all his relatives, and that he would stop bothering her if she would stop reciting the charm.

What is unclear in my account, and in my actual knowledge of the situation, is the role Ummu's own character and actions have played in creating her plight. From Hammadum's own point of view, and from that of other members of his family, it is Ummu's own behavior that is setting his family and hers at loggerheads. In any case it is impossible to say in any objective way what the "best" strategy for Ummu should have been or should be now, for this depends greatly on whether she will have any children with Hammadum, and on whether she could have children with another man if she left Hammadum. There is no way she can know this. In this respect her predicament is the same as that of any young married woman who has not yet had any children survive. They all must act in great uncertainty. Should she stand up for her rights? Should she try to ride out this difficult time in silence, in hopes of ultimate vindication when she has a child? Should she leave the marriage and try for a better one? But how can you know in advance what a "better" marriage would be? Her brother, in talking over Ummu's plight with another sister, said with a sigh, "Ummu just wasn't fated to have a good marriage."

Old Age and Irony

Traditionally, I have been told, the stages of a woman's life are signaled by changes in hairstyle, but the only significant change I saw while I was with the Fulani was the one that occurred at menopause. By this change in hairstyle a woman indicates to everyone else that she now considers herself old, but what this means for the individual varies considerably from person to person. Old people are normally treated with a good deal of respect and deference in Fulani society. Early in my first field trip, however, I accidentally included an old woman in the background of a photograph I took of a small girl, and the young men found it extremely funny that this old hag should be in a photograph at all, a photograph that would be taken all the way back to my country and be looked at by people there. This incident was my first experience of quite another view of aging and old age. The view of old people as ridiculous or laughable is held not only by the young men, but by members of all age groups, including the aged themselves. Middle-aged and elderly women repeatedly insisted that they were ugly or unattractive, and would get upset if I tried to photograph them; they would indicate the youths of the community and tell me that they were the ones of whom I should take photographs to show my people.

I think that Fulani women get their sense of being valuable as people from basically two things: being beautiful and being useful. Both men and women are quite concerned about their physical appearance, but, as in our own society, the canons of beauty for women seem more narrowly defined than those for men, and a woman's looks often have a far greater effect on her life than a man's looks do on his. The reason is that in her youth a woman's security and happiness depend largely on her being pleasing to men; men, on the other hand, would deny (officially) that it was important to be physically attractive to women, and they would be right. Far more important are the esteem of their peers and their ability to support themselves and their dependents. Women don't have this latter responsibility because they don't really have dependents. But though most women have at least some beauty for a while, beauty does fade. People talk about this in quite a matter-of-fact way. One morning a friend about my age and I met a woman whom we greeted and with whom I shook hands. My comrade, however, refused to take her hand and jokingly called her "trash" (bonDo, literally "bad," "spoiled"). She laughed and said that he was "trash," and we continued on our separate ways. When we were out of earshot I asked him what the meaning of this little incident was. He told me that he used to screw her (a fairly vulgar word) but that he didn't any more because she was old. I myself found her an attractive woman; she was thirty-five years old. Later that day I spoke with her about something else, and she mentioned to me that her husband had dropped her. Husbands don't leave their wives, so what this means is that he had stopped spending the night with her when it was her turn. The woman's explanation for this was simply that she was getting old and he didn't like her any more.

Being useful is for most women the major source of being valuable, and it is chiefly by doing women's work that women make themselves useful to their husbands and children. Although having a pleasant disposition or being able to cure certain ailments are also useful in their way, they are not sufficient to keep a household going. The concept of usefulness implies subordination: a dominant person is not usually thought of as useful but as the one to whom others wish to be useful. The Fulani frequently use the word "useful" in conversation, and the expression "to be useless" is often applied to lazy people and old people, particularly, but not exclusively, women. The old lady whose photograph I had accidentally taken during the first weeks of our stay said to me one day, after we had been there about six months, that she was dead. "No, you're alive," I insisted. "No, I'm dead. I'm useless. A person who can't do any work is dead," she said. The woman who feared that her husband had dropped her not only no longer felt beautiful, but also, I suspect, felt useless, because she had not given him any children.

A man's sense of being valuable, of contributing to life's purpose, does not normally come from being useful but from being capable and powerful. These two ideas are expressed by a single word in Fulfulde, *waawude*, which means to know how to do something, to master a skill, a thing, another person, or even oneself. This ability is displayed in the way that gives men the greatest pleasure when they are not only able to provide for their own families, but are also able to honor their visitors with style and to help friends and relatives in need.

If we look carefully at the data I've just presented concerning a man's and a woman's sense of being valuable, a very important qualitative difference emerges. For the woman, the sense of value rests in a way on her being, because it depends on her looks and on the immediate work that she is doing. For a man, on the other hand, the sense of being valuable rests to a much greater degree on having—on having the strength and the resources to do what you want, but not necessarily on actually doing it. This is not an absolute distinction but it nonetheless does play a large role in shaping people's subjective experience of growing old. Perhaps the most immediately obvious and important point is that a woman's ability to accomplish her goals in life is in general much more dependent on her physical condition than is the case for a man. A woman's satisfaction lies primarily in her work itself and in its immediate results, while for a man, though his work is not without intrinsic satisfactions, the work is one of a number of ways to obtain the wherewithal to satisfy needs. Another way, the most important one today, is having children who are old enough to do the work. A man whose children are doing the work he formerly did is in a radically different position from a woman whose children are doing her work. For the latter person is no longer "useful," and feels that way, whereas a man whose children are working for him is, and feels, at the height of his powers in the sense that he has more resources than ever before to take care of his needs and those of his dependents. So a man's power to realize his goals goes up while his actual physical condition declines, due to the strongly maintained ideology that seniority and fatherhood are legitimate and compelling bases for authority, and to the fact that those in authority effectively control most of the wealth of the society (the food supply on which everyone depends).

What is it, then, that makes an old man feel old? It is not his declining physical powers, but rather insubordination in one form or another. It is not that he is getting older that is troubling (except when he becomes quite decrepit), but that those under him are getting older and are thus in more of a position to take care of themselves. In addition, there usually comes a point when an old man's ability to control his passions lapses into feebleness and impotence. Much Fulani humor is based on the fact that an old man may see this point as being located in quite a different place from where everyone else sees it. The ability to perform sexually and beget children is actually crucial, for if a man fathers a son at age sixty or sixty-five, he will have an able-bodied person to work for him when he is in his eighties.

One eighty-year-old man told me that his wife was divorcing him, and he was very unhappy about it. I told him that he could always get another woman, but his reply was that if he were really able to get another woman his wife would not have left him in the first place. It was because he was old that he could do nothing about her leaving him. The fact that he had cattle was not enough by itself to keep her. Her departure was upsetting, then, because it made him feel old; it shattered the illusion that he was running things and made apparent the disparity between his wealth and status and his actual ability to do things. It is also highly usual for old men to feel that they have not been given their due, and to become increasingly sensitive to slights to their status.

There is thus a good deal of irony in the predicament of old men in Fulani society. Being older than another person, either in generation or in absolute years, is the one unquestioned source of legitimate power in that society. Yet to utilize that power one has to do more than just occupy the status. One has to have presence, force of character. Part of what this refers to is the sheer physical ability to be up and around and responsive to people, and in control of one's own needs and expressive behavior. So long as a man is capable of this, he is able, in some measure at least, to maintain congruence between his behavior and the aura of authority which surrounds his position. But for the Fulani, and for old people generally, I think, there is greater and greater effort (or will) involved in maintaining consistent behavior in the face of greater fatigue, pain, and weakness. It was my impression that not only did old people suffer more from aches and pains and chronic diseases than did young and middle-aged people, but also that their suffering was more frightening to them because it presaged not merely the end of their lives but, more importantly, the end of the self-control on which their sense of being human is based. The irony of the old men's situation is a fact of life that is apparent to all and is perceived as funny by those a safe distance away, with ambivalence by those closely sharing life with such a man, and with some bitterness by the man himself. The irony of the irony is that even this bitterness is muted, for its open expression would again be a sign that he had failed to master his feelings.

Old women suffer aches, pains, and the fear of shame just as much as men do, but the element of irony is much diminished with them, if not entirely absent, for they do not have to justify a role of authority. People speak of feeling pity and compassion for their old mothers, but not for their fathers: this emotion is felt by a protector for a dependent, and thus would not accurately describe how most people feel toward their old fathers. Where an old man spends much of his time alone or with other survivors of his ever-diminishing cohort, an old woman, as we have seen, spends hers with women of all generations and with young children. Thus, even though she may call herself "dead" or "useless," no pretense is involved in her playing the role of dependent which has always been her lot to some extent anyway. Her female beauty, which can be thought of as a counterpart to male charismatic authority, faded long ago and is not a significant part of her security or her sense of who she is. Thus women share a sense of participating together in a life process that even being useless cannot obliterate.

There is considerable ambivalence felt toward old people, as we have seen. I think that this is due in part to the great fear of death that the Fulani have and in part to the fact that the infirmities of age make the Fulani have feelings of disgust that they must suppress. Though the man's way of being useful in life and the woman's way are different, if they reach extreme old age they both become equally useless. They have done what they were capable of doing, and now they are finished. A Fulani proverb compares a man to an old pair of pants: "When one pair of pants has been used to make another, what's left over cannot become pants again." That is, in an extraordinary blending of the notions of tailoring and of wearing pants (being mature), once you have raised a son ("been a pair of pants") and your son has raised a son ("been a pair of pants also") you are too old to do it again. As we have seen, however, being finished or being useless does not imply rejection or lack of compassion.

5

INFANCY AND
EARLY CHILDHOOD

My goal in this chapter is to give as full an account as I can of how FulBe and RiimaayBe treat infants and small children. It is my contention that the child-rearing practices of these two subgroups are essentially the same and that their effects on children are usually the same. Therefore it will be a prime concern to show what the practices are, what their range of variation is, and how children appear to respond to them.

Now, how does one actually show that two things are the same or different? This seems like a logical impossibility at first, since whether you judge two things to be the same or different depends completely on the respects in which you choose to compare them. What I am looking at primarily here are the basic, repetitive actions of mothers and other caretakers that have to do with feeding, cleaning, carrying, protecting, curing, toilet training, playing with the baby, and so on. There is a certain amount of variation among individuals with regard to how skilfully, carefully, or lovingly they do these various things, but I don't think the variation can be said to be between the two groups in which I am interested. Because my study involved both careful and casual observations of a limited number of families and individuals, I was not able to quantify anything except in quite a rough and ready way. To try to compensate for lack of quantification, and to enrich the reader's impressions, I will present many brief vignettes and anecdotes as I go along. This will establish both the kind of data I am using and the manner in which I draw my inferences, and at the same time it will give the reader enough information to check my interpretations and to try out his or her own hypotheses.

I said in a previous chapter that women seem ever to be involved in food preparation, regardless of what else they might be
doing, including caring for children. For women with young children the point could perfectly well be made the other way around:
they always seem to be caring for the children, regardless of what
else they might be doing. There seems to be nothing women do
from which babies and small children are excluded. To me it
seemed very much as if women's work were all of a piece, and the
primary source of this impression was the fact that no matter what
they were doing, babies and children were always part of the
scene, and their needs, impulses, curiosity, and acts were always
responded to by the others present. From an occidental point of
view, babies can be a nuisance, and their needs and behavior can
and do get in the way of other activities their mothers and caretakers want to do. Among the FulBe and the RiimaayBe, however, people do not usually see it that way; on the contrary, to
watch babies, to play with them, and to care for them is for most
participants, it seemed to me, a fascinating and absorbing way to
pass the time. What frustrated mothers and caretakers was not the
amount of time they had to spend with babies, but rather the times
when a baby was colicky or sick in some other way, so that nothing the mother could do for it seemed to make it feel better. Those
were the only times I had the sense occasionally that strong irritation or even anger might be building up in the mother.

Birth and the First Two Months

A birth in the community is experienced as a major event. Relatives and neighbors all pitch in with help of various kinds, and
during the first week of the infant's life the mother–child couple
are treated with the utmost care and consideration. When the time
for giving birth seems very close, the woman normally has someone with her all the time. Her husband will usually leave the hut,
and a female relative of his will sleep each night in the same hut as
the woman (when having her first child, the woman usually returns to her father's or mother's home, and remains there for about

two months after the birth before returning to her husband). The reason for this companionship is not so much to give the woman physical help with the birth when it comes, but more to be a safeguard against the dangerous forces that are at large in the world and to which women who have just given birth, and their newborns, are highly vulnerable.

I did not witness any births—men in Fulani society generally stay away from where births are taking place, though they are ready to intervene in case of emergencies. I was able to visit a number of families, both FulBe and RiimaayBe, who had babies less than a week old, and I followed events closely in one FulBe family from a few hours after the birth until the naming ceremony for the child one week later. The mother was a neighbor of ours in Petaga, and though I knew everybody very well I think my visits during the first hours following the birth made people feel uncomfortable.

Women generally give birth in their houses and without assistance. In the case of the birth just mentioned, the woman gave birth to a son, her fifth child, at about 7:00 A.M., and her companion didn't wake up until it was over. When the baby emerges from the womb it is important that it come out on the ground. The contact with the earth establishes a connection of some kind between the child and the place; it is my impression that this is to ensure that the earth will be welcoming to the child (though people did not put it to me that way). For instance, whenever an infant comes to a new place, people pick up a little dirt from the ground and rub it on the child's forehead, "to show it the earth (*hollude leydi*)." When children eat dirt, grownups say that a person will always come back, no matter how far away he goes, to the land whose dirt he has eaten. The afterbirth (*baawol* or *minyiraaDo*) is usually buried in the earth right where the baby touched it when it was born.

Though everybody in the community is mentally ready when the baby is born, no obvious physical preparations are made. I think the reason for this is, once again, the protection of the mother and child. People avoid calling attention to the pregnancy and birth until it is absolutely necessary. For example, once the child is born it is necessary to light a fire that will burn continuously for the first week of its life. This is to heat water (plain and medicinal) for washing, steaming, and infusions, and perhaps has some other significance as well. In any case, the fire is not allowed to die out until the naming of the child, which normally is held on the eighth day of its life. But people make no special collection of wood for this fire until after the child has been born. In the case of the birth in Petaga, the first thing I noticed on getting up that morning was the sound of the baby's grandfather's voice yelling at another of his daughters to go and get wood, and then, when I peered out of my hut, I could see an unusual number of women coming and going from the hut where the baby had been born.

As soon as a pot of water has been heated the baby and mother are washed. In our neighbor's case, it was the mother's mother who took charge of these matters and who washed the baby for the first time several hours after the birth. She also set up woven mats as screens just outside the hut to provide a place for the mother to wash herself, which she did several times during the first day. The fire was burning near the eastern end of the bed in the hut, and the grandmother sat on the ground with her knees partly drawn up just beyond the bed at the extreme eastern end of the hut with the pot of hot water beside her. She held the tiny baby on her insteps and leaning against her shins while she washed him over and over with soap and warm water. Her mood while doing this was one of tenderness and quiet joy, and it was shared by the other members of the family, particularly the older siblings of the newborn. The grandmother had seated herself so that the water she used would fall on the ground directly where the afterbirth was buried. I was told that hot water would be poured on the spot from time to time to prevent the afterbirth from rotting. During the following days the baby was always washed on that spot, and from time to time I saw the mother take a little ladle-full of water from the pot that was always boiling and pour it on the ground there.

During the first days following the birth the mother was always extremely careful in how she sat, how she oriented herself and the baby, with regard to the cardinal points. FulBe beds are always oriented east–west, and the proper way to lie on them is cross-ways, the man on the west side facing east, and the woman on the east side facing west. Much of the time people lie on them any old way, and don't pay much attention to the division between the man's side and the woman's side. But in times of danger and vulnerability, as when people were sick, or when a woman had just given birth, I always found that people observed these customs scrupulously. For example, not only was the mother always seated on the eastern half of the bed whenever I visited her, but she generally kept her baby's head pointed to the door, and when he was lying on the bed it was always to her west. Another form of protection that is never omitted is a piece of iron, usually a knife. For the first weeks, and sometimes much longer, the baby will always have a knife, or at least a scrap of a knife blade, lying nearby. When the child is asleep, for instance, the knife will be placed near his head. The mother, too, carries the same protection. Whenever she goes out of the house, to wash or urinate, for instance, she carries her *garjaahi* (straw-cutting knife) tucked into her skirt at all times. And she is never allowed to be alone at all during the first seven days after giving birth. A companion goes with her to the bush when she needs to relieve herself.

The frequent baths given the newborn may contain medicines for diseases we would recognize as well as for attacks from witchcraft. The newborn boy I've been describing wore a little chip of the *kahi* tree on a string around his neck. This purpose of this, people said, was to protect against "mouth" (*hunduko*), which is not a disease but rather is a danger incurred by the baby when people say certain things in its presence. If anybody praises the child, says he or she is good-looking, healthy, or (especially) fat, this is very dangerous and could lead to the child's death. In fact, when visitors to a newborn made any comments they were usually uncomplimentary, such as, "Have you ever seen such an ugly baby?" Parents would be upset and even scared at a remark we would call complimentary, for they would assume the person intended harm to the child. I was frequently not able to figure out what diseases people were talking about, for many native terms do not in fact refer so much to entities, but to conditions, like fever, chills, vomiting, diarrhea, or pain, or to parts of the body, like head, heart, or stomach. For example, there is a much-feared killer of small children during their first rainy season. Its true name, which people fear to pronounce, is *jontere,* which means fever, so people call it *omre* instead, which seems to be the name for a disease that afflicts cattle in the rainy season but which is normally not fatal. My own hunch is that the disease is malaria, but the

Fulani think there is a special relation between omre and the small antelope called lewla. Mothers abstain from eating lewla meat during the child's first year, and further protect their child if they can by procuring them a little bracelet of lewla skin to wear during this precarious period. The lewla, incidentally, is rarely eaten by anybody, since to get one you would almost necessarily have to shoot it. The Fulani do not practice archery, almost nobody has a gun, and very few people hunt. I have not been able to figure out the connection between this animal and a fever that kills young children.

Children are so highly valued, as we have already seen, that when a child dies people's first interpretation often is that someone or something wanted it badly enough to "take" it. Thus many strategies for protecting infants can be seen as attempts to outwit those "others" who want the child. The two basic strategies are to disguise the child and to have the child already "taken" before anything else can get to it. Practices such as rolling the child in dung soon after birth to make it unattractive, or holding the naming ceremony on a different day from the usual one, exemplify the first strategy. Such children often have nicknames like "Birigi" (cow turd) or "Juggal" (horse picket). People who want to protect their child by having it already "taken" arrange to have someone— very often a blacksmith—mark the child in some way so as to establish his prior claim. Thus blacksmiths will commonly pierce the child's ear or scarify the child's cheek. From then on the blacksmith is said to "own" the child; in the case of a girl, if she survives, he must be consulted and eventually given a gift at the time of her marriage, for it is thanks to his power that the child lived.

In the days between the birth and the naming ceremony all people for whom this birth is significant—and this would be all adults in a FulBe village—pay at least one call on the new mother and child, and often bring a gift for the mother (gifts for the child come after he or she has been named). There is a special term for bringing such a gift (*wosude* the mother with something); the gifts women bring are prepared food, such as nyiiri and milk, while men's gifts are usually unprepared food, such as a sheaf of millet, salt, ram, kid, bull calf, or money. There is also a special term, *dambude dimDo,* for spending the day with the new mother during this same period. Its literal meaning is to "shut in" or "confine" the mother.

I won't describe the FulBe naming ceremony itself in detail here because I have already given a fairly lengthy (though still incomplete) account of it elsewhere (Riesman 1977: 58–63). It is important to emphasize, however, that the *indeeri* as held by RiimaayBe is quite a different ritual from the FulBe one. The two rituals (both have the same name) are practically identical with regard to the infant, who is washed, has its head shaved, and is carried outdoors and back in three times if a boy, four times if a girl. The sacrifice of a goat simultaneously with the pronunciation of the name is also done the same way. What does not happen in the RiimaayBe indeeri that is central in the FulBe one is the giving back and forth of the *beDi* (sing. *mbeDu*, winnowing fan and calabash cover). These exchanges have to do with the organization of the lineages in the region, and the definition of the new child's place in that organization (Riesman 1977:60–61). At an indeeri for a Diimaajo child, the goods distributed are all foods—cola nuts, millet, and meat—and they are distributed not according to families or lineages, but according to caste or locality: so much for FulBe, so much for blacksmiths, so much for RiimaayBe of this village, so much for RiimaayBe of that one, and so on. The child is thus symbolically localized in space and by caste, but not as a member of a corporate group larger than the nuclear family. Though this obviously has no particular effect on the child at the moment that it is happening, the meanings underlined here are in fact crucial elements of people's sense of identity as adults, as we shall see.

The fact that most child-care activities are simply a part of women's ongoing life while they cook, weave, do laundry, chat, do one another's hair, and so on, means that women not only have company and possible emergency assistance most of the time, but also have guidance, commentary, and criticism. All women caring for their first babies will have had years of experience taking care of babies already under the watchful and sometimes severe eyes of their mothers, aunts, cousins, or older sisters. The other women around them will immediately notice, comment on, and perhaps strongly criticize any departure from customary behavior on the part of mothers. I think this helps to explain the great homogeneity of practices among both FulBe and RiimaayBe. Deviations hardly have any chance to develop so long as most of the work of child care takes place in the public arena. The main differences to be found are of two sorts: on the one hand, there is a difference of

general ambience between the FulBe and the RiimaayBe since, as
I've already mentioned, they differ noticeably in their apparent
introversion versus extroversion, their loudness and overt ex-
pressivity in conversation, their degree of self-control versus
spontaneity. The second kind of difference is individual and idiosyncratic, concerning the frequency and exact nature of various
medicinal and protective treatments given the children. These
variations are of course all overlaid upon individual differences of
temperament that are probably largely genetically determined,
such as sensitivity to various sensations, irritability, intelligence of
certain kinds, and so on.

During the first weeks of life babies are held during nearly all
their waking hours, and even when they are asleep they are not
necessarily put down. There is no effort at all to get babies to sleep
or to form any particular habits of sleeping and nursing. During
those weeks mothers have no other work than to nurse and care
for their infants and to get back their strength. For forty days they
are considered religiously impure and cannot pray or fast. In principle their husbands should not have intercourse with them before
the end of that period either, but people told me that nobody rig-
orously abided by that rule. I don't think new mothers have any set
time that they are supposed to start their normal household rou-
tines again. It was my impression that they picked these up gradually as their strength came back, starting about ten days to two
weeks after the birth.

A mother gives her breast to her child whenever he or she
seems to want it throughout the nursing period. Here are some
examples taken from my field notes to show the various ways in
which the child's wants are noticed and responded to.

(1)

Diimaajo. Bukkari (twenty-five days) was asleep on a wattle bed when I
came in the middle of the morning. Suumaay, his mother, was mixing
gappal (an uncooked dish of millet flour mixed with water, red peppers,
salt, and soured milk) with her hand in a calabash. The baby then began to
wake up. Suumaay's grandmother told Suumaay to pick up the child, but
it seemed to me she had already been starting to. The boy nursed at both
breasts. While nursing he coughed and spit up a little. His mother lifted
him away from her breast and held him over one knee, face down. He
sounded as if he had a cold, so I asked if he did. His mother said yes. Then
she finished nursing him, and let him lie across her lap on his back. He was
wide awake and kept looking around. He is wearing a string around his

neck with a little charm tied near his Adam's apple. When I ask about it, the mother tells me it is to protect against coughing (probably whooping cough). After a few minutes the mother shakes the child gently, almost as if he were a gourd in which she was churning butter.

(2)

Diimaajo. Kajjata (twenty-three days) was sleeping on a bed in the family courtyard when I arrived. Her mother, Dikkoore, was nearby, pounding millet. The latter's mother-in-law, the baby's paternal grandmother Daado, picked up the child to show me (it was one of my first visits to this family). After a few minutes Kajjata begins to cry, so the mother takes her and nurses her, while Daado takes over pounding the grain. Dikkoore gently shakes the child after it has nursed, and then gives it back to the grandmother while she herself resumes pounding the millet. Daado kisses the baby several times on the lips, but Kajjata starts to fuss and so she ties her onto her back in the typical African manner, with a rectangle of cloth. The mother leaves to seek water, but the baby continues to fuss; bouncing her, whether on the grandmother's back or around in front, does not seem to help. "Shush," she says, and gives the child her own breast.

Notice that the grandmother had no compunction about waking up the baby to show me when I arrived. This illustrates well the point made earlier that people are not especially concerned to get the child to sleep, either for its good or for their own convenience. Second, it is an example of the non-sacred character of sleep generally. Unlike in our society, being asleep is not a statement to the world: "Do not disturb." On the contrary, a person would normally be quite upset on learning that a visitor who had come and found him asleep had left again without waking him. Third, in a few respects, children, even babies, are treated as if they were adults. Here, the child is woken up to greet the visitor; when the visitor is a joking relative (e.g., cross-cousin) to the child he or she may "tease" the child by insulting it, or taking something from it. Finally, adults do not use "baby talk" or other deformed or simplified language to speak to children, but talk to them in an adult way well before they expect them to understand anything.

(3)

Pullo. I spent some time this morning over at Hapsatu's. She was there with her baby Alu (one month) and with her daughter Amnata (age about six). Amnata was playing with the child most of the time, while her mother worked outside pounding millet for gappal. She held the boy under the armpits and jounced him up and down in front of her face, his little legs bouncing against her thighs. Then she would put her lips to his, and the child would suck at them. She explained that the child really wanted milk, but he was sucking her lips in the meantime. I asked her if he was sucking her tongue or just her lips, and she said her lips. This struck me as a very sensual scene, and when Amnata drew her lips away from Alu's, her mouth was red and glistening; she looked at me as if she had just eaten an ice-cream cone. She was not at all self-conscious, however, and in fact was quite willing to show me how it was done, using Alu to demonstrate.

Amnata seemed to be trying to get Alu to sleep, but he did not want to. I don't think it was because she was bored or wanted the freedom to do something else, but rather it was a kind of play or experiment. Every few moments she would lay him down on the bed. She would lay him to the west of her, with the head toward the door (just as grownup women would). She would lay him on a piece of cloth, and cover him with another piece, but soon he would start to cry. Almost instantly she would pick him up and begin jouncing him on her lap again as before. I have no idea whether he liked this or not, but at least he didn't cry. Yet Amnata was sure that he liked this game, just as she was sure that he wanted milk and so gave him her lips as a substitute.

(4)

Diimaajo. The new mother, Dikkoore, has her mother's sister Altine, her father's sister, and her father's mother with her when I arrive at about 9:30 A.M. It is my second visit to the family. Dikkoore had come home to her own family's house to give birth and spend the first several months of her child's life. The great-grandmother has the baby, Mayrama (twelve days), on her back at first, but then gives her to Altine to hold. The baby is fussy and Altine keeps telling her niece that Mayrama wants to nurse, but Dikkoore does not respond. Is it that she feels uncomfortable in my presence? [My subsequent visits suggested not, for she continued to be slow to respond to what people told her to do.] Finally, fifteen minutes after having been told to nurse her child, she does. She has a serious expression on her face, and carefully holds the child's head up to her breast.

(5)

Diimaajo. At 11:30 A.M. when I arrive, Hoyraandu, the baby (in her second month), is asleep on the bed in the courtyard, but she wakes up when I sit down. Her mother gives her the breast, and then starts to play with her. Then she passes her to her mother-in-law, the mother of the child's father, so that she can separate corn from chaff. The grandmother thinks the baby is sleepy and gives her back to the mother to put down. But once lying down on her back (people never lay a child on its stomach) she keeps moving around; finally the mother picks her up and again gives her the breast. Hoyraandu doesn't seem interested; she just wants to play.

(6)

Pullo. When I arrived at the village around 2:45 P.M., I found the baby Muusa (in his second month) and his mother Hapsatu visiting at Raamata's house near their own. Hapsatu (about eighteen years old) is twisting strands of flax into string for use in weaving straw mats. Muusa, however, is being difficult and so Hapsatu brings him back to her own hut, since she wasn't able to work on her flax. I leave around 3:30 to make some other visits, and then return to Hapsatu's again at 5:30. Hapsatu tells me she began the first pounding of millet for supper when I left, and she still hasn't finished. I assume that Muusa has prevented her, so I ask, "Why not?" "Just because I'm lazy," replies Hapsatu.

Hapsatu is with her mother Aadama, to whose home she had returned to have her baby. Aadama tells me that they can't cook *basi* (medicinal broth) tonight because they don't have any fire or matches. I give her some matches. At my arrival I found Muusa asleep, but he was waking up just as Aadama was entering the hut. She picked him up and sat him in her lap; after a few minutes he began to have a bowel movement. Aadama quickly put him on her shins for him to complete his movement. Then she cleaned off his behind with a twig and called to her daughter to come and nurse him. Hapsatu was pounding millet outside the hut at the time and didn't want to come. "Bring him," she said, but her mother wouldn't budge. Finally she put down her pestle and came and got him. She brought him back outside and nursed him for about five minutes while her mother fanned the fire for heating up the basi. When Muusa had nursed to contentment and was lying in his mother's lap gurgling, his grandmother told Hapsatu to bring him back in so that she could give him his basi.

The basi is a little hot right now, so Aadama feeds it to her grandson by dipping her fingers into the pot, and then dabbing her fingertips on his lips so that the liquid goes in drop by drop. When the broth has cooled down enough, she places the child on her insteps facing outward and leaning back against her partly drawn-up knees. She takes a small, split gourd for a ladle, places it to the child's lips, and pours the medicine into him little by little. She laughs at his willingness to drink it, and says, "He's drinking so he can go pee." When he has drunk enough, Aadama picks him up and puts him on her back to carry, completely covering him with a cloth.

In this episode we see a very typical situation, namely the passage from holding the child to helping it have a bowel movement to nursing, to giving it basi, and other combinations of the above. The following descriptions of the same family, from notes taken the previous week, show even more fully the way in which caretakers shift from one sort of treatment to another, depending largely on the baby's own needs, but also on the adults' concern to make sure the child gets enough food and medicine.

(7)

Pullo. When I arrived at 4:45 P.M. Hapsatu was here alone working at weaving her straw mat under the shelter erected just beside her grandmother's hut. Her baby (in his second month) is away being carried on his grandmother's back while she visits a friend. When Aadama returns soon after, Muusa is asleep on her back. Her daughter tells her to put him down, but she replies that if she puts him down now he will wake up, while if she continues to carry him on her back he will stay asleep until they have been able to prepare supper. She goes out, still carrying the baby, to try to head off the calves from getting to their mothers and drinking all their milk, and to start a fire for cooking basi. Hapsatu continues to weave her mat. When her mother returns she tells her again to put the baby down, and Aadama repeats that the child will wake up if she does, but she finally puts him down anyway. Hapsatu goes out to milk the goats, but comes back almost immediately because the kids got out of their pen and have sucked their mothers dry. She and her mother work together for a while at the straw mat, a task they carry on intermittently all day long. Muusa's eyes blink open a little but he isn't quite awake yet.

I ask the women if they have pounded millet for supper yet, and they reply that they are not going to today, but will eat leftovers from their midday meal. Ten minutes after having been put down, Muusa is fully awake and Aadama picks him up and holds him a few minutes. She passes him to Hapsatu to nurse and continues to work at the weaving herself. Muusa has a little bowel movement on his mother, who passes him back to Aadama and tells her to help him to finish. His grandmother takes him and places him on her insteps in the same position as for administering basi. She makes little kissing noises to encourage the process, but nothing further comes out. She gives him back to Hapsatu so he can nurse some more. As he sucks he makes little choking sounds, or stifled cries, as if he were working hard.

He stops nursing briefly and his mother dandles him a little. Then he gives his little stifled cry again and she offers him the breast. "He's full," says his grandmother, but he does nurse a little more. "He's full even before he's had his basi," says Aadama. She takes him and holds him in a sitting position, supporting his head. She remarks that he burped, and that he will be spitting up any moment now.

Hapsatu and Aadama prepare Muusa's basi mixture. Last year Hapsatu had had a baby who died after living only two weeks. This year, when her new baby Muusa began to spit up, they obtained the basi ingredients from some RiimaayBe women, and it seems to have helped reduce his vomiting. The women tell me that when they mixed the basi with milk, Muusa would spit it up, whereas if they mixed it with butter he would keep it down. So they add butter to it just before giving it to him to drink. After stirring in some butter, Hapsatu goes off to the well to draw water and leaves Aadama to administer the medicine.

Contrary to expectation, Muusa has not spit up. Aadama checks the basi by taking a few sips of it, concludes that it has cooled down sufficiently and starts to give it to the baby. Muusa struggles against the liquid, but not as violently as some babies I've seen. When she has completed the dose, Aadama first shakes the boy's head, then pulls each of his limbs with a shaking motion, a little as if they were jump ropes. Then she picks him up and shakes his whole body a little, with a sort of rolling motion between her hands, like an upright ninepin held between the palms. Finally she puts him on her back and kneels down, rocking and moving around to soothe him. He seems quiet and contented now. Aadama says he will go to sleep soon.

(8)

Pullo. When I arrived at 11:15 A.M., Muusa (in his second month) was lying half awake on a mat on the floor while his mother worked on the mat she is weaving. After a few minutes she picked him up and gave him the breast, without his having made any obvious demand. I asked if he had spit up any today; Hapsatu said that he had a little. But just then Aadama came back from getting water at the well and said that in fact he had thrown up a lot today because she had not made basi. And for this reason as well he would not achieve satiety. Muusa has stopped nursing and is now lying stretched out upon his mother's legs, his feet toward her torso and his head resting on her knees, while she continues to weave her straw mat. He is quiet and I can't tell if he is asleep or awake, so I ask. Aadama tells me he is wide awake. Hapsatu picks him up again and gives him the other breast to nurse from.

When he has finished, his grandmother says she wants to give him an enema. Hapsatu seems reluctant to have her do it, but hands him over to Aadama and picks up her weaving again. Aadama fills a rubber bulb with water and squeezes it into the baby's anus as he lies crosswise on her outstretched legs. Then, holding him by the buttocks and the torso she gently jiggles him for about a minute. After that she puts him in a sitting position crosswise on her shins, with his feet dangling over her left shin, for him to have his bowel movement. Soon he does. Then she faces him the other way so that she can give him a little water to drink from the palm of her right hand, and finally she washes him all over with plain water.

FulBe and RiimaayBe both give enemas quite frequently to their small children. People who lack the rubber bulb will often simply use their mouths to push the water or infusion into the anus. There is considerable idiosyncratic variation with regard to how often and for how long a child will receive such treatments. For example, while nearly all mothers give basi, different families have different recipes, as we have seen; people are willing to share the made-up basi with others, but not the recipes. But some people administer basi only a few times to their children, while others do it regularly for several months. It is possible that the family of Muusa (numbers 6, 7, and 8 above) were not used to giving basi to their children, but as one baby had already died, and as Muusa apparently vomited to an unusual extent, they sought help from people who were experienced with it. Some people do not give enemas. The mother of Alu (number 3 above) claimed not to know how, but she said that if she had the knowledge she would do it. There seems to be a striking contrast, from a Western point of view at least, between the child having the initiative to nurse, to play, and to go to sleep, while parents quite autocratically choose the moment to administer basi or an enema (often employing basi), or to wash the child, even if the times chosen have in turn been affected by the infant's condition and behavior.

Early Childhood Until Weaning

We have seen in these vignettes of newborn infants and their caretakers a very high degree of attentiveness to the baby's needs. There always seem to be people around a baby who are quite aware of what its current state of being is, though caretakers do not always react to that knowledge immediately. This way of phrasing what we have observed slightly distorts the lived reality, however. Even at this early age, and to a much more evident degree later on, I think that people are responding to the child as a source of vitality, desire, and will. They don't normally say of babies "he needs to nurse," or "he has to defecate," but use phrases like "she wants to nurse," or "he's looking to go pee." In addition, before long one begins to hear people saying, "he wants to be picked up," "she wants to play," or "he misses his sister." Holding the child under the armpits facing you and jouncing it on your lap (see number 3 above) is a very common way of playing with young children. When the child is a little bigger the person playing with it may even throw it slightly into the air on the upward bounce, and catch it again coming down. This play is called *womnude,* which literally means "to make dance." One of the many Fulani proverbs about friendship and kinship uses the image of this play with the child to suggest that a true friend is willing to help your relatives, and not just you alone. Literally translated, it says, "It's the mother's friend who will make the baby dance (*giDo yaaye womnata BiDDo*)."

(9)

Pullo. When I first arrived half an hour before noon, the baby, Aysatu (three months), was asleep. Shortly she began to stir; it seemed to me she was having a bad dream. Her mother Hiidi picked her up right away, grasping her in the typical Fulani way by one upper arm just below the shoulder, and then swinging her over from the bed to her lap to nurse. The baby was not yet fully awake. When she seemed to have nursed to her contentment, I motioned to Aysatu to come to me. Hiidi asked me if I was going to "make her dance." I said yes, and took her and jounced her on my lap for a few minutes. But I was not yet a familiar visitor and suddenly the child became frightened. Her mother obviously expected me to give her back immediately, so I did. Aysatu quieted down as soon as she began to nurse again.

(10)

Diimaajo. Maynmata is trying to do Suumay's hair and entertain her own baby Hajjiratu (about six months) at the same time. Though the baby keeps crying and seems to want to be held, this does not appear to irritate the mother in the least. She stops the hairdressing every now and then, and tries to get the baby lying in her lap to take one of her long breasts by herself so that she can have her hands free. Hajjiratu wouldn't accept that arrangement, so for a few minutes Suumay sat up and Maynmata played with her baby; then she put her across her lap the other way and tried to give her a breast again. This time it worked, for a short while anyway (five minutes). Soon the baby begins to get restless again: "*Moy fiyi ma?* (Who hit you?)" says her mother. Suumay, who has moved to a sitting position, picks up Hajjiratu and plays with her, jouncing her slightly (*womnude*) and patting her on the back. Hajjiratu quiets down.

Mothers make this remark ("Who hit you?") very frequently to their small children. Its implications are important and fascinating to elucidate. First of all, it is only used when in fact no one has hit the child, when the child's discomfort has not been caused by a person. At times, as in the case of Hajjiratu, it is not clear just what the matter is; often, however, an adult will say "Who hit you?" when the child is crying because of some accident, such as falling down. The main implication of this usage seems to be, then, that the only "legitimate" reason for crying is that someone harmed you. If older children cry because of getting hurt in some way, people make fun of them unless the injury is very serious. People offering moral support to others discourage them from crying by telling them that it's a waste of energy, it won't do any good. This applies even to the tears of grief, which everyone thinks of as perfectly understandable but nonetheless useless. For the Fulani this is not a teaching, as one might at first think, that evil in the world comes from humans alone, but rather that crying is a form of communication. For the Fulani, then, it does not symbolize raw emotion, but contains messages that only humans (and certain spirits including saints, the Prophet, and God) can understand and react to. In addition, this example gives us an important clue as to how the Fulani view the human person. As raw expression of emotion is useless, it is also meaningless. It only becomes a message when it is addressed to somebody, and when such a communication is appropriate. The human way, then, is to transform whatever is involuntary and accidental into something intended. Intention only can occur when people are acting in relation to other people who share the universe of meanings in terms of which messages can be interpreted.

Another point is crucial to notice here. We might interpret such remarks by mothers as being a form of early training of children. I don't think this is the case, any more than talking to the children in adult speech, rather than baby talk, is training from the parents' point of view. After all, a baby of six months would simply not understand the meaning of a sentence like that in the first place, and what it would understand—the tone—is comfort and reassurance. If the mother were trying to train the child not to cry "when it wasn't supposed to," then she wouldn't respond with nurturance to the child's tears. This interpretation is corroborated by the change in response to mockery of older children when they cry. But if mothers are not trying to train their children at that age, why do they say anything at all? What are they saying such things for? I think it is their way of remaining human to themselves and to those around them when having to deal with a being who is not fully human yet, who does not understand the things that are happening in human terms at all. The mothers are acting their culture, presenting their culture, but not at all with the idea that their audience understands the language.

(11)

Diimaajo. Hawwa (nine months) now sits up and has two lower front teeth. But she has been sick with fever these last few days; she has largely prevented her mother Pendal from working. Today, for instance, Pendal went to her field with Hawwa, but was unable to do any weeding because Hawwa *jaBaay* (lit. "didn't accept," i.e., wouldn't go along with what her mother wanted). Her shots are sore, and she has an infected ear (because of being *tufaaDo,* pierced for magical protection) and a boil on the back of her neck. Just now for no apparent reason she started crying and her mother immediately picked her up; she thought an ant might have bitten her. She gave her the breast, saying, "*Feewi, feewi jonkay. Lobbo!* (It's all better, all better now. That's a nice girl!)" Hawwa gradually quieted down, but won't be separated from the breast.

Before going further, I want to put us on guard against reading our own meanings too quickly into the data. The use of bottle feeding in the United States encourages us to think nursing equals feeding. It is undeniable that nursing is the sole means of getting food for these infants, but they get much more than that. It emerges clearly from these data that Fulani mothers not only give their children the breast whenever they are hungry, but offer it to them when they cry for almost any reason. Sometimes they offer it to them because they feel like it, or because they anticipate that the child is about to signal for it. It is clear from mothers' explanations of what they are doing that in many instances their action has nothing to do with whether the child is hungry or needs food. The child may be in pain from a cold or teething, or may be sleepy and irritated, or may have gotten a fright from falling down or a goat charging through the courtyard. Mothers try to sooth all these troubles by nursing their children. And not only mothers! Grandmothers may offer their breasts to babies or to recently weaned older children; in some cases this actually stimulates a flow of milk.

We can see, then, that nursing is definitely a kind of communication between mother and child that goes both ways. Both participants have unconscious, somatic responses as well as conscious ones to the gestures of the other that enable the interaction to flow smoothly. This communication is usually sustaining and comforting on the part of the mother. Even when adults travel to see their mothers people express what they get from the visit by saying, "So-and-so went and sucked at his mother's breast" (cf. Riesman 1977:122). As the child gets older he or she begins to experiment with this relationship; during the first five years or so there are many playful moments. Here is an example. One afternoon, while on a regular visit to a Diimaajo family, I found the child, a fourteen-month-old girl, asleep and the mother away at the market. Soon after I arrived the mother returned. The child woke up "as if she sensed her mother's presence," I wrote. Her mother sat down and nursed her, and then the girl got up and went into the house to play. The mother remarked that her daughter had made her let down her milk and then had gone off without really nursing. I wonder, now, if this was one of the ways in which that girl was already getting a certain sense of power or efficacy in human relations. Since the mother could hear that the child was beginning to get into mischief in the house, she went in to check on her. My notes continue, "Then she picked her up and carried her back outside, playfully growling into her stomach. Kajjata was half laughing, half crying. Then the mother dumped Kajjata in her grandmother's lap and began to pound millet. Kajjata seemed happy. She calmed down immediately and sucked for a little at her grandmother's breast."

Another implicit message that seems frequently communicated in the nursing relationship is that the child rules or owns the mother. The mother may offer the breast spontaneously to the child, but the latter can request to be nursed at any time and the mother cannot refuse. There is evidence, in fact, that the milk children get from their mother belongs to them by right. If a child's mother gets pregnant while she is nursing, the child must be weaned right away, because the milk that forms in her breasts at the same time as the new fetus is believed to belong to that baby. For the older child to take it is a kind of theft from the younger one; not only that, the milk of the new child is believed to be actually poisonous for the older one, and causes a common illness of children this age called "weaning disease." Mothers are concerned about weaning, then, not for the psychological health of their children, but for their very survival.

New Foods, Weaning, and Continuity in Mother–Child Relationships

Whether or not there are objective grounds for considering basi a food, for the Fulani it is a medicine and can be forced on children, quite the opposite from how parents offer foods. We have seen that mothers offer their breast to children in a wide variety of circumstances, but the children are never forced to take it, nor are they forced to eat other foods. There are no foods specifically prepared for children; children are simply given little tastes of certain foods adults eat from quite an early age. Butter, cow's milk, or goat's milk may be given as early as the first week, and *bita,* a thin millet gruel often flavored with lemony tamarind pods, baobab fruit pulp, red peppers, or sugar (or various combinations of these) may be tried after a few months of life. In addition, children of this age, as seems to be the case universally, use their mouths as a way to explore the world immediately around them. Now let us examine some instances of children eating and drinking foods other than mother's milk. I present the first scene in much detail to give the reader a feel for the complexity and variety of what goes on as a large, extended-family group of RiimaayBe prepares the evening meal. Most of the children described are still nursing, but other things go into their mouths as well.

(12)

Diimaajo. A whole crowd of women and children are in the courtyard near the kitchen at about 5:00 P.M. as the final cooking for supper begins. Jeenaba (seven months) is sitting on the ground and playing happily, more or less together with Aysata (six months); they each have something in their mouths. Jeenaba has been playing with a tiny bell made from a little mentholatum container with a pebble in it; she puts it in and takes it out of her mouth, but Aysata keeps trying to get it from her. She had it for a while, at which point Jeenaba picked up a lump of cow dung and started chewing on that. Now Pendiri, her mother, who had been sifting flour while others pounded, is nursing her. Aysata is still sitting and playing comfortably in the dirt. Pendiri continues to sift, sometimes using both hands, while her daughter sucks at her breast.

Bukkari (eight months) is crawling around. His mother Salaamata gives him a drink of water from a cup. All this compound's children get drinks from cups these days if they want them. Bukkari is now playing with the little bell and ToBaa, a little girl, rides a "donkey"—a pail lying on its side.

Now Jeenaba is sitting on the ground at her mother Pendiri's feet, while the latter holds Mayrama (five months) in her lap while that baby's mother, Dikkoore, makes the fire for supper. Pendiri plays with Mayrama, who is delighted, while Habbata, the mother of ToBaa, holds Jeenaba. When Salaamata comes by the two women together womnude ("make dance") Jeenaba briefly.

Jeenaba and Aysata are again on the ground side by side. Someone has given Jeenaba an old ladle, made from half a split gourd and encrusted with yesterday's sauce, to play with. Aysata plays with tassels on a shirt she has just been given, and with the little bell, which has been taken away from Bukkari. Bukkari starts to whine, so his mother, Salaamata, stops pounding and picks him up.

At 5:30 P.M., Dikkoore is coating the cooking pot with mud prior to putting it on the fire. Pendiri is still playing with Mayrama, while Habbata has picked up Jeenaba, Pendiri's daughter, who was beginning to wonder where her mommy was. Habbata jokes with her, saying, "Aren't I your mommy? Aren't I as good as your mommy?" Shortly, amid general crying, there is an exchange of babies. Jeenaba goes back to Pendiri, Aysata to her mother Baylo, while Mayrama is taken by her stepmother (mother's co-wife).

A calabash of cobbal has appeared from somewhere, and the women are all sitting around and drinking it. Habbata is now holding Aysata, while the stepmother continues to hold Mayrama, who has started to cry. Dik-koore, Mayrama's mother, is in the circle, but doesn't make any move-ment to get her. Finally the stepmother gives Mayrama to Dikkoore to nurse. Bukkari is making complaining noises, and his mother gives him some cobbal when the gourd ladle comes around. ToBaa is given a little of the cobbal in a wooden bowl to eat by herself.

(13)

Diimaajo. Dikkoore, who had one baby she was still nursing and another recently weaned, found herself without water one morning. No water-sellers had come by, and so she was getting ready to go to the large well near the center of town. Just at that moment, however, her three-year-old daughter said she wanted to eat. Dikkoore had some nyiiri but no hoy. The daughter would not eat the food without sauce, and Dikkoore was wondering what to do when a neighbor came by to ask if she had been able to get water yet. Dikkoore said no, and asked in turn if the neighbor had any hoy. The lady said she wasn't sure, but that she had put some on top of the bed-canopy and didn't think anyone had taken it yet. Dikkoore tied her baby onto her back, took a small calabash to use as a bowl, and dashed off to the neighbor's house. She was back in a few minutes with the little cal-abash half-full of hoy. She took the bowl of nyiiri, placed the dish of hoy on top of it, and placed them on the ground in front of her daughter. "Now, eat well until you are full," she told her, and went off to get water, carrying her baby still on her back and a large earthen pot on her head.

(14)

Diimaajo. Amie, a little girl, had a calabash of cobbal. Another little girl (about six years), who had been holding Hawwa (fifteen months) for the past twenty minutes or so, gave Hawwa some of this cobbal. Then Amie took the cobbal away and Hawwa began to cry. Maysi, Amie's mother, told her daughter to let the baby have some more cobbal, since she wasn't going to eat any more anyway. But at that moment Pendal, the baby's mother, came along saying she didn't want Hawwa to eat cobbal. "It'll make a hole right through her stomach and she'll have the trots something terrible," she exclaimed. She said that she had bita put aside for her and that was what she wanted her to eat. But when she brought the bita to Kumbo to give to Hawwa (since she herself was busy cooking the midday meal), Hawwa just cried and would not take it. Pendal told Kumbo not to try to force her. It happened that Maysi was just setting off to the market to sell cobbal she had made, so Pendal bought some of it for Hawwa and Kumbo is now mashing it together with milk and water.

A few minutes later Kumbo finished mixing up the cobbal. By now Hawwa seems to have forgotten she wanted some, but when Kumbo set the calabash of it in front of her Hawwa started to cry. Kumbo picked her up and set her on her lap, then started to feed her cobbal. Hawwa stopped after one ladle full. "Why did she stop?" I asked Kumbo. "She's full," she replied. Now Kumbo is eating the cobbal. At this point another little girl sitting nearby started to cry. Kumbo rushed over and said, "Hey, look! Here's cobbal," but Raamata didn't want any. In the meantime, Hawwa was starting to have trouble opening a peanut. Pendiri, who happened to be passing by, noticed the problem and helped her to peel it.

What is the quality of the relationship·between the child eating the food and the person who gives it in these examples? In the last two, especially, I sense a strong continuity between nursing the child and feeding it other foods, in that the mother or caretaker tries to satisfy the child's requests as quickly and completely as possible. In some cases the mother even goes against her better judgment: she thinks a certain food is bad for the child, yet if the child wants it, the mother gives in. These observations, then, seem to confirm the interpretation that the child rules or owns the mother. Actually, however, that strikes me as an ethnocentric interpretation, for that is what such behavior might mean in our own society. Among us, there often develops a sort of battle of wills between parent and young child, but I do not detect that situation among the Fulani. On the contrary, they interpret the parent's ability to satisfy a child's wants as a strength, not a weakness. There is a Fulani saying which goes: "There are two things a father must not say—'I cannot,' and 'I don't have any.'" In addition, Fulani conceptions of the nature of the child, of human nature generally, are different from ours. For a fuller understanding of their behaviors it is necessary to take these notions into account.

A person's desire for something, as the Fulani understand it, seems to be a partially independent aspect of the self. This desire is aroused by the sight, smell, or perhaps even thought of food or some other desired object, such as clothing, a radio, or even a beautiful woman. This desire is called *goddi*. When you satisfy it it is said you "remove the goddi (*a itti goddi*)." But if the desire remains unsatisfied, or is frustrated, then someone has "cut the goddi (*taYi goddi*)." These expressions suggest that goddi is like an emanation from a person that attaches itself to the desired object, so that if you successfully remove it the goddi returns to its owner, while if you cut it this deprives one of some part of oneself. To have one's goddi cut is a dangerous situation. I don't know what it does to children, but I was told that it would cause a pregnant woman to abort her child, while in a man it would make urination painful. People's sense of the danger of cutting goddi emerges clearly in their belief that you must remove the goddi of djinns when cooking, by making little offerings of food to the four directions.

In the next three examples, the focus is on children who are in the transition between breast-feeding and eating the foods of adults. Here, too, we can see the parents' concern to satisfy the child's wants, and at the same time what looks like an absence of pressure on the child to conform to any particular standards of food preference, manners, or cleanliness. The parents present to the children what they think is good or proper, but they do not appear to force them into conformity.

(15)

Diimaajo. Pendiri is spinning cotton late in the morning at her house. Her two youngest children, Saydu (four years) and Jeenaba (sixteen months) are here, as well as Aysatu, a little girl of five or six. The boy has been sick a lot of the past year but seems in better health today. He and Aysatu are wrestling playfully, Saydu laughing joyfully each time he is thrown by the girl, who is much bigger and heavier than he is. She always throws him gently, holding him as he falls so as not to let him hit the ground hard.

Jeenaba sits on or stays close to her mother. Every few moments she wants to suck. Pendiri verbally discourages her, but makes no physical effort to stop her (the baby doesn't yet talk). Pendiri keeps telling the kids that Saydu is going to start crying soon. Aysatu will hit him or hurt him soon. Still, they have been horsing around for a long time and he hasn't cried yet. "I'll be darned if he isn't going to cry any moment," says Pendiri. Pendiri sends Jeenaba off, carried by another little girl, to look for her older sister Ndewri (twelve years). Jeenaba doesn't object at all to going, and even seems pleased. She is gone ten or fifteen minutes, but then comes back without having found Ndewri, who wasn't where she had been said to be. As the girl who had carried her slips away, Jeenaba begins to whimper. "It's you she's crying for," says Pendiri to the girl. Jeenaba goes back to sucking at her mother's breast while Pendiri serenely continues to spin cotton.

I asked if Jeenaba was getting milk. Pendiri said she gets a little from nursing, but that it is not enough. She has to have bita too. Does she eat nyiiri? I asked. Yes. How about meat? We don't have any meat, said Pendiri. Pendiri is trying to get Jeenaba to stop sucking her breasts. "Ow, my breasts are so sore!" she exclaims to me. She offers the child some bita, but Jeenaba isn't interested. Then she calls to Saydu, who is somewhere outside, to come and finish the bita. She tells Jeenaba to hurry up and eat before Saydu comes and eats it all up. Jeenaba is unmoved by this. Then she calls, "Here, kitty kitty, come here, come and bite her," as if there were a cat there, but this too has no obvious effect. Jeenaba continues to whine and try to suck. Suddenly, of her own accord, Jeenaba crawls across her mother's legs to the bita, takes off the cover, and starts to play around with the gourd ladle. After a few minutes of this, Jeenaba starts to eat, using her left hand to hold the gourd. Her mother shows no reaction to this. Saydu comes in and says he wants some too. Pendiri sends him for another gourd ladle, and now both children are drinking the bita. That the children drip the porridge on the mat they are all seated on does not seem to bother their mother. Pendiri only got a little annoyed when Jeenaba, in playing, splattered some bita on the cotton she was spinning.

But suddenly Saydu and Jeenaba are fighting over the bita. Jeenaba feels that Saydu is taking her bita, for Pendiri has called it hers, and she whimpers and pushes him away with her hands. Saydu struggles to keep eating. Pendiri tells Saydu to stop, but he says, "I will not stop." Then she takes his gourd from him and puts it on the bed-canopy. He goes and gets it. Pendiri meanwhile removes the bita from in front of Jeenaba to the other side of her, far from Jeenaba. Saydu comes back from getting his gourd and is about to sit down to eat some more, when he discovers that the bita is no longer there. He looks around, sees it, and gets up to go to it, stepping across his mother's outstretched legs. "Don't eat Jeenaba's bita," says Pendiri. Saydu reaches for the calabash, apparently oblivious. Jeenaba starts to cry. "Don't eat her bita," repeats his mother. "You can go and get nyiiri, after all." Saydu takes a gourd full and drinks it, then puts down the gourd and goes out. Jeenaba, at her mother's breast again, calms down.

(16)

Diimaajo. Aysama (three years), the next-to-last child of his mother Suka, is almost completely weaned at this time. He sleeps at his mother's mother's house and spends the day with his mother. He tends to be fearful and clingy, and his mother and grandmother seem to try, at times, to get him to go with other people and not cling so much to his mother. Several times this morning these women tried to persuade him to go off with other members of the family. When his older brother Hasan (by a different mother) left after breakfast, they told him to go with him, but he refused. The same thing happened when his father came and went off. Then when a young neighbor named Muusa came in they told Aysama to go with him "to see what your father is doing, what he is going to give you." Aysama remained unmoved. Finally, with much cajoling, his grandmother got him to go with her to get some guavas. They gave him a mbuudu. Soon they returned. While they were still outside the door, Aysama suddenly began screaming, ran in and collapsed on his mother's feet. He had been frightened by a uniformed soldier who had come by to say hello. Now he is peacefully sitting on his mother's knees, eating guavas; his younger brother Haaruuna (one month) is lying on her lap, asleep.

(17)

Diimaajo. Daado and Ditta, a mother and her grown daughter, have been talking about the former's granddaughter, Talel (four years), who still to-day refuses to stop nursing. She doesn't nurse from Dikkoore, her mother, any more, but she frequently sucks at her grandmother Daado's breast. The two women say that this is why Talel is not getting fat. She drinks from the breast and then does not have enough to eat because she refuses to eat well. The only thing to do, they agree, is Talel *sana Noge*. In other words, a moodibbo will have to be asked to recite certain verses from the Koran while spitting on some of the child's food; this should stop the child's desire for the breast.

When I asked Dikkoore, the mother, whether Talel had been given *lekki enentere* (medicine for "weaning disease"), she told me to ask the grandmother. Which I did. Daado told me that she had gotten an egg from a young chicken, cooked it in coals, then gave it to her to eat. I asked if she had bought it or asked for it. She said that she had asked for it from her own mother. Had Talel or Dikkoore taken any other medicines, I asked? Daado said no; one was all a person should have, for if you had more than one it could cause you to be sick.

The Fulani do not appear to believe that the ground is dirty. Children not only pick up things from the ground and put them in their mouths, as we have seen, but they eat dirt itself. Parents see this as perfectly normal. What must be avoided, on the other hand, is food coming from the wrong people, people who are possible dangers to oneself or to one's relatives.

(18)

Diimaajo. Aysata, Baylo's four-month-old daughter, is just beginning to sit up. Shortly after I arrived this morning her mother gave her to me to hold. I did for a few minutes, but then she began to cry. Baylo took her back and put her down on the ground facing me. She hasn't budged, but looks at me now and then. She also immediately began to eat dirt. Baylo seemed interested, but made no attempt to stop her. An old woman who was making gappal in the same courtyard said that no matter where she went now, she would always come back to Djibo, since she had eaten the earth of Djibo.

(19)

Diimaajo. Bukkari (eight months) is sitting on the ground beside his mother while she pounds millet with several other women. He has been eating lumps of dirt. When he puts sticks in his mouth people take them out (this is what people here will usually call *tuundi,* "filth"), but they let him put his face on the ground and lick the dirt, despite the fact that the surface is covered with goat droppings. The women say that eating dirt is *da sukaaBe* ("children's custom"), as is playing horse with millet stalks when they get bigger.

(20)

Pullo. Little Aamadu (fourteen months) is sick. He drinks so little milk right now that his mother's breasts are painfully full. Just now he is eating some dirt. Jeewo, his grandmother, noticed and told her daughter Aasaare, the child's mother, to take a piece of straw out of his mouth. The women had said that his mouth hurt and that a bit of cola nut would help. They had none, but I had one in my pocket which I offered to them. They gave a piece to a little girl, his cousin, to give to him, but he wouldn't take it. He just let it fall from his hand. Then his mother stuck a little piece in his mouth, and he chewed on it. He has two lower front teeth, and others are coming in; this is perhaps why he is sick right now. Then, after his grandmother had chewed her piece of the nut for a while, she spit a little of the juice directly into his mouth. This was to make the pain in his mouth go away.

(21)

Diimaajo. Today all the children except the baby are away playing. The baby, Kajjata (three months), is asleep; the mother, Dikkoore, is beginning to cook the evening meal; and the grandmother, Daado, is spinning cotton and chatting with me. I asked her if she worried about the children while they were wandering around, and if they knew what they were supposed to do and not do. Daado said that they knew not to get too close to the edge of deep pits, and to get out of the way of bikes, mopeds, and cars. What about eating? I asked. "*Be njaBataa* (they wouldn't accept that)," said Daado. They won't eat anywhere except with their own relatives. If they get hungry they come back and eat. Why not, I asked. Because some people are bad, said Daado, and they might give the child something that would cause it to die. If we find that a child has eaten where he shouldn't, "*min piya Dum faa yi'a bonnde* (we'll hit the kid till he knows that it hurts)." Daado said that they were very careful to tell children where they could eat. This danger is not present in water, however, since, according to Daado, everyone drinks from the same water pot; hence a person isn't going to put anything bad in it.

(22)

Diimaajo. Maama is the ex–co-wife of Faatumata. She continues to live in the same compound, but has been abandoned by her husband in favor of Faatumata. Today, at about noon, she came up to the four-year-old daughter of Faatumata, RuGiyatu, and gave her a little gourd ladle full of gappal; then she walked back to her house. Faatumata saw her bring it, but said nothing. RuGiyatu smiled, took the gappal, and set it down on the ground near her mother. I do not know what happened after that, but I wonder.

More generally, the crucial point is that children learn who they are through coming to know their relatives and their place in the network of relations into which they are born. How children learn to identify with their parents, especially with their fathers, since identification with the mother is much easier to see, and how the sense of what it means to be who they are as members of a group gets expressed to them, will be discussed in the following chapters.

6

LATER CHILDHOOD

Weaning is often a difficult period both for children and their caretakers, yet all the examples given tend to show that it does not involve a significant change of attitude toward either children or their behavior. Children are not permitted to nurse—though mothers differ with regard to how abruptly this rule is enforced and how rigidly—but they are not expected to have "grown up" or to "understand" or to accept this change willingly. It is when children begin to develop *haYYillo* (social sense) that adults in turn change their expectations and behavior. This can be noted in all aspects of life. Between the ages of five and seven, children, especially girls, begin to be given their first responsibilities. As food preparation and handling is so central in women's lives, it is easy to find many instances in this domain to illustrate these points.

The sharing of food, at least under certain circumstances and with certain other people, has a very high value for the Fulani. We have already seen some hints of this. But here again we have to watch out that our own notions of what it means to share don't get in the way of understanding its meaning for the Fulani. Let us now examine a few episodes of sharing, or failing to share, more closely. These will shed light on how Fulani interpret the giving of food in different contexts, on how the meaning of children's acts changes as they get older, and especially on how adults change their way of responding to children once the latter are believed to have acquired social sense.

(1)

Diimaajo. Mayrama (thirteen months) is not quite able to walk yet. She is in great spirits, staggering around holding on to things. When I first arrived this morning she immediately offered me the little calabash she was holding and that she was eating peanuts out of. I took it from her and then gave it back. She offered it back to me again. This went on a number of times. She would also put whole peanuts in her mouth, chew them shells and all a little, then spit them out into her calabash and offer them to me. Then she went around the room playing some more.

(2)

Diimaajo. Cingiti (six years) got herself some cobbal from where her mother had stored it and sat down with Saydu (three years), a cousin, to eat it. But then she started whining, saying, "*sukkara, sukkara.*" Finally her mother got her a sugar cube—she admitted that the cobbal was very sour (*cobbal lammi sanne*). Cingiti at first tried to feed Saydu by holding a gourd ladle of cobbal to his lips, but Baylo said she should let him eat on his own. The two children then sat facing each other over the cobbal calabash, and passed the ladle back and forth, but they didn't exactly take equal turns. Cingiti took a ladle-full and drank it all down in a several mouthfuls, while her mother criticized her (the proper way is to take just one mouthful at a time, regardless of the size of the utensil). Cingiti responded with a throwing motion of the index finger—an insulting gesture—while continuing to drink. Several times Cingiti tried to take the cobbal from Saydu by force, and Baylo criticized her each time (though I unfortunately didn't record her exact words). It was clear to me in watching this scene that Baylo really did not expect Cingiti to behave differently. Nor did she think that what she said would have much effect. But Cingiti looked funny to me, like a little wild animal, as she gulped down the cobbal, peering over the rim of the ladle with defiant eyes.

(3)

Diimaajo. Jeenaba (twenty months) is sitting on her mother Faatumata's lap with a little tin of powdered milk. She was giving it out to the other little children, especially to one little girl named Kajjata MaccuDo, who is distantly related. Jeenaba's older sister, RuGiyatu (five years), was trying to prevent her from giving the food to Kajjata, but Jeenaba kept insisting. Finally another little girl held RuGiyatu's hands so that she couldn't block Jeenaba anymore. After giving some to Kajjata MaccuDo, she also gave some to Jeewo Naaba (eight years), her eldest sister, and to RuGiyatu. Faatumata, the mother, told her to give it, but did not need to insist. She had told RuGiyatu to let Jeenaba give the powder to her friend, but without using any force herself, and she said that RuGiyatu should let Jeenaba give the milk to the person *mo mbeelum hawriti* (whose soul meets with hers). Later she explained, when I asked about that expression, that when people are friends, you say the one has *nanngi mbeelu makko*, or *nanngi haqqillo makko* (grabbed the other's soul, or grabbed the other's mind).

(4)

Diimaajo. Later in the same visit, RuGiyatu was whining for something to eat. Her mother said she had nothing and told her to go get a mbuudu

from her father for lacciri. RuGiyatu said, "What if he is not there?" "Ask
the moodiBBe he usually sits with, then," said her mother. RuGiyatu
went, but came back saying they were not there. RuGiyatu's face as she
whined for something to eat was half smiling, it seemed to me, but in any
case Faatumata was not visibly irritated. She got down some of the lacciri
she had made to sell and gave her a gourd ladle full. "*Beydu* (more)," said
RuGiyatu. Faatumata took out a large pinch with three fingers and added
it to the calabash. She told her to get water for it. But then after she got the
water, Faatumata seemed to think that her daughter needed some milk
after all, so she got down some milk put aside to sour and added it. But
then little Jeenaba wanted some too; Faatumata gave Jeenaba a gourd ladle
and RuGiyatu a metal spoon, but Jeenaba cried that RuGiyatu was eating
too. Faatumata told RuGiyatu to stop and let Jeenaba eat, but RuGiyatu
wouldn't stop and Jeenaba kept on crying. So Faatumata picked up Jeenaba
and nursed her, while RuGiyatu finished the lacciri.

(5)

Diimaajo. Early in my research I asked one of the mothers how she responded when her child was called on to share food. She told me that if
your child is eating and another one comes along, you ask your child to
give him some. But whatever he does is then up to him. If he gives some
to the visitor, fine; if not, then you just let him eat and you promise the
other child you will get him some too.

The examples just quoted seem to bear out the generalization
offered by this woman. Caretakers may tell their children what
they should be doing, but they don't make them do it. If the children don't go along with the adult request, then it's up to the adult
to find some other solution that satisfies to the extent possible all
the children concerned in the situation. As the following instance
shows, however, parents respond very differently when the child
is old enough to know better.

(6)

Diimaajo. Amnata (thirteen years) came in with a calabash of *buuru*
(deep-fried bread). Someone said that Maani (co-wife of Amnata's mother)
had stopped her as she was coming by and asked her for one. Amnata
didn't give Maani the dish and say, "Here, take one; they're Suka's (Amnata's mother's)." Instead, she gave one to Maani's child Sali (about three
years) and told her to give it to her. But it was hot and Sali dropped it and
Maani then refused to accept it. On hearing about this, Suka got mad at
her daughter and said, "*Ko woni naalu meereewu ngu!* (What kind of hope-
less moron are you!) Go back and offer her the calabash and let her take
one from it," which Amnata then did. When I questioned Suka about the
incident later, she said that she and Maani were *fuu gootum* ("all one"), and
both were Amnata's mothers, so Amnata was wrong to hold back something of Suka's from Maani.

One of the striking aspects of this incident is that it presents a contradictory teaching to the one in which the mother insisted that her daughter be allowed to give the powdered milk to the person to whom she felt like giving it. In the present case, we are tempted to explain the daughter's "error" as expressing merely spontaneous loyalty to her mother and a withholding from a person she didn't like. For the Fulani, then, proper behavior toward relatives means that, regardless of their actual feelings and inclinations, kin should give each other the impression that they believe themselves to be "all one." The daughter showed bad manners also by using a child, in that context, as a go-between. Children are, in fact, constantly being asked to carry messages or objects from one adult to another, and particularly when the latter would find it awkward, for reasons of propriety, to talk face-to-face. This is precisely why she should not have asked the co-wife's daughter to take the bread, because to do so, when face-to-face communication was possible and normal, could only be an affront to the other person.

There is a more subtle point here that is of even greater importance for the theme of this book. If the daughter had been of age six or less, she would not have been considered to know any better. If the co-wife, Maani, had gotten upset about such behavior, she herself would have been the one at fault for taking the child's act as socially relevant. But why is the act of someone with sense more socially relevant? It is because "knowing better" in fact means nothing other than knowing who you are as a participant in the networks of relationships to which you belong. For the Fulani this is tantamount to developing the feeling of oneness with your most important relatives. It is only when a person has this "sense" that choice has any meaning; the very idea of a goal implies a personal identity in terms of which some acts are more valuable than others. Amnata's mistake was serious because it showed that she did indeed "know who she was," her mother's daughter; therefore her act could be interpreted as expressing something of her mother. Suka realized this immediately. Her reprimand focused on what behavior was proper, but its urgency was due to the fact that Maani would implicate Suka in her daughter's act.

The extreme language Suka used to bawl out her daughter is common. Both FulBe and RiimaayBe yell at their children from time to time, and criticize and insult them in strong terms. Kids seem quite used to this treatment and appear to absorb it without flinching. In most instances they do not take it too seriously, for two reasons: first, no matter how strong the insults, they do not have the wounding quality they would have if uttered to an equal. The children know their subordinate place and receiving insults is simply one of the normal features of that status in society. Second, the children can tell that the tone of voice is not one of real menace, hatred, or dislike. On the contrary, it often seemed to me, at any rate, that there was an affectionate exasperation in the voice, as there must have been in Aunt Polly's when bawling out Tom Sawyer.

Everybody seems to feel that beating children is a good way to teach them things. Despite this unanimity of opinion, I never actually saw a real beating occur. Beatings were often threatened. The insult "*a hanyan!* (You'll shit!)" implies that the speaker intends to "beat the shit out of" the kid, as we would say. Perhaps most children, by the time they are old enough to be beaten, are also old enough to know how to run away from an enraged adult. Here are a few examples of adult violence, or threatened violence, toward children.

(7)

An adolescent Pullo boy once explained to me why his father, a good friend of mine, had hit him. The reason was that he had been entrusted with a calf or other livestock to sell at the market and was to buy certain things with the money. Instead he "ate" the money by spending it for his own amusement. The boy told me that he thought his father was perfectly justified in hitting him; the two of them had gotten along well prior to the incident, and were on good terms after it as well.

(8)

Pullo. I was helping the village chief by taking down and translating into French a letter he needed written. We heard the noise of children shouting outside, and someone told the chief that two little girls were fighting. At this he dashed out of the hut and hurried over to the hut beside which they were struggling. He picked up a thin stick from the ground and switched the girls with it, swearing at them all the while. The two girls ran off. The chief picked up some pieces of dried cow dung and flung them after them. The people gathered in the hut where we had been working all laughed at the show. I couldn't learn for sure why the chief got so mad or why he even intervened, for he didn't usually do that sort of thing. I suspect the reason was that the two girls, though of about the same age, were of different generations; it is a very serious offense for a "younger" to insult or strike an "elder." When he returned to the hut, slightly out of breath, we went back to work without discussing the incident.

This interpretation is supported by a number of other situations I observed where children were reprimanded for hitting an "elder" relative. Some adults, however, took the matter more seriously than others.

(9)

Diimaajo. Just now a very interesting play fight occurred. Salaamata (eight years) slapped Talel (four years) from behind and Talel turned and slapped back. Then they started giggling and slapping at each other. Daado, Talel's grandmother, grabbed Talel and tried to prevent her from slapping Salaamata. Another woman present seemed to take the slapping a little more seriously, saying a person shouldn't hit her *goggo* (father's sister), "or she'll enter hellfire." Talel got away from Daado and, still giggling, slapped at Salaamata some more; she, dog-paddling, slapped back. Then the other woman grabbed Talel, insisting that she mustn't slap her goggo, and Talel began to cry. Daado immediately took Talel back from the visitor and gave her the breast. She took a few minutes to calm down. The three grown women joked some more about how Talel would surely enter the fire for having slapped her goggo. Dikkoore (Talel's mother) laughingly said, "Oh, she's already been in it a long time!"

(10)

Diimaajo. At one point in the hairdressing session described in the previous chapter, the ten-year-old boy of the woman doing her friend's hair got into mischief. He was fooling around by trying to shinny up one of the poles supporting the roof of the verandah under which the women were sitting. These roofs are fairly low, so that it is possible for adults, standing on tiptoe, to place things upon them for storage away from children, goats, dogs, chickens, and so on. This boy, nearing the top of the pole and wildly swinging his hand about to grab the roof, knocked down a small sauce pot that had been placed there. The pot had some water and old sauce in it, and it fell onto one of the hearthstones used for cooking and broke, splattering people with the contents. Startled, the boy's younger brother began to cry.

"You're the one who's going to be hit next," said Maynmata, the mother, to the older boy. She was sitting on the ground with her friend's head in her lap, while her baby sat on a nearby mat. She ordered the boy to bring her a stalk of millet (to hit him with). "You'll not have it," sassed the boy. The mother then asked a little girl who happened to be walking by to give her the stick she was carrying. The girl did so, and Maynmata tried to hit the boy with it from her sitting position. He merely dodged out of the way, including behind me, to avoid the blows. Maynmata lambasted him for his orneriness, but he kept of range and she could not reach him. Soon he went off, singing.

Just before I took my leave, about half an hour later, I asked Maynmata whether she would have hit her son had I not been there. "Does a person dare hit his child in front of somebody else?" she asked. I asked my question again, and the mother said that the boy had damaged things and therefore deserved to be hit—yes, she would have hit him.

(11)

Diimaajo. Salaamata, about two years old and recently weaned, was playing with a dish of millet grains in the house. Her mother, Saajo, was not there and one of her baby twin sisters was being taken care of by a little girl caretaker, the other by another. Salaamata spilled some millet on the floor; she picked up some and instead of returning it to the dish she put it in the container of millet that had been already sifted. At that moment the mother, who was about twenty years old, came in and made an exclamatory sound, covering her mouth with her finger. Then she got mad at her daughter. She picked up a millet stalk to use as a switch. Salaamata started to cry. When Saajo raised her arm to hit her, one of the little girl caretakers, about twelve years old, put her arm in the way, saying, "*suro, suro* (calm down, calm down)." Salaamata just stood there and cried. Her mother laughed at her. She raised her switch again to hit Salaamata, and this time I intervened to prevent her just as the little girl had. Salaamata still stood there crying. Saajo told her to get out, but she wouldn't go. Then she told Buulo, a weaver who was winding his bobbins outside the house, to call Salaamata. Finally she struck her daughter lightly on the neck and shoulders and drove her out. Outside, Salaamata went and stood crying beside the two caretakers, who had gone out by then to help pound millet. "*Taa woyu mi fiyete* (Stop crying [or] I'll hit you)," says her mother. After about ten minutes the girl quieted down. Her mother said she didn't know why she was crying. "*O woyi pereeje tan* (She's just crying 'bricks' [i.e., for nothing])," she answered, when the weaver Buulo asked why. At one point she started up crying again, and her mother said, "*Taa woyu mi filante bonbon* (Stop crying; I'll look for a piece of candy for you)." This seemed to make Salaamata feel better.

This episode seems to contradict many of the generalizations I have been making so far in this book. The mother gets mad at a child who cannot yet be expected to have "sense" and makes the child cry. Not only that, she almost seems to enjoy doing it, and shows no evidence of empathy for the girl. This woman was, in my opinion, a more immature and hot-tempered person than most mothers, but I think there are people like that in any society. I didn't know any other women who were as rough and unfeeling with their children as Saajo seemed to be. But her living situation was a little different from that of the vast majority of people in that her husband was a government worker. She lived in a larger house than most people, and did not do her food preparation with other women, either relatives or neighbors. Instead, her husband's salary enabled her to pay people to help her with pounding millet, getting water, and so on. Thus, unlike most young mothers, she was not surrounded by other women of all ages most of the time. Such people would surely have stopped her from tormenting her child long before she actually did. Or, had her grandmother, who was often around, been there at the time, she would have stopped it too (I saw her intervene on other occasions). Had Salaamata been over six years old, however, Saajo's behavior would not be considered wrong, though the sheer vehemence of it would still be unusual.

The other grownups of the community not only serve as a check on each other, as we have seen, but also take direct parts in the teaching of children between the age of getting sense and adolescence. For example, they often put children through informal tests. The following episode is a variant of a very common pattern.

(12)

RiimaayBe. I have been sitting with these men in the shade of a great tree for about an hour while they chat, snooze, and weave cotton cloth, and have been half asleep myself from the heat and my own fatigue. At about 11:00 A.M. two boys ten to twelve years old are returning from the pond with their fishing poles. They haven't caught any fish, but they are both carrying bunches of water flowers they have gathered that are good to eat. A man calls out to one of the boys to come and give him one of his flowers. Immediately the boy starts towards him while detaching one of the flowers from his bundle. As he approaches, the man says, "Okay, that's good. Go along now." He didn't really want a flower, but was just testing the child to see if he would respond properly. But the boys actually did not get off that easily. Two other men called the boys over to them and each took a flower, one from one boy, the other from the other.

It is very likely that Maani, in the episode described above (number 6), was putting her stepdaughter to a test of this same sort. Let us examine more closely, now, the ways in which children learn these behaviors and attitudes they are tested for. On the one hand we want to discover what the adult conceptions of them are; on the other we want to glimpse, if we can, the learning process itself in operation. The former is a lot easier than the latter. In the last episode, for example, we could say that the elders are teaching the boys at least two things: first, the necessity to show deference to elders, and second, the requirement that one share whatever goods one has with others. In earlier episodes we have seen that knowing who your relatives are and treating them properly is of utmost importance. But are those the messages that get through to the children? How can we know what effects such practices are having on them? The purpose and the effects of beating are particularly interesting to consider in view of our modern rejection of the "spare the rod, spoil the child" belief. I think that the goal of beating is not so much to inflict pain as a punishment, but to make the child afraid. Afraid of what? Whereas we would want to make the child fear to make the "same mistake" again, the Fulani want him to develop fear of the adult. That is more important than any particular behavior. Many grownups explained their actions in this way, and both children and adults often used the concept of fear to explain why they refrained from doing something (cf. Riesman 1977:131). This also helps explain, perhaps, why violence was often threatened but infrequently carried out. It would be actually used only when the adult had reached his or her limit of tolerance, or when the child seemed to have lost his fear.

Children of course are learning things in some sense from the very first days of their lives. They learn much practical knowledge, including speech itself, well before they have acquired haY-Yillo. We have seen that children go everywhere that their mothers go and have almost complete freedom to explore their immediate world. They also learn how to learn, by imitating things their parents do, and they are encouraged in this. From a very early age, for instance, children do dance movements. I have seen little girls dancing who couldn't talk yet. People don't seem to worry if what the children are practicing would not be appropriate for their gender once they have grown up. Many boys, both FulBe and RiimaayBe, play at cooking when they are small (younger than four or five). Older boys are sometimes commandeered by their mothers into helping with food preparation or child care if the mother has no other helpers at the time.

(13)

Pullo. Burayma, about two and a half years old, doesn't seem to mind when his mother dashes off and back trying to milk the cows before the calves get to them. He had a little calabash of baobab fruits and played with it, humming and talking to himself. When his mother got back from milking, her son told her he was cooking and she should come and eat. His mother laughed and said, "Praise the Lord" (which really means approximately, "Well, I'll be darned!") and something I didn't catch, and went into the hut. Her son followed her, trying to catch up, saying, "Here's the sauce, here's the sauce," and fell over a chicken in the doorway. He didn't cry, but just got up and brushed himself off. His mother went back to pounding her millet, and Burayma continued with his cooking too.

(14)

Pullo. This morning again I find little Burayma cooking. He says he is cooking nyiiri. His mother tells him fine; make cobbal too. A male relative comes up and chats with the mother and myself for a while. He notices the way Burayma is playing and says he shouldn't be playing at cooking, that's women's work. I ask him what a boy of this age should be doing. The man replies, "He should be making model cows out of clay, he should carry a herdsman's club on his shoulder, he should be pasturing cows." I think he is joking.

(15)

Pullo. When I arrive at about 4:30 P.M., Hapsatu and her son Usel (eleven years) are pounding in two mortars in front of their hut. Little Booyi (six years) is playing at cooking, and her baby sister Aysatu (fifteen months) is with her. Booyi plays with much concentration, manipulating a large assortment of broken or battered utensils, bits of mud, and cow dung. As the only thing boys usually pound in a mortar is leaves for dyeing their shepherds' cloaks, I ask Usel what he is pounding. "Supper," he replied. His mother explained that he was helping her cook supper, as she was tired. Usel did not seem at all embarrassed by my asking him what he was doing. His older brother Bukkari (about eighteen years) is sitting next to me as I write. I ask him if he had ever pounded, as Usel is doing now. He replied that he had pounded a little in Winnde, a nearby village containing the main mosque of the area. "For your moodibbo?" I asked. "Yes." But he had never pounded for his mother.

The way parents teach changes once children have passed the threshold where they should have haYYillo. Prior to that point, children are watched patiently and are not always corrected. When parents do correct children, they usually do it gently and in an encouraging way. But once the children should have social sense, adults show very little patience and chew out and threaten children who make mistakes of various kinds, and particularly children who are sassy or disobedient. We have already seen in passing a few examples of both situations. It is interesting that all children seem to go through a stage (which adults recognize but do not have a name for) of being sassy, disobedient, and just plain stupid. Here are some episodes that illustrate these generalizations more pointedly.

(16)

Diimaajo. Faatumata, having just been shat on by Umaru (three months), asked her son Alu (three years) to get her a bit of millet stalk to clean up the mess. Alu didn't understand very quickly what she wanted, but she patiently asked him again and again for the millet stalk until he found the right thing and brought it.

(17)

Diimaajo. (Talel, at four years, seems to be on the border between having sense and not yet having it.) I noticed this morning that Dikkoore was giving Talel instruction in Fulfulde. Talel said *hanki* (last night), and Dikkoore corrected her, saying *"nyenden wi'etee"* (you should say, "the other day"). Then Talel repeated it after her. Later Talel was talking about a certain Kumbo, and Dikkoore asked her if she knew who Kumbo's father was. Talel said she didn't, so Dikkoore said, "Well, do you know Ummu's older brother?" It wasn't clear whether Talel did or not.

(18)

Diimaajo. Talel (four years) greeted me this morning calling me "Jooro Amnatu." Amnatu being the local name for my daughter Amanda, *Jooro Amnatu* means "Amnatu's chief," a formula used to name a woman's husband. *"baaba Amnatu wi'etee wanaa jooro Amnatu,"* said her grandmother Daado, who was sitting out in the sun. ("It's Amnatu's dad you're supposed to say, not Amnatu's chief.") Then she said that "Talel's getting old" and that she was a "little talking sack."

(19)

Diimaajo. Jeenaba (twenty months) and RuGiyatu (five years) are both learning to greet me. Jeenaba sticks out her hand for me to take. Today when I said, *"RuGiyatu, a nyalli e jam?"* she replied, *"jam nii."* (Standard greeting formulas meaning: "How are you today?" and "Just fine.")

RuGiyatu is humming the song Yimata composed recently that everyone is humming these days, and does the concentrated, shoulder-hunching dance that goes with it.

Faatumata, their mother, gone for a few minutes to get her mortar, comes back to find a foreign goat drinking the *kambulam* (water in which millet has been washed) together with one of hers. She slaps it and drives it away. Jeenaba slaps the other goat, and Faatumata says, *"a fiyan mbeewa ma nga? accu mbeewa ma yara* (You're hitting that goat of yours? Let your goat drink.)."* Jeenaba stops.

A *gariibu* (Koranic novice student) just now helped Faatumata chop a log, and she thanked him. A typical formula would be, *"Alla hokke moYYere* (May God give you good things)." RuGiyatu said, *"Alla hokke suudu lobburu* (May God give you a beautiful house)." Faatumata laughed and said it wasn't what you were supposed to say to a man. *"Alla hokke debbo lobbo"* is what you should say ("May God give you a beautiful wife").

(20)

Diimaajo. Soon after I sat down Dikkoore staged a sort of demonstration for me: she told Kajjata (seventeen months) to go and get her the calabash "over there" (by the entrance gate). Kajjata started out, but seemingly in

the wrong direction, and Daado said, "She doesn't understand." Dikkoore
pointed out that Kajjata was going around a goat which happened to be
barring the most direct route. Kajjata went around the goat and around
behind my back and then headed for the calabash. Dikkoore continued to
talk to her, encouraging her, praised her when she picked up the calabash,
and practically cheered when Kajjata actually gave it to her. Kajjata also
got more and more excited as she approached her mother. She has been
walking less then a month, and so sort of staggered a bit and almost fell
over her feet for the last few steps. Dikkoore gave her a big hug, saying,
"*lobbo* (beautiful)," and she and Kajjata both beamed. Dikkoore remarked
that Kajjata couldn't talk yet, but already she was capable of being sent.

(21)

Diimaajo. Dikkoore told Talel (four years) to push one of the logs a little
further into the cooking fire; Talel picked up the end of the burning log,
but seemed suddenly stupid and didn't know what to do next. Her mother
yelled at her instructions like, "Pick it up with both hands," and "Push it
in," but Talel, standing there holding the stick, wiggled it a little and said
she couldn't. Her mother swore at her colorfully, but told her to give up
trying and come and do something else. As she was nursing her baby at
that moment, she told Salaamata, her seven-year-old helper, to come and
do it.

(22)

I am visiting my friend Huseeni, a man of about thirty, who has been ill
for several days, perhaps with hepatitis. While we were chatting in his
house at about 3:00 P.M., his daughter Vingt-Et-Un came in. She is about
nine years old and may have come looking for something to eat. Huseeni
sent her out with 100 francs to buy fifteen francs worth of cobbal and
ten francs worth of milk (soured). "You mean fifteen francs worth of
milk. . . ." said Vingt-Et-Un. "Huh? Get off it," said her father. "I said
fifteen francs worth of cobbal and ten francs worth of milk." "Do I get to
keep some change?" asked Vingt-Et-Un. "Just get going and bring back
the change," said Huseeni. Vingt-Et-Un looked for a container to get the
food in. All she could find was a dirty enameled bowl. "But this bowl is
dirty," said Vingt-Et-Un. "Well, get some water and wash it," her father
told her. When the girl came back with the food about ten minutes later,
Huseeni asked her if she knew how to *diibude* (mash and mix solid food
and liquid into a smooth consistency). "I know how," said Vingt-Et-Un.
"Go serve yourself some water, then, and mix it up," said Huseeni. When
she had finished, Huseeni got her a Fulani wooden spoon and told her to eat.

What struck me in this sequence was that Vingt-Et-Un seemed
to be playing dumb a little, as if she couldn't use her own head, and
this seemed to have the purpose of getting her father to relate to
her. There was just a tinge of flirtatiousness in this. On further reflection concerning Vingt-Et-Un's behavior, I now have an alterna-

tive interpretation of its "dumb" quality, for I have seen something like it in other girls and boys of that age responding to their parents. These children suddenly seem to lose their normal competence and sense around their parents. The fact is, children of this age are highly capable in many everyday tasks, and in the absence of their parents they act with the self-confidence of people who know everything. The "dumbness," I think, is their way of expressing, largely unconsciously, the contradiction inherent in being a child of that age in Fulani society (and perhaps in all societies). Along with practical competence the children develop social sense, but it is precisely this latter ability that paradoxically reveals to them their lowly position in society—dependent, "socially incompetent." They are learning mentally to clothe the emperor. Several families that I knew well had children living through these difficulties during my fieldwork.

(23)

Diimaajo. When I arrived at about 3:30 P.M., I found the family sitting in the shade of the east wall of their house. Faatumata was holding her baby on her insteps to have a bowel movement, and she asked her daughter Jeewo-Naaba (seven years) to get a mat for me to sit on. Rather than obey her mother, Jeewo-Naaba just continued to do what she was doing, and her mother bawled her out for that. A few minutes later Faatumata asked her to gather up some dirt from the ground and bring it to clean up the baby's mess with. Again, Jeewo-Naaba just sat there. Again her mother bawled her out, saying things like "Look at that! Here I am talking to you and you act as if you hadn't heard a word!" She began to wash off the baby's bottom with water. Moving in a lethargic way, Jeewo-Naaba took a bit of board and used it to pick up a small quantity of dirt. She brought it to where the baby had made its mess on the ground and dumped the dirt over the excrement.

"Well? Don't just stand there; pick it up!" exclaimed her mother.

Jeewo-Naaba didn't react, so Faatumata scraped up the excrement herself, pushing it onto the board with a bit of millet stalk. Then she handed the board with its load to her daughter to dump in the compound's latrine. Jeewo-Naaba took it and headed for the latrine, but on her way she accidentally spilled a little of the dirt among the people sitting by the house.

"Just look at that!" Faatumata exclaimed again. Jeewo-Naaba stared back expressionless at her mother, while Faatumata glared at her with a hurt, almost helpless look.

A little later in the afternoon, when Faatumata was starting to pound millet for the evening meal, she was hampered by the baby's getting in the way. She called Jeewo-Naaba to come and get her. Her daughter washed her hands and then came up and stood near her mother and the baby.

"Well, pick her up!" said Faatumata.

Jeewo-Naaba smiled self-assuredly and picked up the baby; her mother continued to glare at her.

During the year, Faatumata and her daughter seemed to be getting along better for a while. Yet towards the end of my stay things seemed to have worsened again.

(24)

Diimaajo. Maama, Faatumata's co-wife, was about to go to the market to buy some millet for the family. With a crying baby on her back, she had come to the door of Faatumata's house and was standing outside, waiting to be given the money to buy the grain and a container to carry it in. Faatumata handed Jeewo-Naaba a calabash and 100 francs and told her to give it to the other woman to buy millet with.

"How much millet?" asked her daughter.

"What's this!" exclaimed Faatumata. "Here I've just given you 100 francs and you ask me how much millet?"

Jeewo-Naaba turned and went to stand by the door.

"Give it to her, for goodness sakes! Here she's waiting with a crying baby on her back and you don't go to her! What kind of behavior is that?"

At last Jeewo-Naaba went out the door and handed the calabash and money to her other mother.

"Lordy Lordy, will wonders never cease!" said Faatumata (*Laa illaaha illallaa, Muhammadu rasuurullaay!* lit. "There is no god but God; Mohammed is his prophet.")

When Jeewo-Naaba came back in a moment later, her mother asked her to hand her a rope that was lying on the ground near her by the door.

"I'm not going to give it," she replied.

Fifteen minutes later everything seemed calm, as if nothing had happened. Yet it was my impression that at the moments when her mother was yelling at her Jeewo-Naaba had really flinched, blinking her eyes downward.

It was very hard to tell how children were feeling after such attacks. I once asked one eight-year-old girl who was a mother's helper in another family and who had just been bawled out, if she felt angry (lit. if her heart was bitter) after the mother had criticized her that way. I wrote in my notes, "She smiled a little and said no, and seemed to mean it." On the other hand, the emotions following a really severe bout of criticism from a tough, old grandmother seemed to be deeper and more painful.

(25)

Diimaajo. When I arrived at Suka's house at about mid morning, I found her fourteen-year-old daughter standing outside the door of the house, with a shawl over her head. She did not reply right away to my greeting, then turned toward me slowly and mumbled, "Good morning." I didn't try to pursue the conversation, but went into the house. Suka was there, as well as her own mother, Yaaye-Suka. After greeting them I asked what was the matter with Amnata. At my question Yaaye-Suka began—or more likely recommenced—her diatribe against Amnata.

"Amnata is no good. Here we are late in the morning and she has not gotten us a drop of water. Not a drop of water in the house and Amnata sits there getting ready to make fried bread for the market. What's the good of that? We'll not see a single penny from that work. She sells her bread and never gives us a cent of the profit. She spends the whole day making the bread and doesn't lift a finger to help with the housework. She just eats and sleeps here, and we never see a cent of what she makes."

What Yaaye-Suka had done now was to confiscate Amnata's materials for making fried bread. She had told Amnata that unless she went and got them some water she was not going to make fried bread that day.

Yaaye-Suka was talking quite loudly enough for Amnata, standing just outside the door, to hear every word. She called her a worthless, lazy child, and said, what's more, that not one of her father's children had turned out any good. "As for her mother's children (Suka's children by previous husbands), only Hawwa Alu and Hureeta Alu are better. Hawwa is better because she gets mad and fights if people impugn her mother's honor; as for Amnata, she doesn't give a damn. Her heart is dead meat; she doesn't even have a heart. Hureeta is the best of the children [she is married to a Koranic scholar in Mali]. Whenever *she* did work she used to give all her money to her father. And instead of hiding what she earned and using it for herself alone, she would ask her father to buy her something when she needed it. For instance, if all the other girls were getting new dresses, she would ask her father to get her one too, and he would."

Yaaye-Suka went on and on, getting quite carried away as she dredged up all the faults Amnata had been committing during her life. Amnata said nothing and did nothing in response, but just stood within earshot, out of sight beyond the open door of the house. Finally Yaaye-Suka picked up a long millet stalk and stormed out the door, yelling at Amnata to get going and fetch the family some water.

About fifteen minutes later, Amnata appeared in the doorway with a large bucket of water on her head and holding a coin between her teeth in such a way that it pressed down on her lower lip. She eased the heavy container off her head to come through the low doorway and carried the pail by its handle as she walked through the room and out again into the courtyard where the kitchen was. She poured the water into the large storage pot in the kitchen and passed back out of the house without a word. She made several such trips to get enough water to fill the pot.

After her last trip I got up to leave. I looked at her closely, trying to discern in her face and bearing what feelings she might be having. I called her name. She looked at me; not knowing quite what I wanted or what to say, I said, "Thank you." Her face looked strange, and I suddenly realized that she was crying inside.

"Don't look at me," she said, and turned her face away. Then she went into the back room of the house.

I never saw such a harsh diatribe on the part of FulBe adults towards children, but I am quite sure they occurred from time to time. I believe that the reason I didn't see them was simply that during my first field trip I spent far less time in the women's workplace than on my second trip. Any close senior relative has the right and the duty to criticize younger relatives who are behaving improperly. As children get older and become young adults, however, their elders generally refrain from using the whip of insults, as this could lead to rupture rather than strengthening of relations. The case of one young man, who was a particularly notorious wastrel, provoked several attempts at direct criticism. The last son of an old, wealthy man, perhaps he can be compared to a spoiled prince. Many people were trying to get him to shape up, but no one had succeeded by the time of our departure. Not a resident of our village, the young man spent several days on a visit indolently lying around in and out of our hut. One evening the village chief dropped in and found the young man stretched out asleep on the floor of our hut. He was an "older brother" to the young man because his father was the older brother of the latter's father. My notes, taken at the time, read:

(26)

Pullo. Burayma has a rather bizarre coiffure at the moment. His beard and sideburns are connected in one continuous line to a fringe of hair that mounts up his temples on either side and comes together on top of his forehead, enclosing his face in a frame of hair. Between this fringe of hair on his forehead and the rest of the hair on his head, there is a shaven space, which is, in the end, what distinguishes this hairdo from any other. The chief pointed to that coiffure and said, in a strongly reproving manner, "Seriously, do you think that is *good*?"

Next morning, I overheard him bawling out the young man. Burayma had spent the whole day yesterday in or near our hut, working on his new shepherd's cloak or sleeping, and did not go to the wells as he had been asked to. Now the chief was telling him how bad this was. Unfortunately I didn't pay attention right away and so missed much of what he said. The gist was that on the one hand he was selling too many cows and, on the other, that he was not taking care of those he had left. If you don't watch out, the chief was saying, you are soon not going to have any cows at all.

Criticism of people who are not close relatives is also very common, but usually takes an indirect form. People use barbed expressions with double meanings, or express sometimes violent

feelings under cover of laughter and joking. The scandal of the
man who kept running after his errant wife even after he had married a second one provoked many such critiques. Most of the
man's relatives were incensed that the errant wife was bringing
such shame upon one of their own people. One way they expressed their feelings can be seen in the following entry from my
journal.

(27)

Pullo. After about three months of absence, Hawwa, the mystery woman,
has come back. I was very curious to see what she was like, and also to see
how she would like me. I found her by accident, as I was wandering
around the village, in Faatumata's hut. Faatumata's mother, Habbata, was
there, making string from strands of baobab tree bark, and Hawwa was
making it too, apparently helping her. Another young wife new to the village was also there, as were some children. Apparently they had been teasing Hawwa, for as soon as I arrived, they asked me to take my gun and
shoot her so that they could have meat. I refused, saying with a laugh that
the Europeans would come and take me away, lock me up and cut off my
head. "Oh, we won't tell," they replied. "Maybe not," I said, "but her
father will." "We'll tell him she went off into the jungle; if we eat all her
meat no one will know the difference." Throughout this conversation ran
a thread of uneasy laughter, while Hawwa smiled with serene haughtiness.
Later on, I got up to go, saying that I needed to look for some wood to
cook tea with. "Oh, I'll get some for you," said Hawwa. "Really?" I
asked. "You'd better not let her," said Habbata, "or her husband will
come and hit you."

Learning to Be a Relative

In *Freedom in Fulani Social Life* (1977) I was interested in the question of how it was possible for people to stand up to what seemed
to me devastating attacks. Here I am concerned more with the
meanings both of the criticisms and of the acts that they reproach.
For example, what is the significance of the sassiness of preadoles-
cent children? A clue to its explanation lies in the fact that I instinc-
tively chose the word "sassy" to describe that stage of childhood.
This term connotes "back talk"; indeed, what we see in children
acting this way is nothing other than an imitation of their parents,
a reflection of their behavior. The little children who say "impu-

dently" to the mother, "You'll not have it!" are copying exactly the tone of voice the mother herself uses when she refuses something to an equal or a child (they probably wouldn't dare say this to their father). What makes the act impudent is merely the fact that it is a child doing it, for it is considered perfectly appropriate in an adult. Thus sassiness is related to "dumbness" because both have to do with the children's developing competence: they have learned to imitate their elders, but must now accept the fact that they have not become their equals for all that. They may know "who their relatives are" as individuals seen every day, but have yet to discover who they are as figures in the wider society and what it means to be related to them. This is a lifelong process. Although the implications for one's personal identity of having one or another group of relatives are relatively fixed, it takes sophistication to understand them. This is partly because with each stage of a person's life, and also as new historical and individual circumstances arise, there are changes in the degree of support, the obligations, and the opportunities for creative action inherent in a set of relations.

I said earlier that for the Fulani, to have social sense is tantamount to developing the feeling of oneness with your most important relatives. When a two-year-old girl hit her baby sister who was only a few weeks old, the adults explained her act as being due to the fact that the child did not yet realize the baby was her relative. It is particularly interesting that the adults neither said that she was jealous nor that she was bad because of her act; she was simply ignorant and still too young to learn. As a result, the strategy was not at all to punish, but simply to protect the younger child from her. In another family I saw a visitor egg on a four-year-old boy to hit his eighteen-month-old sister. His mother told him not to, but did not stop him by force. On the other hand, the boy's older sister, who was twelve, did physically restrain him. When the visitor left I asked the boy's mother if the woman's action had bothered her. "No," she said, "because the older should hit the younger, but not the younger the older. We never permit the younger to hit the older." In fact, the boy was within his rights to hit his sister, because "she had been bothering him." There is a game played with much delight by boys (girls don't play this game) between the ages of about three and ten that seems dramatically to represent this contrast of right between elder and younger. The game's structure is a little like that of musical chairs, in that a round of play designates the slowest person. The boys sit or stand in a circle and, on signal, all try to put their fists one on top of the other. The one to put his fist down last loses. But the loser is not eliminated; instead, all the other players make a fist with their middle knuckle protruding and then rap the unfortunate one on the top of the head. Play then immediately proceeds to the next round. That fast and slow stand for elder and younger is almost self-evident, and the interpretation has linguistic support in that to say So-and-so was "born first" people commonly use the same word as "to precede" in time or in space. It is significant, in comparison with, say, musical chairs, that no one is eliminated. Being at the bottom does not mean you are out; on the contrary, you are still valued for playing the game.

(28)

Pullo. During yesterday's rain, while a number of people of different ages were sheltering in our hut, Adulkarim (eighteen years old, a classificatory grandfather to the little boy) called Usmaanu to come over to him and play the fist game. The kid, only about two years old, didn't want to; he probably didn't want to get hit on the head. Adulkarim said, "Come here and let me hit you." Then he formed his hand into a fist, whistled softly over the knuckles and rapped the boy gently on the head, but not all that gently. He did this a few times, while the child withdrew further and further, then the adolescent gave up with a little laugh. The little boy seemed to be trying to be brave.

My reaction to this scene at the time was to feel angry at this bully for teasing the child so roughly. I saw the adolescent as a quite insensitive person who just didn't know how to relate to children. I saw him tease the same child on several other occasions as well. Today, I would stick by my earlier intuitive reaction to these incidents, but I see them in a slightly different light. Adulkarim, standing in the relation of grandfather to the child, had the right, as would cross-cousins, to tease him. This was neither the expression of anger, nor an irrational, sadistic outburst. On the contrary, the sheer fact of playing this game with the child is a kind of "staging" of the notion of relationship. After all, the obvious way to indicate relationship is by nurturing, as mothers do. Teasing a person produces a paradox: you are a relative but you are doing "bad" things to the person. While grasping such an idea would be far beyond the little boy, participating willy-nilly in the game gives him practice in trying to be brave and induces him to develop a more complicated, differentiated view of the people to whom he belongs.

In contrast to this, for older siblings to hit younger ones without good reason is not condoned. In the following example we can see the emergence of a different issue—not that of right, but that of maintaining the relationship.

(29)

Diimaajo. Jeewo-Naaba (eight years) and her mother Faatumata are still as much at odds as ever. Jeewo-Naaba has been hitting her sisters, and Faatumata says she *Bawli yonki sanne* (she's very black in her spirit). *"neDDo mo rimaay rimdaaka yi'i bonnde, na haani accude minyiiiko* (A person who has never given birth and who was born without siblings will see bad times, [so she] ought to stop bothering her younger sister)." Faatumata later explained that a person without children and/or brothers and sisters has no help—whoever wants to can hit him, whereas they wouldn't dare hit a person with much family.

Many proverbs make this same point, such as this one: *"liBeede wo Bureede, daaseede wo Bureede saare* (To be thrown is to be bettered, but to be dragged on the ground is to be outnumbered in relatives)." Demonstrations of this harsh reality are constantly occurring. The most glaring examples arose when foreigners of low status occasionally camped for a time in the village. There was a Bella family that camped with the FulBe of Petaga several months out of most years. Bella are the former slaves of the Tuareg; like RiimaayBe, then, they don't have lineages, and they don't even have the benefit of historical connection with particular FulBe families. This family made its living by tanning leather, carpentry, and some metal work.

(30)

Pullo. The little Bella boy has just appeared at the doorway. *"Foo foo* (Hello)," I said to him. "Don't greet him," said Faatumata Muusa, "he's just a Bellaajo. He will steal your things." Then Kajilde, who is making butter behind me, said, "Get out." But he came in, and now is standing by the door looking at me. Now Faatumata is telling me to get my gun and shoot him. I have seen this kid quite badly treated by the young FulBe kids also; they tease and torment him, and hit him. The Bella seem to the FulBe to be a lower species, yet they are allowed to camp in the villages.

The essential lesson to learn, then, has a circular quality. The only people you can really depend on in life are relatives, but this is true only so long as everyone believes that it is and acts upon it. What makes this lesson so difficult to teach and to accept is the inevitable pain in these relationships. Countless proverbs reiterate this point in vivid images. They seem to be trying to prove, by the evident truth of their denotations, that their connotations are equally and inexorably true. The following two sayings exemplify this forcefully. "*Suudu baaba wo saayo kebbe* (One's relatives are a cloak of nettles)." The idea is that they cling to you and hurt you, but they also prevent others from grabbing and harming you. The second proverb needs no comment: "*BoccooDe mboogondura de pu-sataa* (For all that testicles rub each other, they don't burst)."

Proverbs are a way of sharpening adult consciousness and of fixing in memory these truths that seem necessary for social life. But it is through play, not proverbs, that these truths are impressed upon the children. Games like the fist game, and teasing by various relatives having the right to do so, are a crucial part of the process by which children come to terms with the complex reality of being a relative.

We have seen many other aspects of this process throughout this study already, namely all the acts of care and feeding of relatives that not only enable people to live but also delimit fairly clearly who is included in "we." Let us now briefly examine yet another part of this process, namely the transmission of knowledge. Teaching of certain kinds of knowledge should not be thought of merely as the transmission or reproduction of culture, but also as a way of defining relationship.

When I asked people how they learned things, such as lore about the bush, some told me that their mother or father taught them, others that they had learned them from their comrades. Both these generalizations are true. By and large children pick up much practical knowledge, including names of plants and animals, from their peers. However, parents may also give this kind of instruction, either spontaneously or when asked specific questions. One young mother told me that when she would be out pasturing the goats she would bring back twigs and grasses that she didn't know to show her father; he would tell her what they were and what they were good for. Another young mother, in contrast, told me that when she used to pasture sheep and goats it was the older kids she was with who would tell her what things were. They even told her that certain plants were good against witchcraft. Her father never talked to her about these matters, except that he got mad when he discovered she had learned witchcraft medicine. The reason was that he thought this would endanger her; because children cannot hold their tongues, she might incur the wrath of a witch overhearing her talk about it. Yet another mother insisted that children learn more from their parents than from their peers. She said that a parent out in the bush with a child will point things out and ask if the child knows what they are; if not, the parent will explain. Kids tell one another things (she used a disparaging word meaning chitchat or storytelling) but parents take every opportunity to tell their kids how things are in the world. In order to make sure a child won't get harmed by dangerous plants and animals, you say, "*nde neDDo meemi Dum fuu maayan* (If a person touches that, he'll die)." Then if the child is out playing with other kids and they see the thing (e.g., a fruit), the one will say, "*Ayya am wi nde neDDo meemi Dum fuu o maayan. Tinn taa en itta Dum* (My mom told me that if a person touches that, he'll die. We'd better not pick it)." The others will accept this and leave it alone. One adolescent boy told me that it was his father who taught him most of the lore he knew. He would quiz his son from time to time, asking him to identify plants, and telling him the ones he didn't know. He also made the boy lie down on his back at night to learn the constellations. Some of them are hard to perceive, and the father would hit the boy to make him see and learn them. The boy felt this instruction was effective—he did come to distinguish the more elusive constellations—and in his way of telling about this I glimpsed affection and admiration for his father.

Thus people may differ widely in the ways in which they learn about the natural world. Their information about sex, on the other hand, comes entirely from peers. All concurred on that point. Parents would never talk about sex, menstruation, and the like with their children, for they would find it extremely embarrassing (*na enni sanne*, lit. "it makes one very shy, restrained"). When a girl first menstruates, she will ask a person with whom she can talk freely, such as a cross-cousin, what to do.

When it comes to knowledge that is powerful or knowledge that concerns social and historical facts, however, transmission is from individual to individual within families. The case of religious instruction is only an apparent exception, for, as we have seen, novices studying with a moodibbo are normally "given" to him so that they become like his children. Interestingly enough, one young moodibbo told me that youths who go on their own to study with such a scholar generally do less well than children who are "entrusted" to him by their parents. The man told me that his father had taken him at age eleven to the moodibbo to learn to read, and told the teacher to beat him almost to death if he didn't learn his lessons. He *was* beaten by this man, particularly at night when he was falling asleep over his studies, and thus he learned quickly and well. But boys who had come of their own accord resented the beatings because they were never "given" by anyone to the teacher; hence they did not learn and went back home before getting very far. This contrast between the two kinds of students underscores once again, I think, the importance for action of a person's sense of relationship to relatives: when a boy (in this case) feels he is "doing what he found," acting in accord with their values, he has more inner strength than does the loner to persevere in the face of hardships. What is more, the role of beatings in this education suggests another function they have in addition to instilling fear as mentioned earlier. They dramatically establish a relationship of superior to inferior within some kind of unity. They are the most powerful expression of both the oneness and the hierarchy of kinship.

But powerful knowledge in any case is shared extremely reluctantly, as we saw in an earlier chapter. There, the point was that two people couldn't have the same knowledge because that would make them equal in power; such a situation was both socially anomalous and unacceptable to the original holder of the knowledge, who would then be superfluous. Now we need to examine what it means to pass on knowledge to another person. During my fieldwork, and for many years thereafter, not having reflected on the question, I simply assumed that Fulani knowledge was lying around to be picked up by interested members of the society, just as we imagine that the knowledge of our own society is in principle available to all through schooling, textbooks, magazines, self-teaching programs, dictionaries, encyclopedias, and many other media. Our most common ways of teaching in schools tend to play down or even eliminate the relationship between individuals, making education appear to be primarily a matter of efficiently acquiring competencies and knowledge by "tapping into" a "pool" which is not diminished by what people take out of it.

By the time women bear children of their own they already have, as we have seen, much experience in practical baby care. But the preparation and administration of medicines and charms are things they learn on the job, from their mothers and grandmothers. While women will gladly give some basi mixture to other women, the secrets of its preparation are jealously guarded. There are common ingredients to most mixtures, but it would be safe to say that the more potent the medicine the more secret its preparation. In many instances the difference between an ordinary and a powerful medicine will not be the physical ingredients at all, but the manner in which they have been gathered from the bush, the time of day they are cooked, the kind of pot used, and many other variable procedures. For example, in some cases when you take a bit of bark from a tree you must leave a certain (secret) offering to the tree; otherwise there will be no efficacy in the product.

Now, the mother who learns these secrets from her mother or grandmother does not at all think of herself as "tapping into" a general stock of knowledge to which everybody accedes as they get older; rather, that knowledge is experienced as part of her family's way of doing things. She receives that knowledge because of her particular relationship to those who have it, and because she has become a mother herself.

The knowledge received from one's parents has an almost sacred quality that knowledge picked up on one's own or from peers does not have. We have just seen the example of children avoiding a plant because someone else's mother told them it was dangerous. A middle-aged Diimaajo man told me that a father would pass on to his son his knowledge of who owned what land and what the boundaries of their fields were. The purpose of this is to enable the son to take a useful part in settling disputes later on. If the father was a respected person, the son will in his turn be able to affirm with authority that he knows the boundary of So-and-so's field because his father knew it and showed it to him. Fathers will test their son's knowledge by asking them to point out the boundaries for them. What gives this knowledge its authority is both who it comes from and the manner of its transmission.

Not only do we find a division between women's and men's knowledge in Fulani society, but also between the knowledge of FulBe, RiimaayBe, and the different groups of artisans. Though the Diimaajo just cited had spoken in general terms about fathers and sons, I think that particular domain of knowledge concerns RiimaayBe more than FulBe, especially in a densely settled region like Djibo. For the FulBe, of course, cattle care is a rich and complicated realm of knowledge. A great deal of that knowledge is not really esoteric; to obtain it, however, one must live with the cattle day in and day out and observe how various techniques are employed as needed. Several families, as indicated earlier, and in some cases even unrelated families, will share tasks of pasturing and watering cattle. This in turn leads to a constant sharing of information and expertise among the youths who do this work. While magical knowledge is carefully guarded within the family, the practical knowledge could be said to be preserved at the level of the ethnic group. By the time FulBe boys are old enough to take care of cattle, they are also old enough to start traveling with them. When they take their herds on transhumance or in search of distant water, the fact that they are in foreign and potentially dangerous territory sharpens their awareness of their responsibility for and dependence on the cattle, thereby enhancing their sense of family and ethnic identity.

We shall consider shortly some other important impacts of cattle on the lives of FulBe youths as compared with the RiimaayBe. For now, however, let us look at one other type of knowledge and its transmission, namely shameful knowledge. By this term I mean information about a family or certain members of it which must not be mentioned because of shame. It would be impossible to list all the possibilities, but a few examples are that a person is a bastard, that a person is a bedwetter, epileptic, impotent, mentally ill, and so on. The status of this sort of knowledge is quite different from that concerning medicines and magic, in that generally everybody living in the community knows it. What is shared between the family members, then, is not exactly a secret, nor is it a power; rather it is the shame itself, and the obligation to keep silent about it. The Fulani have many proverbs concerning this reality. I will quote two of them because their implications for human relations are interesting and enlightening: "*mo duwaaki suudu anndaa to ndu siirata* (You don't know where the house leaks until you've taken shelter in it from the rain)." "*duroowo paaBi kam anndata laYooru* (It's the frogs' herdsman who knows which one limps)." Both these proverbs contrast the knowledge of the outsider and the insider, suggesting that fine as things may look from the outside, once you get to know the people they have their problems and weaknesses just like anybody else. The question then arises, once *who* gets to know the people? And what notion of knowing is implied?

The knowers are first of all members of the family themselves, but they are also people who become linked to the family in other ways, particularly through marriage and friendship. Thus knowing implies relationship—a belonging of some kind—and vice versa. It also implies both a seeing of people with their faults and a complicity in not revealing them. Having this kind of knowledge of one another in Fulani society, and probably in all human relations, creates a feeling of closeness and we-ness. In Fulani society, it is a we-ness from which no one escapes (except by leaving the society altogether). By being a family member, or a spouse or even a close friend of other people, you are known as having a bond (enDam) with them. You are one of them.

The FulBe have a factor affecting the links between them that the RiimaayBe almost completely lack, namely cattle. Not only does the daily life of FulBe differ markedly from that of the RiimaayBe because of taking care of cattle, but also the fact that cattle are individually owned and inherited, yet normally herded collectively, has a profound effect on family relations, especially between fathers and children. In chapter 3, I emphasized the value of cattle for FulBe survival. From the FulBe point of view, however, the main reason why cattle are valuable is that they permit people to live as FulBe, to maintain a FulBe identity (cf. Riesman 1977:159). The FulBe idea of nobility depends on ownership of cattle not only because cattle are wealth, but even more because they are what we would call "old wealth," coming from the past, by way of the ancestors. They are a kind of proof that those people really existed, and they make palpable the link between them and the families existing here and now. Though cattle do not "beget children" in FulBe thinking (a common concept among people using bride wealth to obtain wives, such as the Nuer), having cattle to use and to pass on to one's descendants is indispensable for maintaining both family line and pride in that line, the ethos of honor that goes with belonging to a prestigious house. Both the line and the ethos are usually designated by the same term, *suudu baaba*; another closely related term for that ethos is *Biingu baabaaku*, which literally means "child-of-father-ness," hence pride in being the child of your father, hence pride in being who you are.

FulBe children begin to learn about these things very young; as soon as their minds are capable enough they begin to pick out the different cattle in the village herds and learn to identify all the animals with their owners. When children reach about age seven their father will deliberately point out which cows belong to them and will explain how they all descend from the heifer or heifers that they received on the day each given a name (this all holds equally for girls and boys). Not just anybody gives the child cattle that day. The father absolutely must give an animal; normally it should be a heifer, but if none are available it is possible to substitute a bull calf which will later be sold or traded for a heifer. The mother and/or the mother's brother may also give animals to the child at this time. A special verb, *sukude*, is used to speak of giving these gifts; I was not able to learn its meaning, though I suspect it is the verb from which the noun for child (*suka*, pl. *sukaaBe*) is derived. People did not say as much to me, but in view of the limited range of relatives who can give these gifts, I suspect that these are a kind of materialization of the child's location in suudu baaba. There is evidence, in any case, that people sense a strong link (we might call it mystical) between the children and their "own" cattle. For one thing, it is significant that cattle and a name are received at the same time; for another, from that time forward everything that happens to those animals is considered to happen to the child. Their flourishing or their dwindling indicate the latter's *dawla* (grace); they indicate the will of God toward the child.

This is all the more interesting in that the male child has no practical role in taking care of his cows until he is an adolescent (never, in the case of women), and usually cannot dispose of them as he pleases until after his first marriage. When talking about cows and their owners people will say "So-and-so's cow," but a person almost never says "my cow." Instead he will say "our cow." This way of talking applies also to wives and children:

people always say "our wife," "our child." This apparently subtle change of possessive is quite significant. Who is implied in "our"? Suudu baaba. The fact that people would not normally use the expression "our husband" (unless they were actually co-wives of the same man) is for once not the result of sexism, but simply follows from the logic of the situation. Wives, cattle, and children all contribute toward the increase, or at least maintenance, of the family line. It is significant that a common term for a woman who has just given birth is *BeyDo*, "augmenter." The other side of the coin is that a woman may call "husband" all the brothers (and even sisters) of her actual husband.

The RiimaayBe use all these same expressions and kinship terms, with the important exception we have already noted of "suudu baaba." In fact, in response to my asking many people what distinguished FulBe from RiimaayBe, a number of RiimaayBe spontaneously answered that they didn't have suudu baaba. For RiimaayBe children the immediate family and the larger circle of relatives they grow up in are no less important than they are for the FulBe, but the lack of suudu baaba and the lack of cattle are important structural differences that affect their lives on two levels. In chapter 9 we shall explore in detail the effects that these different social experiences have on people's self-concepts and personality development. Here I will simply summarize the nature of those experiences.

On the level of everyday relations RiimaayBe children find that the people who are "like them," people who belong to their families, are in fact heterogeneous both in occupation and in ancestry. While nearly all men grow millet, we have seen that most practice a variety of secondary occupations as well. At the time of my fieldwork there were still some old people living who spoke the languages of the people from whom they were captured. For FulBe children the adult world appears more homogeneous and interrelated, both through kinship and through the common interest everyone has in the well-being of the herds. In RiimaayBe experience, each man works only for himself, though he will occasionally participate in collective tasks; there is no equivalent to the tending of cattle for them. In addition—particularly significant for males—children receive neither family name, lineage membership, nor wealth as a heritage from their fathers (under slavery servitude was inherited from the mother, and nothing at all from the father). At best a boy might hope to receive some secrets when his father is on his deathbed, but this is never sure, especially if there are a number of sons. On the level of the wider society children learn, more or less rapidly depending on where they are living, what the place of their families is in the hierarchies of power and prestige. They learn through stories and proverbs, through tellings of historical events, through diatribes and insults against bastards and offspring of slaves of slaves, and through actual encounters between FulBe and RiimaayBe, the range of meanings of the terms that label themselves and their families.

In these last two chapters I have intentionally presented much anecdotal material so as to make it possible to attempt phenomenological interpretations of Fulani childhood experience. Any event occurs in several contexts at once, and can furnish material for reflection on numerous questions. I have striven to preserve this quality of the realities that I have been describing partly to show as precisely as possible how I get from observation to my particular interpretations and partly so that these materials can be used by scholars with other interests and questions than mine. Two major conclusions, it seems to me, can be drawn at this point. The first is that FulBe and RiimaayBe do not differ with regard to the ways in which parents and other caretakers handle children during the first four to six years of life. There is variation from one family to another, but I claim that this is idiosyncratic rather than systematic between the two groups under study. It follows logically from this conclusion that the personality differences we have delineated between the FulBe and the RiimaayBe cannot be caused by the child-rearing practices used for those early years.

The second major conclusion is that, in addition to the adult personality differences themselves, the social environments in which the children of the two groups grow up differ in internal structure, types of work people do, and sociopolitical status in the global social system. Children begin to be able to understand such meanings only in later childhood, as they develop haYYillo. An important component of education, we have noted, consists in drawing on children's haYYillo so that they learn "who their relatives are." This implies both identifying a group of people that one belongs to, and accepting a number of obligations or moral imperatives that vary with circumstances and with the particular relationship concerned. While these injunctions are essentially the same for FulBe and RiimaayBe, the actual models to imitate and emulate are significantly different. Viewed from the outside, then, the essential tasks of parenthood seem to be to take care of children so that they survive their most vulnerable years, and to convince them as they grow older that they do indeed belong to their parents, that their future is with them, and that they are relatives.

7

CHILD DEVELOPMENT IN FULANI ETHNOPSYCHOLOGY

We saw in chapter 5 that during the first few years of life the child, whether Pullo or Diimaajo, boy or girl, is as if continually bathed in an amniotic fluid of warm human bodies. Not only that, the child is a constant center of attention. Whenever children move, get hungry, or need to relieve themselves, somebody notices, and even if they are doing nothing at all somebody might very well be looking at them, want to hold them, cuddle them, or play with them. It is very unseemly for youths and men to be interested in or have anything to do with small children in public, but when among family even a Pullo father may enjoy sitting with a child on his lap listening to the cattle bellow in the twilight. I never saw either women or men roughhouse or wrestle with children as parents sometimes do in our society. While grownup "joking relatives" sometimes used a little violence in their teasing, parents never did so when they played with children; perhaps this was due to the very strong taboo against younger hitting elder.

The picture that emerges from these data on early childhood among the Fulani is extremely positive in the light of clinical and psychoanalytic psychology. It struck me, for example, that according to Erik Erikson's criteria for healthy childhood, as set forth in *Childhood and Society* (1963) and in other essays (e.g., Erikson 1953), the Fulani treatment of children was as good as could be imagined for creating a strong sense of "basic trust" in a child, that is a deep, inner sense that one is good and that the world can be relied on. Similarly, the manner in which children learn to control their bowel movements and deposit them in the right places seemed not at all to put in question their autonomy or provide occasions where they might feel shame and doubt of their own powers. Finally, the behavior of older children and of adults offered convincing evidence for this conclusion, since just about everyone I met exuded a degree of self-confidence and zest for life that are unusual in my experience of Americans. Though I did meet a few people afflicted with mild or acute psychoses, I did not come across any who seemed neurotic.

Now, if my observations are accurate, and if there is indeed a connection between the "good" early childhood experiences of the Fulani and some of the characteristics these people display as adults, we still have to ask: How has this state of affairs come about? Several possibilities, not necessarily incompatible with each other, suggest themselves. It could result from the fact that Fulani tradition contains knowledge of human behavior which our science is laboriously rediscovering. Perhaps the Fulani share our criteria of what a good childhood amounts to, and they are trying to create a solid psychological foundation upon which their children can grow. Or perhaps they are quite unaware of what they are doing—in our terms—but use those methods because it is the ancestral way that they blindly follow. In that case, Fulani practices would have to be explained as the evolutionary end result of an unconscious natural selection of behaviors. All these hypotheses arise naturally out of the framework for interpreting human relations which I have been using thus far. It is one that I believe to underlie both American common sense and many schools of Western psychology. What we must do now is look at childhood and child rearing from a Fulani point of view. If we can discover what the Fulani concepts of childhood and parenthood are, and their ideas concerning why people turn out the way they do, we will have the materials to evaluate our hypotheses. The results, however, will surprise us. We will be led to conclude that the hypotheses may be irrelevant because the Fulani frame of reference is such a different one from our own.

First Find Your Child a Good Mother

Toward the end of my first field trip I asked the head of the lineage we were staying with what the duties of a father toward his son were. He answered that the duties of a father to his son were five. The fact that he could say right away how many there were and could list them in a logical order suggests that this knowledge is shared by many in a formulaic manner, but I didn't have the time to check on this in the field. "The father's first obligation," said the lineage head, "is to seek out a good mother for the child." This remark seemed like an excellent corroboration of what I had been thinking on the basis of my observations of Fulani child rearing: parents feel that mothering is extremely important and believe that for the child to turn out well he or she must have a good mother. But, as it became clear later in the conversation, that interpretation of the statement is entirely wrong. What the lineage head meant by the phrase "good mother" was simply a woman who comes from a "good" family, that is a prestigious and influential family. Even the woman's actual character or personality were not considered of primary importance.

The first point to notice here, then, is the absence of the idea that parental behavior shapes the child's character. This is not an idiosyncratic finding. Indeed there is overwhelming evidence that Fulani do not imagine that parents have this kind of influence on their children's character. Invariably when I argued with people and tried to explain to them how we Americans viewed the role of parents, they would explicitly contradict such an argument. Once, for example, another man and I were discussing why it was that a certain person was "bad," in the sense of often failing to exemplify Fulani ideals and causing trouble and dissension between his family and others. My companion did not in this case make the argument that the person was bad because of the moral qualities of his parents, for the latter were in fact among the most respected people in the community. He simply refused to see that the way the parents brought the child up could make the slightest difference. His view was that God gives a person the character he has. The father has the obligation to try to correct his child if he sees him doing something wrong, but it is God who determines whether or not the child listens.

Altine, a young woman who had no children herself, strongly denied the idea that how the parents acted shaped the child's character. I had told her that many people in my own society chose not to have children. I added that, in my opinion, this was a good thing because if they did not want children and yet had them anyway, they would not like them. Consequently they would take poor care of them and the children would turn out no good. Altine didn't agree. She said that regardless of what you did the children could turn out bad—and bad children were certainly numerous these days. And in any case she couldn't imagine not wanting children at all, for "without children, you have no *wuro* (household, home)," and eventually you are alone.

A mature woman, in a conversation I had during my second field trip, corroborated the idea that the mother was all-important in determining how the child turns out. Certain young men were "bad," she said, "because their mothers are bad." "Do you mean because they brought them up badly?" I asked. "No," she replied, "it's that the mothers are bad and the children drink this through the milk. The milk that is nursed is the milk that comes back." This last sentence is a proverb that means that the qualities which the child gets through the milk it nurses at the breast are the qualities it will manifest when it grows up. It is clear from these remarks that what this person meant by "bad mother" was not at all that the women were bad at being mothers, but that they had bad moral qualities. We can say, then, that the Fulani deny that it is either the parents' actions or the parent as model that shapes the child's personality. They do not all quite agree on how badness and goodness are transmitted from parents to children, in that some emphasize lineage while others emphasize mother's milk, but it would be accurate to say they believe these qualities to be transmitted in some natural way, or to be God-given, rather than to be shaped by culture or learning.

It will be helpful at this point briefly to analyze some of the terms that Fulani use to talk about character and personality. There is, in fact, no word that easily translates our concepts. Here, as is so often the case in the study of another world view, the difficulty of translating our terms is not just an obstacle but can teach us much about another way of thinking and about our own as well. I think of the English terms 'character' and 'personality' as meaning almost the same thing, namely those qualities that exemplify and determine a person's way of behaving in all kinds of situations. But the former term emphasizes the morality of the person while the latter one has more to do with how the person affects others in interaction. In Fulfulde I know of two terms which are used interchangeably, *tagu* and *jikku*. While I have not yet been able to discover the etymological root of *jikku*, *tagu* comes from the verb *tagude*, to create. That word applies only to the works of God, and cannot normally be applied to things humans do. Thus this term means "the way a person is made," and can be used in many contexts where we would use the terms character or personality. Notice that the very vocabulary here seems to preclude the idea that humans would shape a person's character.

There are several other words which refer to the personality from the point of view of outsiders. *Sifa* simply means description. It is a word you would use if you wanted to ask of one person, "What is So-and-so like?" You say, "What is his description?" Another common word referring to how the person interacts with others is *haala*, speech, a word with very broad meaning and diverse usage. People often explain their like or dislike of someone by saying they like or don't like his or her haala, or way of talking. This can refer also to a whole range of things, from the sound of the voice to the content of remarks. It is my impression, though I can't document it at present, that in Fulani thought haala would be considered an aspect of tagu.

Charm or charisma is another attribute of the person as perceived by others. Both the Fulani and ourselves consider it important for success in life, or at least for a life above the level of mediocrity. The important point for our study is that while we would consider that quality to be an aspect of one's personality, in Fulani thinking it is not. Their term, *dawla*, refers to a magical kind of power which can be freely given one by the Creator, but which one can seek to augment for oneself by magical and religious means. Dawla brings one popularity, but it also brings success in one's enterprises. The concept thus resembles in some ways our notion of grace, because once you have it even God, who gave it to you in the first place, is favorably disposed to you. The terms *weli-hoore* (sweet-head) and *weli-tiinde* (sweet-forehead) are used where we would use the term "fortunate" or "lucky." They are not exact synonyms for dawla, but are often used to describe a person who appears to have it. They are ineffable attributes of people that make them attractive to others—including to God. Certainly neither they nor dawla are qualities one could get by training in early childhood or through experience at all.

Most Westerners probably do not think of charm as a quality that a person gains through childhood experience. On the other hand, we tend to attribute to that experience a number of other qualities (or their negatives) deemed important for success, such as self-confidence, industriousness, optimism, perseverence, or ambition. For the Fulani, however, not only would these qualities be aspects of one's tagu and thus have nothing to do with childhood, but also they would have nothing to do with success either. This is a crucial point for understanding the difference between Fulani psychology and ours. While both the Fulani and ourselves would admit that optimism or a tendency to be depressed are qualities of one's personality, the Fulani, contrary to ourselves, do not in the least see the personality as affecting one's eventual success or failure in life. I shall take up in the final chapter the question of why our world view differs from that of the Fulani in this regard, for the answer may shed useful light on our own culture. But the fact that Fulani find character traits irrelevant for success is probably a major reason why they do not perceive parents to be shaping their children's personalities in childhood.

Whatever the explanation for it, this "non-perception" presents us with a puzzle, for most of us believe in the importance of good mothering for producing people with healthy personalities. The puzzle is, how and why do the Fulani do such a good job of taking care of their children when they categorically deny that good parenting has anything to do with how the child will turn out as an adult? Before facing that question directly, we can fruitfully look at it indirectly by comparing the implications for our folk psychology and theirs of the methods used by parents to make children do something or stop doing something. Looking back over the vignettes describing how parents deal with children before the age of reason we find that adults don't make children do things at all. We, on the other hand, often do make children of that age do things, or struggle to; hence we assume the same must be true for parents elsewhere. Is there any American parent who has not forcibly taken a toy or some other object away from a child? Are there American parents who don't do at least one of the following: make a child eat something; make a child stop playing; make a child share with another child; make a child go to bed; make a child stay alone or with some other person? The list could go on. We have seen that among the Fulani adults don't use force this way. They are horrified when they hear of people elsewhere doing it. If Fulani adults want children to do something or stop doing something they will try to persuade, distract, or cajole them, but if the children don't give in they will not force the issue; they will desist. We have noted already many instances that support this point, but I would like to present one example where I was a principal actor, for the occasion taught me a dramatic lesson in Fulani psychology. At the time this incident occurred my wife and I were very familiar to everyone in the hamlet, and children ran in and out of our hut the way they would with any relative's hut.

(1)

I was chatting with an adult friend in my hut in the FulBe village, and a child was playing on the ground. He had some object of mine (I don't remember now what it was) that I wanted back, but he wouldn't give it to me. I then began to try to take it by force; this frightened the little boy and he looked as if he might start to cry, but he hung on to the object for dear life. My friend spoke up at this point telling me to be nice and let the child play with the thing. I interpreted this remark as interference and taking sides with the child, and I wasn't a bit ready to be mollified. I made another unsuccessful effort to take the thing from the boy without actually hurting him, and probably expressed to my friend my fear that the kid might break the thing—and besides, I needed it. At that point, my friend let me in on the secret. He told me that the child was now frightened and would surely give me back the object if I appeared to let myself be calmed by the adult. That is in fact what happened. My friend went on to explain that what he had just done with me is something adults do all the time with each other when they are trying to get children to obey them without having to use force or inflict pain. No one wants to strike a child, but with this system of mutual assistance an adult can threaten a child in the presence of others and know that they will intervene.

In actuality I never saw anyone as angry at a small child as I felt on that occasion. But I think that children learn several important things from seeing a little play such as the one my friend unexpectedly induced me to act in: they learn that they can rely on the community to support them regardless of what they have done, and they learn that an adult who is important to them and gets mad at them is not mad for keeps, but can be soothed by a few well-chosen words from other people in the community.

While this strategy could strike us Westerners as ingenious, it would not quite be quite the same if we used it in our everyday life. The reason is that it is not a teaching strategy, not a strategy designed to teach the child to obey, or not to play with certain things. Rather, it is an ad hoc strategy used to deal with an immediate problem perceived by the adult, such as "I need that spoon now to stir the sauce." It is crucial to realize that we can only understand Fulani behavior in situations like these if we leave behind several almost axiomatic notions we hold about early childhood, namely that the characteristics a child displays then prefigure those that will be displayed later, and that in any case the way the child behaves is largely determined by the parents' care and training. These typical kinds of Fulani treatment of children make perfect sense in the light of the contrary Fulani assumptions that a child's behavior is bound to be quite different from that of an adult and that in any case the parents' way of caring for and training the children have nothing to do with the kind of people they will turn out to be. Fulani parents just don't feel the awful anxiety of many American parents when they see their two-year-old behaving in a way that would be most shameful in an adult. American parents will feel that they have got to get rid of Victor's thumbsucking, or that Jane must learn to sleep all night in her own bed, because they fear that it must be something they, the parents, are doing that is making the child act the way it does. There is a philosophical point of profound importance here. To the extent that my characterization of how American parents feel is accurate, our responses to such behavior express to our children the disturbing idea that anything of value they have is what we have put into them, and that they have no essence that is truly their own from which they can offer a spontaneous contribution to the world.

In the light of this analysis we can see that, strange as it may seem, two opposing tendencies common in America—to live through one's children or to withdraw involvement or interest in them—rest on the same premise: what the children are in themselves is either nothing or of little significance; hence their importance, if any, lies in what they manifest about the adults who shaped them. The fact that I can talk about these implicit meanings of some of our ways of acting doesn't mean that I am free of them. I am trying to live my life to some degree in accordance with the values which I came to appreciate among the Fulani, yet events now and then forcibly remind me to what degree I am caught in the web of my society's values. A poignant and revealing example of this occurred during my second field trip.

(2)

My four-year-old daughter, who would sometimes accompany me in my work in Djibo, one day accidentally broke a small sauce pot she was playing with at a house we were visiting. I was immediately upset and embarrassed, and saw her accident as a reflection on me. The woman whose pot it was insisted that it was nothing and not to worry about it. I took her reaction to be sheer politeness and decided on my own that the proper thing would be to replace the pot as soon as possible. It didn't occur to me not to be emotionally involved, and my feelings felt entirely natural at the time. Yet looking back on the incident I can see that my having had these feelings reveals that I felt partly responsible for my daughter's behavior; I saw it neither as her own responsibility nor as a simple accident. This attitude amounts to my denying, without realizing it, that she was an independent center of will and action; it seems to have been based on the tacit premise that it was I who made her the way she was and hence it was I who was the cause of what happened.

A day or so later I went to the blacksmiths' quarter, for it is the women of the blacksmith families who are the potters in the Jelgoji. I had become friendly with one of the potters and thought she would be pleased if I bought a pot from her. When I got to her compound she was sitting with two friends, a Pullo woman and a woman of the woodworker caste. The women were surprised that I would want to buy such a pot, for they couldn't imagine why I would want one. They got me to explain what it was for. When I did, all three women immediately exclaimed that I mustn't do that, I mustn't give the people a new pot to replace the one my child had broken. "Why not?" I asked.

"Because they would be very upset, and it would displease them a lot," the women replied.

I was completely baffled by this, for I thought I was being very proper by making this gesture. "Why would they be upset?" I asked.

"Because all children are the same," they said. "People don't distinguish between their own children and other people's children, and they would resent it if you did. No one can stop children from getting into mischief, so no one takes what they do seriously. Children have no heart; they don't bear grudges. If they are fighting one moment they are friends the next, while a grownup, if he is offended, never forgets. That is why grownups never try to decide who is right and who is wrong in children's disputes; they just stop the kids from fighting. Probably the worst thing a child could do around here is kill a cow or a horse, but even then a parent would never ask the child's parent to pay. After all, his own child might do the same thing to someone else one day."

My analysis of my own feelings in this incident has brought out that I, and other Western parents who would share my reactions, tend to perceive my children's character and behavior as the product of my influence on the children; thus we implicitly deny them responsibility for their own way of being, any essence of their own. Yet wouldn't it follow from the fact that the Fulani do not enforce particular behaviors in small children, nor punish them for acts which would be reprehensible in an adult, that the Fulani also do not consider them responsible for what they do? That would indeed be a correct conclusion, but with a slight shift in emphasis that makes an important difference. The Fulani believe that children are not responsible for what they do because it is in the nature of children to be irresponsible, to lack self-control and social knowledge. This idea does not at all amount to denying, as we Americans do, that children cause their own behavior. The fascination children have for the Fulani, and the pleasure they get from being with them, come from the fact that to them children have an essence or character that adults perceive as inviolate and as developing on its own quite apart from parental training or influence. In the Fulani view, children grow up under parental care, but not *because of* parental influence.

Yet the Fulani consider training and education to be very important. They probably value more highly than we do the learning of politeness, good manners, and proper social etiquette in relations with people in different kinship and social categories. Doesn't this fact contradict the major point I have been trying to demonstrate, that the Fulani believe people are born, not made? No, it does not, and to understand that we must look at another significant contrast between our thought and practice and theirs. We have seen that in Fulani thought there is an important difference between children younger than five or six and children older than that, namely that the older children have haYYillo. We in our culture implicitly recognize this difference at about the same age too, as can be seen from the differences in the techniques used by professional teachers of kindergarten, first grade, and second grade. But what we do that the Fulani don't is make a deliberate attempt to train or induce children to behave in certain ways long before they have reached this "age of reason." Now, I am not saying that Fulani parental behavior has no effect on how their small children behave; on the contrary, I have argued above that there are significant effects. What I am saying is that Fulani do not perceive what they are doing with their small children to be education, training, or formation of character, whereas American parents do tend to perceive their actions that way.

Let us look now at some implications of this contrast for Western and Fulani notions of how a child develops into an adult in society. The first of these is that we believe children can and should be trained to act in certain ways before they have developed smartness—in fact some of us probably fear that if we let children get smart before we start to teach them, it will be too late to inculcate the very qualities we desire them to have. The Fulani, on the other hand, hold the opposite view that it makes no sense to try to teach children anything before they have become smart, before their eyes have opened, as they say. Other differences that flow from this one immediately begin to appear. We seem to view education, at least in part, as an involuntary process for children, for we teach them things before they have the intelligence to accept or reject the teaching. This is clearly related to the idea discussed earlier that the child's very personality is in some measure made by the parents, and it is also related to our use of force in general on very young children. Many of the very words we use to describe this process also contain these implications of its involuntary nature and the use of force: inculcate, instill, habituate, socialize, enculturate, and sometimes even condition, engineer, and so on. Among the Fulani it is only after children have intelligence that adults begin to expect something of them.

Interestingly enough, the Fulani draw a clear distinction between social sense and quickness of mind. I once mentioned to a mature man my impression that a young man we knew, whom I considered extremely sharp, was intelligent (I used the word haYYillo). My companion did not agree at all. "Sure he is smart," he said, "but he is not intelligent." For the Fulani, as we have seen, the very concept of intelligence includes as an essential component the ability to be sensitive to social contexts and to choose the most appropriate course of action from a variety of possibilities. Learning, in their view, is closely connected with the idea of choice. In fact, the Fulani term which best translates our word "to learn" is the verb *jaBude*, "to accept or agree to something," which connotes an active taking of the thing or idea offered to you.

Fulani Concepts of Child Psychology

A possible misunderstanding may have crept into the reader's mind by now. Fulani deny, I have been arguing, that parental behavior in early childhood shapes the child's personality. This does not mean, however, that they believe parents have no effects at all on the child. In fact, there are a few influences we should now consider. These are of essentially two types (my own division), magical and psychological. We have already come across some of the magical influences in the taboos and certain other health care procedures mothers employ on their children. Here are a few examples to remind us. Many mothers pull the limbs of their baby just after administering basi. This manipulation is simply part of the procedure, and is meant to help the proper development of the limbs. No mother would eat lewla meat, as we have seen, for the spirit of the animal could then gain the power to make the child sicken and die. Similarly, it is considered dangerous for a child to have contact with the mother, and particularly her milk, beginning in the last months of her pregnancy with her next child and continuing after the birth of that child. The protection against this is to have the older child eat an egg, cooked directly in the coals, from a chicken that has not yet had any offspring.

If breast milk should drip on a little boy's penis it is believed that he will become impotent. Should breast milk fall on a girl baby's vagina, her husbands will divorce her quickly; she won't be able to stay married. In the first days of the child's life, before the milk has come to the mother's breasts, the mother will dip her finger into milk or butter and then feed the child drop by drop by putting her finger on the child's lips. One mother told me that the way in which this is done affects the manner in which the child's teeth come in later on (this is important because teething is always painful and often a very perilous time for the child). If the mother used one finger, the child will get one tooth at a time, two fingers two teeth, and so on. In addition, certain character traits of the mother can be transmitted through this mode of feeding: if she is talkative or taciturn, the child will acquire those traits, as well as the mother's tendency to eat quickly or slowly, as the case may be.

(3)

Diimaajo. Faatumata is shaving her five-year-old daughter RuGiyatu's head. RuGiyatu is not making a scene, despite the pain. Now and then she says "*a warii kam* (you're killing me)"; the blade is dull. Faatumata told me about the belief that if a person who has never had children shaves a little hair from the head of a child, she will have children while the shaved child will die, as will any subsequent children the mother has. She told me that her older daughter Jeewo-Naaba had a little patch shaved off her head last year—she made a patch on RuGiyatu's head the size of a nickel to show me—but she wasn't worried about it because Jeewo-Naaba had been ritually protected by a charm since shortly after birth. It is characteristic of this procedure that Jeewo-Naaba was not aware of it when it happened and could not say who had done it.

Faatumata also says that if a person cuts a little bit off your wraparound or your sandal, he can use it to *huuwude* ("work," put a spell on) you. If he picks up some dirt from your bare footprint and mixes it with a certain medicine he can *weDDude* you (magically force your departure); by throwing the mixture away he can get you to leave the area for ever. Faatumata checks all her clothing from time to time to make sure it has not been tampered with. If your clothing has been, you must either throw it away or get a moodibbo to *tuutu* it (say a charm and then spit on it) for you. Then it is safe to wear.

(4)

Diimaajo. This morning on Ouagadougou Radio Suka and Yaaye Suka heard the weekly Islamic broadcast in Fulfulde. The preacher was saying that if a son goes away to Abidjan and works and spends everything he earns on women and drink, and so on, and then finally comes home and brings nothing, he will say that thieves stole his goods from him. But this is not true; it is his parents' curses which have prevented him from becoming a somebody. Because even if his parents have not actually uttered the curses, the mother's breast will do it of its own accord, as will the father's chin or beard, even if the parents don't open their mouths at all. Apparently this is a widespread belief here, and this wasn't the first time they had heard the idea. Yaaye Suka went on to say that the breast or the beard could have the reverse effect also: if a parent cursed a child who was normally a good person, but just cursed him in momentary anger, the breast would say, "*Kaari, walaa hawla!* (Let there be no words!)", and the curse would be deflected into the bush and would not have any effect.

I included the passage concerning shaving the child's head and tampering with a person's clothing—or even footprint—to point out a parallel between "normal" magical influences and certain parental powers. To produce magical influences operating at a distance a person generally needs some "piece" of the victim, yet parents seem capable of exercising similar influences without any such article. The power that parents have to curse (and to bless or protect) their children offers further evidence that in Fulani thought parents and children automatically have something of one another's substance.

Children, however, do not thereby seem to have any equivalent power over their parents. It would be astonishing if they did, given all the social energy that goes into maintaining the ideology of precedence by age and according to who gave birth to whom. On the other hand, certain acts of small children do have special significance. They are like signs for grownups to read. Perhaps this is another reason why parents interfere so little with what children do prior to reaching the age of reason.

(5)

A Diimaajo woman remarked, "When a child sweeps, it means a guest is coming or somebody is about to give birth. When a child carries a doll on her back, she has seen her (unborn) younger brother or sister. If a child gives someone a straw, the person will have a child. If a child picks up a handful of dirt and gives it to you, you'll get an eye infection. When a child looks back over his shoulder, he is calling his younger sibling; it means his mother has become pregnant."

In addition to many ideas such as these concerning magical influences of people on one another—and parents on children specifically—I have occasionally heard people make comments that sound like genuine psychology to my ears. We have come across a hint of this already in our discussion of hitting and threatening children by adults. For example, the man who told me to calm down and let the little kid have my object also remarked that the child was frightened and would give it back to me soon. In people's talk about how people influence one another generally, fear is by far the most frequently cited effect. As I have showed elsewhere (cf. Riesman 1977: 195–196), fear is closely related to shame and is not necessarily a bad emotion. It is important, for example, to fear

God. People often criticize one another by saying, "So-and-so doesn't fear God," or will directly exhort a person to fear God. Similarly, parents, particularly fathers, should be feared. In fact, children rarely fear their mothers, but quite normally do fear their fathers.

(6)

Ngurunga, a Diimaajo man in his fifties who has had many children, says that *towtude suka* (keeping distant from the child) will make the child fear his father, and thus obey him later on. If a father plays with his children, they will never do what he says later. Ngurunga says with Alu (his three-year-old son) he doesn't care if Alu obeys because by the time Alu is big enough to be useful he (Ngurunga) will be dead.

In fact, Ngurunga did play with Alu a lot; I often found him with the boy on his lap. But this was the first of his children whom he had treated in this way; he had kept his distance from the earlier ones. A similar insight to his is expressed in the following comment by a young mother who knew the chief and his family quite well.

(7)

Diimaajo. Aadama, Yampoka's mother, says that the people in the "court" (this refers to the chief of Djibo's family) don't hit children; the reason she gives is that the children are not required to do work. You hit a child who refuses to do what you say, but if you can do it yourself or can get someone else to do it, then you don't need to hit your child. You just stop asking.

In our own psychology we place a lot of emphasis on positive reinforcement. We often claim that people do their best, learn the most, and so on, when they are motivated either by the intrinsic pleasure of the activity, or by the reward they gain from it in money or some other social value, such as esteem. Do the Fulani have such an idea? If not, might they nonetheless unconsciously make use of rewards for correct learning on the part of their children? Once when I brought up this topic with one of the families in my study, we had the following conversation.

(8)

Diimaajo. I asked Faatumata whether the parents did or said anything when a child had done something good for them. Faatumata said they wouldn't say anything, though some people might say *foofoo maa* ("thank you"). Her husband, who was resting in the back room (it was windy and rainy so Faatumata and I had come inside), spoke up saying that if parents praise a child it means he is dead. It is only after a child has died that parents will say how good and helpful he or she was, but if the child is alive, parents say nothing and let others do the talking. "If you have a new car and show it to people, are you going to say how beautiful it is?" asked the husband. "Of course not. You will let other people admire it. It's the same with children. You don't say anything and let others praise them."

But praises uttered by outsiders can themselves be very dangerous if they are not worded properly, because of the risk of *hunduko* ("mouth"). For example, if a person says to you, "*wuuy! suka ma na wooDi* (Wow! Your child sure is beautiful)," you might reply, "*hunduko ma soppu fuudo maa* (Your mouth points right to your asshole)." It is quite different if a person comments on a possession of yours, such as a new article of clothing. In that case you reply, "*Alla wann ndamma balDe ma* (May God make your days secure)," or "*Alla hokkare ko wooDi* (God give you something beautiful)."

If you want to praise someone's child (to avoid the dangers of hunduko) you can say, "*wuuy, Bii maani na barkini; huunde fuu ko o wi'aa imo jaBa* (Wow! So-and-so's child brings blessings; no matter what he's told to do, he will do it)," or something like that.

I asked the man if children would actually hear people praising them. Oh yes, he said. They will hear their praises if they are good, and they will hear their criticisms if they are bad. Besides, children don't need to be told by their parents that the latter like (or dislike) what they are doing, since they know what pleases and displeases them.

These remarks correspond very well to what I was able to observe generally. When children had reached the age of reason parents mainly seemed either to talk to them in the imperative mode or to criticize them. I have presented many instances of this. But is a child capable of comprehending the reasons for the parents' lack of praise, what we would call verbal rewards? Wouldn't this constant barrage of orders and insults make the child feel unloved? And doesn't the remark about the car suggest that children are thought of almost as possessions, not as people in their own right? For the Fulani I think the answer to each of these questions is the opposite of what it would be if we were observing these behaviors in our own society. The reason is that there is a very significant difference between their basic assumptions and ours concerning the parent–child relationship.

Among ourselves, parents are producers of children who are independent social entities. For the Fulani, parents and children form a unit and parents do not see themselves as producing their children for "society" to consume, as it were. Their goal is not to create their children's character, but to maintain their relationships with their children. The man who keeps his distance from his child is not trying to shape the child's character, but to shape their relationship.

All American parents sometimes ask themselves, "Am I doing a good job of bringing up my children? Did I do a good job, or have I made some terrible mistake?" How children are brought up and educated is a vital issue in this country because we believe that it is a person's character and education that will make all the difference for his or her success and happiness in life. But behind this recognition of the importance of character and education for success lie two deeper and yet more obvious, more taken-for-granted, premises. The first is that people are made, not born. Virginia Satir, a family therapist, entitled her book about raising children *Peoplemaking* (1972), and this title captures very concisely what both laypeople and social science professionals believe the job of parents is. The second is a corollary of the first, namely that a person, once made, is above all a product. As such, the individual comes on the market completely finished, as it were, and with a lifetime guarantee. Depending on the qualities of the particular "model," individuals join or compete with others to fulfill their own purposes. The confluence of these two ideas, namely that people are made what they become by their parents, and that character and education are essential for success, is a primary cause of the anxious, almost hysterical concern many American parents have for achieving the "right" childhood, and the most up-to-date training, for their children.

Throughout this chapter, however, we have argued that Fulani do not perceive parental care practices as shaping their children's character. If we look closely at the magical and psychological effects that we have just reviewed, we find that the former are like a direct transfer, through food or inheritance, of the very substance of the parent, and hence of parental qualities. The psychological effects, on the other hand, have nothing to do with the child's qualities, but rather with the nature of his ongoing relation with the parent. In our own psychology, the very idea of giving a reward—including the reward of love itself—implies that the giver and the receiver are *not* a unit, but rather are separate entities. Fulani thought and behavior, on the other hand, become perfectly clear when we recognize that parents and children share the assumption that they are a single unit. While it might be possible to interpret Fulani parent–child relationships in terms of rewards and punishments, costs and benefits, and the like, to attempt this would only obscure the nature of that relationship as experienced by the participants.

I don't think that the man's example of my feelings about my car means that he (or other Fulani) think of children as objects and possessions. Rather, he was just trying to find a way to make me understand something I was obviously having difficulty with. I don't know whether children between age six and adolescence know about the idea that if parents praise them that means they are dead, but I doubt they do. On the other hand, I am quite sure that the lack of verbal praise or specific rewards for what they do does not in the least make them feel unloved. In fact, though children obviously felt hurt at times from being yelled at by their parents, I found not the slightest indication that any of them underwent a long-lasting feeling of being bad, guilty, or unloved. We have seen instances where children felt their parents' hitting them was justified and actually beneficial. Parents, for their part, are quite aware that all kids go through a stage where they don't appear to hear a word you say to them, and whatever you tell them to do they get wrong or do the opposite. Hence they don't assume that the way children act at age six or ten is the way they will be forever, and they don't despair or get angry to the point of bearing them any ill-will. It is clear, then, that hitting or bawling out a child does not mean, either to the child or the adult, that the adult does not love the child. The meaning of such acts—as is true for any acts— depends on the context. For the Fulani, given that such acts are normal in all families, and that they occur in a context of the child's complete acceptance in the family and oneness with it, they are probably generally understood as an aspect of parental love. In any case, no one ever seems to take them to indicate withdrawal. Such a gesture on the part of a parent is almost unthinkable.

We can see, however, how antipathy gets expressed in the relations between women and children of their co-wives, where rivalry, jealousy, and hatred can all exist. A co-wife who wants to annoy her rival's children has a number of subtle means at her disposal, particularly in connection with food. There might be occasions where she could get away with serving them bad food or insufficient food, and she could also tell the children whenever they came to her hut that she was out of whatever it was they wanted. Such acts are powerful messages. I never actually heard any bad stepmother stories, but we have a powerful description of this kind of behavior in a recent autobiography of a Pullo of Cameroon (Bocquene 1986), who talks poignantly of how he and his brothers, whose own mother had died, were treated by their father's new wife. In addition, this is a common theme in Fulani fairy tales.

The Task of Parents

Fulani parents are supposed to teach their children good manners, but good manners amount to the proper imposition of self-control. Manners are not themselves the expression of personality, but the fact that one has accepted them (i.e., learned them) is considered proof of one's good breeding. For the Fulani, then, successful bringing up of a child is not a matter of parental technique—of doing—but of being. If you are a moral person and come from a good family, then your child will have received these qualities at your breast and will have the intelligence to accept what you have to say. Once you have raised your child and provided a material start in life and the benefit of your wisdom, you have fulfilled your duty as a parent. Now it is up to the child to decide whether or not to follow the same path you did, to "do what [the child] found" or not. It would never occur to you to think you had failed or made some mistake if the child chose not to do so, for it was not you who made the child in the first place, but God.

From a Western perspective, this ethnopsychology of the Fulani that I've been presenting sounds terribly old-fashioned. Should we seriously entertain the hypothesis that a person's character is received through the mother's milk? This idea is absurd, and besides many apparently normal people have grown up with little or no mother's milk. Or is that what is the matter with them? The silliness of this thought reinforces the point that throughout this discussion it has not been our aim to compare Western and Fulani psychology to see which has the better hypotheses accounting for personality formation. Rather we have been seeking to discover some of the implications of these psychologies. These implications have been of two sorts: on the one hand we have been examining what concepts of human nature, human growth, and parental roles must be presupposed if the psychologies are to make sense. On the other hand we identified some of the consequences for feeling and action when parents who are convinced of one psychology or the other raise their children in that conviction. I have argued that in terms of some major Western psychologies it is not Western practices but Fulani ones that should provide children with the soundest foundation for a healthy personality. Applied to the American situation, this assessment entails a paradoxical conclusion: If it is true that the way parents handle their children in early childhood shapes the future personality of those children, the children are adversely affected when parents believe that that is the case.

We return now to the major question that we left hanging earlier. At this point we can phrase it as follows: If the Fulani are not only unaware that their child-care techniques help ensure the psychological health of their children, but in fact adamantly deny that the practices have a significant effect on their personality development, why are they expending so much care and effort? We have seen that it is very hard work to be a good Fulani mother; her whole rhythm of life is subordinated to that of the child, whose care and safety require her constant attention, and all the household tasks are made harder because the child is always on her back and may interrupt whatever she is doing at any moment.

I hope that the reader will have already realized that there is something a little crazy about the question as I have phrased it. I am being a bit perverse here to indicate the unspoken assumption that the only reason a person would hug children, play with them, comfort them, and so on, is that those acts are known to have a beneficial, long-term effect. There are unfortunately some American parents who are so alienated from themselves that they are crazy in just this way; their own pleasure in their children, and their love for them, get undermined by reinterpreting everything they do with or for the children as "for the children's future good." All of us, however, are touched by and perpetuate such craziness to the extent that we act towards our children not according to ethics, nor out of the immediate feelings we engender in each other, but with the goal of engineering in them some quality of character or attitude that will be useful to them later on. This sort of orientation to the future seems quite absent, as we have seen, from the Fulani ideas and practices we have examined.

To understand the reason for this difference, let us look first at ourselves. I mentioned at the very beginning that we believe a person's character and education are vital for success; I also mentioned one premise that underlies this belief and that we have been discussing at length, namely that people are made, not born. There is an additional premise that seems so basic to us that we view it as a given of our existence, as in fact it is. The premise is that when our children grow up they will lead a life largely independent from us. Believing this, parents have no choice but to plan for separation and to devise some way of remaining related to their children—that is, continuing to have some effect on them—at a distance in time and space.

This observation, which may seem self-evident, takes on its importance in the light of the contrast between our life-situation and that of the Fulani. The latter are raising their children in the expectation that most of them will stay at home or nearby for life. We are so habituated to the idea of grown children living their lives apart from and independently from their parents that it is not easy for us to become aware of the subtle ways in which this enormous difference in our expectations about life affects our attitudes toward children and our psychological ideas. Fulani parents are not in the least trying to produce or manufacture a human being who will eventually and independently exemplify and embody their ideals. Rather, they are caring for a child because that child is one of them, a relative, and will always be so. The very structure of Fulani society, as is generally the case in small-scale traditional African societies, consists in the relations that relatives and the groups they constitute maintain with each other.

Incidentally, it is because these societies are so constituted that it has seemed quite reasonable to take kinship as the central object of study in much Africanist anthropology. The focus of such research, however, has rarely been the experience of life in society, but instead the rules of marriage, residence, inheritance, and the like embodied in the kinship system, and the logic of the system's structure. It was only many years after completing my fieldwork that I came to understand why the Fulani kept replying, "We are all one," whenever I would ask them to explain to me how their kinship system sorted them into different lineages. When people said that to me I used to think it was just a way of getting me to stop asking bothersome questions, but I now believe it expresses an important truth about the Fulani experience of human relations. In the light of my analysis here we can see that being "all one" means sensing that one is kin to everyone implied by that phrase, such that one shares life and all its vicissitudes with them.

There is other evidence that the feeling of relationship in Fulani society is the feeling of being one, and that this in turn means sharing in the same fortunes. I heard a number of proverbs expressing what it means to be a relative. One of them goes, "The blood of the head can't bypass the neck." In other words, relatives are like the head and the neck in that just as the qualities of the head's blood must affect the neck too, since these are inseparable, so whatever happens to a relative must happen to yourself also. One man explained this proverb by saying, "Whatever happens to one of your people happens to you." A second bit of evidence can be found in a key term used much in daily speech. The very word for relationship or bond in the Fulani language, enDam, is also the word for mother's milk, which is, in fact, its base meaning. This seems to imply a sort of continuity of being among people who are related, and it may have some connection with the Fulani belief that people imbibe their character in the milk from their mother's breast. At the same time, the double meaning of the term for mother's milk should give us pause; were we too hasty in condemning a while ago this Fulani notion about how people get their character?

The care, love, and effort that Fulani mothers invest in their children are, in the Fulani view, simply inherent in the mother–child relationship. That is a relation that sustains both the mother and the child, and for the mother it is a major source of meaning and identity. Similarly, the relation between father and child is a major source of a man's meaning and identity, despite the many differences between that relationship and the mother–child one. For example, both mothers and fathers feel pleased and honored when people address them—as they often do spontaneously—as mother or father of So-and-so. Sometimes those forms of address stick, and the parent in effect gets a new name which is commonly known and used. In bringing up a child, both the mother and father wish for nothing other than that the child live and remain their relative, their son or daughter, with all the meanings that implies. The assumption is that the child who perceives that he or she has been treated well by the parents will want to continue to be a relative to them, to maintain the meanings of that shared relationship indefinitely. It is here, if anywhere, that there could be an ulterior motive in Fulani parental behavior, for while the Fulani reject, as we have seen, the idea that their practices shape character, they do feel that if they act properly as parents their children will indeed want to remain close to them throughout life. Many splits between parents and children are interpreted as what the parents had coming to them for improper or cruel treatment of their children, particularly on the part of men.

For ecological reasons, at the least, separations between relatives are often necessary in a person's lifetime. People usually undergo them, however, as personal quarrels or conflicts, despite the ideal of remaining together that is so important (cf. Riesman 1977:38–42, 214). After all, the breakup of a group of relatives is a break in the very fabric of society, since the social order is constituted not by larger institutions, but by interactions between relatives. As we might expect, then, an enormous effort goes into maintaining those relations in a stable form. The Fulani are well aware that being a relative is not in fact the automatic result of biological kinship, but is a way of living with others that involves both hard work and frustration. "Being together is not easy" is a phrase that I heard many times during my stay with the Fulani. Being a relative means showing deference and obedience to parents and elder siblings; it means visiting and talking with all relatives who share life in the same village as you; it means paying visits to relatives living elsewhere either just to see them or on the occasion of an important event, such as a death or a naming ceremony; it means calling on your relatives for help when you need it, and helping them when they do; and it means offering moral and material support to your children even while they begin to take on the job of maintaining you in your old age. Thus in a sense there is no gap between being a relative to your children when they are infants and being a relative to them throughout the rest of life. That is life itself, and it never stops.

8

SELF, IDENTITY, AND PERSONALITY

At this point we have reviewed most of the data we need in order to explain the differences we have described between the typical personalities of the FulBe and the RiimaayBe. But throughout the presentation thus far I have been deliberately vague in my terminology, sometimes using the word personality, sometimes character, sometimes self. We now have to clarify just what it is we have been discussing; in so doing, we will also actually be sketching out a theory of the personality and its formation.

While I have used the terms character and personality nearly interchangeably, I think of the self as a concept of a different type. George Herbert Mead's thinking about this concept has been extremely useful to me, though I do not follow him exactly. For Mead (1964), the term "self" designates what other psychologists often call personality. It consists in two aspects, the "me," which is the impressions of the person that others reflect back and which the person then sees as "me," and the "I," which is the agent who both responds to the "me" at any given moment and creates and modifies it through action. The terms "I" and "me" have been helpful to many scholars because they keep in our minds the fact that the person is both an agent and a bearer of qualities attributed to that person by others.

In what follows, however, I will use the term "self" to designate the agent, that which acts and undergoes experiences. It is very close and possibly identical to what Mead called the "I." For Mead and for the rest of us, the crucial problem of the self is how the part of it that he calls the "me" is created. I think he is right in saying that it emerges through the relationship between self and other, but it will be useful to name and examine several distinct aspects of that "me" and to see how they are constituted. These I will call the identity, the personality, and the sense of self. Though I use these terms with their ordinary meanings, some explanation is still in order.

One's sense of self is roughly equivalent to the "I"'s impression of the "me" at any given moment. For Mead, the "I" could never see itself. Rather, in any act it created a "me" in its wake, as it were, which it could then perceive after the fact. In my view, however, while I agree with Mead that experience and memory are essential to developing a sense of self, that sense is nonetheless quite immediate. As the agent (the self) acts, it has a sense of itself. One may be surprised by what one actually does at any given moment, but that doesn't imply that one lacked a sense of self. Whatever sense one had may start to change as a result of the new experience, but the person might equally well call what happened a fluke in an effort to preserve the same sense of self as before. Thus our sense of self includes some qualities that are relatively permanent, and others that change constantly with circumstances. Anyone's sense of self at a particular moment is too complex to describe completely, especially since it includes inchoate elements like the feel of one's body from within, the feel of walking, eating, picking up a baby, and so on. Nevertheless, in particular contexts different elements of the sense of self become primary and these can be usefully specified and described. For example, to feel that one is dominated, powerful, sexy, fatherly, Diimaajo, or American, are all primary senses of self one might have in different situations. Direct experiences of emotion, on the other hand, are not; it is their implications that are. For instance, sheer fright is not a primary sense of self, but feeling that one is "going to pieces" or that one "has a grip on oneself" are different senses of self which one might experience while undergoing fright.

It can be seen from these points that the sense of self is a symbolic construct. A person's sense of self at any given moment is built entirely out of the available meanings concerning situations, feelings, actions, and so on. Thus we can see that it is partially determined, or limited, by the common understandings shared by the actor and other members of the society. An excellent example of how it is shaped by cultural context is provided in Michelle Rosaldo's (1980) account of the particular sort of diminished sense of self that young Ilongot men have prior to taking a head.

The sense of self is entirely subjective to each individual. Other people have no direct access to it. Yet the fact that it is built out of a shared system of meanings implies that other people's thoughts are in fact major constituents of a person's sense of self. How do we incorporate the thoughts of others? We do it mainly as we become aware of our identity, which is initially entirely constructed by others. Identity, I will argue, is the single most important component of the sense of self.

Perhaps the main reason for this is that one's identity exists long before one's own consciousness of it does. This is because everything important to people has identity, not just humans. A particular object's identity consists in how it is located in people's categories of understanding, and how it is established as a unique item in terms of those categories. Human identities are an extension of this principle. They are indispensable for social life because they enable the members of a society to identify a particular human body with an actor who has a certain history and place in their system of social relations. They are indispensable for a more obvious reason as well, which is that one is a human being only when one is aware of one's identity as human in the terms of a particular culture. That is the sine qua non of being an "actor" at all. It follows from this that, initially at least, we cannot know our identities without knowing how we are known by others. Thus we must come to understand our personal histories and how we are located in society's system of relations, and must construct an image of our identities from that. Adult members of a society, in turn, have to ensure that the new members coming in through birth acquire such an image of themselves.

This point helps us understand, I think, the Fulani practice of treating infants as people in some respects, particularly in how one talks to them. It is not that adults are trying to educate the child at that early age, as we have already seen, but that they are establishing, almost like a verbal cocoon, the identity through which the metamorphosis of the child into a human will occur.

While each identity is unique, by definition it shares features with the other identities to which it is related. In the United States the nature of these shared features is quite indeterminate. Thus they can include nationality, race, gender, kinship relations, geographic proximity, school attendance, occupation, hobbies, club memberships, and so on, almost indefinitely. This plethora of possibilities was designated by Erik Erikson, correctly, I think, as the cause of a major developmental crisis of adolescence: "identity versus role diffusion." Here is a perfectly possible sentence describing a perfectly possible situation: "John is an aspiring physics student and art student by day; three nights a week he is a companion to his retarded younger brother to help out his family; in the afternoons and on Saturdays he is a champion tennis player; Saturday nights he is a jazz pianist in a bar." This list is both amazing and yet not unusual. Notice in particular that it seems perfectly natural to say "John is" all of those things, as if each one of them could be in itself a complete identity. The fact is that none of them is a complete identity, from the actor's point of view, nor does any particular combination add up to an identity. For an identity is not a label; on the contrary, it is the conviction that it is indeed oneself as a complete human being who is acting in the world (cf., in this connection, Erikson's notion of "selfsameness"). To do things without this conviction is merely to play roles, to go through the motions. Camus's "stranger," for example, did not feel it was really he himself who did things; nor would he accept any interpretations of his actions that attempted to unite the many fragments of his life. In view of my point that one must have human identity to be an actor, it is quite significant that Camus's Meursault sensed affinity not with human beings, but with the inhuman universe.

One's identity affects the sense of self profoundly in two ways. One of these we have just noted in the hypothetical example of John and the fictional character Meursault, who fail, or run the risk of failing, to know how they are known by others. As we shall see when we examine the implications of this study for contemporary American society, the consistency or inconsistency in society's messages about one's identity can facilitate or hinder the forming of a clear image of it; this outcome in turn affects how solid one's sense of self can be. Second, the actual content of these societal messages, if consistent, is usually taken on by the individual as a basic, enduring aspect of his sense of self.

The reason why small children do not have a sense of self—or at least an enduring one—has to do with their total dependence on caretakers and their lack of memory. The two aspects are related in that a part of that dependence consists in the very organization of the child's daily life by its caretakers, who do whatever planning is needed. As G. H. Mead says, "A child is one thing at one time and another at another, and what he is at one moment does not determine what he is at another. That is both the charm of childhood as well as its inadequacy. You cannot count on the child; you cannot assume that all the things he does are going to determine what he will do at any moment. He is not organized into a whole. The child has no definite character, no definite personality" (1964:223). Evidence that the development of some kind of memory capacity is involved here can be seen in children's capacities for learning (and forgetting) languages at different stages in childhood.

We have just seen that our identities are initially entirely constructed by others even before we have any awareness at all, but that each of us then takes on an identity and transforms it in the process of incorporating it into an individual sense of self. The personality, on the other hand, develops in a different way and must be distinguished conceptually from the identity. It, too, is constructed by the person's entourage, but as an interpretation of behavior, not prior to it. At bottom, while identity is the person's location in a social structure, personality is the persona, the symbolic medium through which one person establishes contact with another. This medium is of course essential for any human relationship, but cultures vary in the degree to which they develop a concept equivalent to "personality." As in the case of identity, all the elements out of which the interpretation of a personality is made must lie within the cultural meaning system (cf. D'Andrade 1984) shared by the people. At the same time a person's actions, like any other symbol, remain open to multiple interpretations. Thus it is to be expected that the actor and each person with whom he or she interacts will all have differing images of the actor's personality.

In the West, for reasons I shall bring out below, personality is an important conceptual tool for understanding and clarifying what it means to be human. But personality or character is not a self-evident organ, like the heart or liver, that appears to have a clearly separable identity from other parts of the body. Psychologists and laypeople alike conceive of the personality as a structure of qualities and dispositions and impute it to people so as to categorize them rationally and to account for what appear to be regularities in their behavior. The difference between being able accurately to say someone has an enlarged spleen and someone has an enlarged ego is that while the spleen can be seen directly (or detected by palpation) and thus measured and compared with those of other persons, the ego, as used in that phrase, is never seen and cannot be measured directly. Instead, it is a quality that we infer from a person's actions. When we use such a phrase in ordinary speech, it is usually not clear whether we are simply summing up a series of observations of a person, or whether we see the quality in question as causing the person to act in a given way. The presence of this confusion can easily be verified by reflecting on how we use adjectives like "nice" or "selfish." In psychology, however, traits of personality, or structures like the Oedipus complex, are generally thought of as determining behavior.

It is also true that a person who has a "big ego" or an Oedipus complex doesn't necessarily know this. Nevertheless, a person who is honest might both know it and strive to act honestly in all circumstances. Does this mean that honesty is somehow a qualitatively different sort of trait from, say, selfishness? That a person would strive to be selfish seems most unlikely; the idea is comical. More likely one would strive to be unselfish. The person who acts selfish or who has a big ego probably would label this way of acting differently: one might claim to be protecting oneself or trying to obtain one's due. Thus honesty and selfishness are not different in type; they are both exactly alike in being character traits known to a group of people and used by members of the group to summarize or explain a set of actions accomplished by another person.

That the actor and observers can disagree as to how one is acting is very important. On the one hand, this possibility for several interpretations follows logically from the fact that actions are essentially symbolic: they intend or mean something. On the other hand, what an action or group of actions means to somebody depends entirely on the context within which it is interpreted.

To say that actions are symbolic is not to say that they are somehow not real. The contrast is rather between happenings that we

see as occurring because of natural laws and those that are the consequences of human choices—even when the choice may be to
"bow to necessity."

The human personality, then, must be first and foremost a symbol too (like the sense of self). Whether viewed from the actor's
point of view or from some other perspective, the personality is an
interpretation of the totality of a person's actions, or at least some
large subset of them.

But suppose a particular personality contains elements that
don't seem to be a matter of choice at all, such as anal compul-
siveness. Where is the choice in that? The point is that in any given
situation no particular item of behavior is automatically induced.
It is true that a person who has interpreted a situation may then
feel there is no choice but to act in a certain way. But the process of
interpreting a situation in that manner still presupposes that there
is a variety of contexts in which it might be understood.

If it is correct that the human personality is indeed a symbol, it
follows that the problem of understanding it is essentially a problem of how meanings are made, maintained, or changed, and of
how people are moved by meanings or persuaded of their validity.
We can then study personality with the help of the many approaches to symbols that have been developed in fields other than
psychology alone, including anthropology, philosophy, religion,
and criticism of all the arts, particularly theater and literature.

It seems to be a common finding in all these fields that it takes at
least two to make meaning. Meaning only exists in communication. Though at times this communication can be imagined and
not actualized, it is absolutely necessary to have had practical experience of communication to be able to do it in the imagination.
The reason communication is necessary is that meaning does not
exist until it has been made intelligible. Hence any meaning must
not only be expressed in some medium, but must also be received
by someone. It is only possible to recognize reception, however,
when the receiver in turn acts in such a way that the person who
sent the "message" can feel that it got through. In the case of
simple verbal messages conveying, say, good news or bad news,
responses expressing pleasure or sorrow clearly indicate this.

But what kind of meaning is personality? It is one of two important kinds of meanings that define the self and that people nor-

mally believe to inhere in the person. More specifically, it is one's realization or portrayal in gesture of the sense of self one has, of the person one believes oneself to be. Thus personality is above all a phenomenon that occurs in direct relations with other people because it mainly concerns those relations. As we already noted, from the observer's point of view everyone has a personality; it consists of the image that others form of the actor by reading, from actions, the actor's sense of self. This process occurs whether or not the actor consciously tries to portray an image of self. The form such a portrayal takes, as we shall see in detail further on, depends on the stock of gestural meanings that are intelligible to most of the people in the actor's society.

While others attribute a certain personality to someone on the basis of the actions performed, what of the actor? What is the source of those actions, and what do they mean to him? I suggest that every action expresses something of a person's current sense of self. The reason for this is that, as I showed above, behavior has no human meaning to people—whether actor, addressee, or observer—unless they can perceive in it the agency of a particular human being (the same point holds for group action). In slightly different terms, if we do not "put ourselves into" what we do, the activity feels meaningless to us. We may feel like robots, slaves, or prisoners. Note that these words *do* express a sense of self, but one that is non-human or subhuman. In the case of being possessed by a spirit, we may not be conscious of acting at all. In all these situations, however, observers will understand the action as being performed by some agent other than ourselves—such as Ford Motor Company, our king, or the Holy Ghost. From the individual's point of view one's personality is the acting out or portrayal in everyday interaction of one's sense of self, the person one believes oneself to be.

Now, it does not follow from this that people others regard as selfish, for example, think of themselves that way. It is the meanings of particular actions we must look at, such as hoarding something or refusing help to someone. People who do such things may, in their own minds, be expressing any of several quite different possible senses of self, such as: "I am alone and weak and need all the protection I can get"; or "I'm too important a person to be bothered by every Tom, Dick, and Harry"; or "I am who I am entirely through my own efforts, so I don't owe anything to anybody." With the help of this example we can see a number of features of this interpersonal communication: actors are not necessarily conscious that their actions are expressing anything at all; actions may express both conscious and unconscious meanings, which may in turn differ from observers' interpretations of them.

On the basis of our analysis thus far we could even define "to know oneself" as meaning to have a mental image of the effects that one's actions have on the world—especially other people. This definition does not exclude error. One's knowledge of oneself might be based on imaginary effects, in which case others would claim that this knowledge was false. Probably everyone is in this situation to some degree, for errors in communication can occur in both directions. People responding to an actor, for example, might well be ambiguous or even incomprehensible themselves. But if there is no overlap between a person's sense of self and others' image of the person, that would be madness. To put this in somewhat more dynamic terms, to get a sense of oneself, one must have an accurate understanding of how one's actions affect others. For this to happen, as we have seen, the others must respond comprehensibly.

We have slipped into a discussion of identity without specifying an obvious but important point, namely that identity, like personality, is of a symbolic nature. Let us look a little more closely at what it is for the Fulani. In that society a major part of one's identity is the family one is born into. We saw in chapter 6 how important it was that children learn "who their relatives are." From our current perspective we might reinterpret this process as people's way of establishing the child's identity. Putting it this way falsifies the reality, however, because it suggests that the parents have a goal—which in fact they do not—of helping the child through an identity crisis.

What is the relation between personality and identity? This is not necessarily the same from one society to another, perhaps even from one social context to another. In the American middle class we have a tendency, in our everyday thinking, to conflate the two. We think of who a person is—or who a person truly is—as being what the person's personality is. The name, the nationality, the family, are accidents of history and might have been otherwise, but the irreducible core of the personality is who the person truly is. In some cases the person's sex is also thought of as an accident, especially if it does not correspond to his or her inner sense of profound identity. Perhaps the reason for this conflation of personality and identity is the hopelessness of piecing together an identity from all the diverse roles we play in modern life. We imagine that we have a better chance of finding and differentiating ourselves in *how* we act rather than in the particular functions we may be fufilling in the social order.

In all societies there is a relation between personality and identity in that for any identity people only consider a certain range of qualities appropriate, and they severely sanction a person whose qualities do not fit the range of the claimed identity. The material presented thus far, and particularly in the preceding chapter, suggests that the Fulani do not at all conflate identity and personality; rather they see some aspects of personality as depending upon identity through kinship, and others as quite independent of it.

It may appear by this point that the main thing I have done is to complicate yet again the study of personality by introducing another, narrower definition of it. It might be argued that the concepts of identity and "sense of self," as I have been using them, merely refer to aspects of what most psychologists include in the concept of personality. It might also seem that "self" is just another synonym for that term. To this I reply that that is precisely the problem with the term "personality" today; it is used to refer to several aspects of a person that are easier to understand if kept more distinct while we think about them. In addition, the reader should keep in mind that this way of thinking about personality is the result of my reflection on how people develop and function in two very different cultures. Thus all the generalizations I have made in this chapter have included as a deliberate goal validity for both Western and Fulani cultures. It would be presumptuous to claim at this point that the theory I am working out is valid for all humanity. But it does have the merit of encouraging and facilitating the comprehension of what we call psychological similarities and differences between people living in radically different social and cultural contexts.

Having examined in some detail the concepts of "sense of self," personality, and identity, let us now focus more directly on the nature of the self. Like the "I" of G. H. Mead which it resembles, it is elusive and difficult to discuss. At the outset I said the self is the agent, that which acts. It is unknowable not merely because of its unpredictability, which is what Mead insisted upon, but because it, like the other aspects of a person that we have been discussing, is a symbolic construct. Thus it is an inexhaustible source of meaning and can appear to take on even radically different meanings in different contexts.

I said earlier that identity was the single most important component of a sense of self. Let us now look more closely at the reason why. Above I emphasized that identity established an individual's uniqueness. At the same time, however, it establishes "sameness" with regard to other individuals through kinship and other systems of classification. What does sameness mean here? This is not something that can be specified in advance, for it depends on the notions of kinship and personhood that are maintained in the culture. In addition, in the light of our earlier discussion of the age at which children "get sense," it would seem that such ideas only begin to be grasped by children in later childhood. Prior to that time, their sense of identity depends greatly on the small number of close, intense relationships they have with family, caretakers, and peers. Their identity at that time, then, would be essentially a function of their sense of being known to virtually all the people with whom they interact every day. Attachment psychologists say that during this period children become attached to their mothers and other caretakers; psychoanalysts say that the child identifies with the mother in feeling somehow a part of her. In the materials I have presented so far I have not made any claims of this sort. But if we look at the child's early experience we can discern the basis for the child's feeling at one with the caretakers because the latter are indeed "extensions" of the child. They do for the child all the things the child is incapable of doing yet independently; in particular they feed, help evacuate bladder and bowels, clean, and protect the child from dangers. Erik Erikson used the term "mutuality" to describe this relationship, and saw it as occurring mainly, but not exclusively, through breast-feeding (c.f. also Winnicott 1964).

Whether or not memories of this period persist in later life, this impression that certain other people are extensions of oneself is one source, and possibly the most important one, of feeling at one with them and thereby participating together in some larger self. It is the give-and-take of everyday communication that produces this sentiment in us, because the same results recur whenever we direct the same actions towards the same persons. This regularity then not only constitutes the self that we are when with those people, but also constitutes that larger self that we make together. Good examples of the experiences I am talking about arise in playing a team sport or playing or singing music in a group. In the latter situation, for instance, we not only feel at one with the other members of the group, but we also create a "new" self together with them and the music—Beethoven's op. 59, no. 3, for instance. The playing of music or games is subjectively akin to undergoing possession (cf. Rouget 1985). Our experience of social life forms a continuum ranging from that of being an isolated self through total absorption in another self, which would be interpreted as possession in many cultures. In possession, one's own self completely disappears and is taken over by some other agent, while in playing music, for example, one's individual self becomes a participant in the larger self being created.

The nature of this self, and thus our sense of self, depend in part on the other players in the group, and in part upon the music we are playing; the latter not only has a particular style, but also may vary or remain constant in the course of performance depending on the genre and complexity of the piece. This point is of utmost importance for the argument of this book. It implies that the psychological processes through which a person can feel part of a larger self are universal. At the same time, the qualities which one senses that self to have are completely dependent on circumstances.

What I intend to do in the chapters that follow is to trace out as precisely as I can the process by which circumstances affect the self in Fulani society. This will then enable us to understand why the sense of self and its expression in personality differ for FulBe and RiimaayBe. Finally, I hope to build on this case study to develop a more general theory that would describe the relations between self, personality, and society for all situations.

9

CONCLUSION

I have sketched an ethnographic comparison of the FulBe and the RiimaayBe that not only shakes our common belief that early childhood is the decisive period for the formation of personality, but also strongly attacks theories such as those of classical culture-and-personality, which claim that personality traits shared by a group of people are formed in childhood by the practices parents use to care for and bring up children.[1] There are no systematic differences in the ways parents and other caretakers handle children during the first four to six years of life that might account for the striking personality contrasts between FulBe and RiimaayBe adults. Within each group I found some variation between households, though more in attitudes than in practices, and there were in some cases variations even for a given mother in how she treated different children, though this I could learn only from what mothers told me themselves of how they had changed. My general conclusion from all these observations is that the child-rearing practices of the FulBe and the RiimaayBe are quite indistinguishable from each other.

I have, therefore, proposed an alternative theory of personality which views personality not as a set of traits or qualities acquired during childhood but rather as the active portrayal—sometimes more deliberate, sometimes more unaware—of a person's sense of self.[2] Personality is an interpretation others make of a person by reading a sense of self from the person's actions. While a person's sense of self is entirely subjective to each individual, it is nevertheless built out of common understandings shared by that individual and other members of society. Its single most important component, I have argued, is identity—that is, how a person is located in the society's system of relations. Although a person's identity is initially constructed by others, it is gradually taken on and transformed by the person as it is incorporated into a sense of self. In contrast, the personality develops not prior to behavior, but rather as an interpretation of it. Whether or not one will be able to develop a clear image of one's own identity, and consequently a solid sense of self, depends in large part upon the consistency of other people's messages in respect to who one is. Although there is a relationship between personality and identity in all societies, the Fulani, as we have seen, never conflate the two. Rather, they regard certain aspects of personality as dependent on identity through kinship, and others as quite independent of it.

This theory does not deny all importance to childhood. Childhood is significant for the development of personality in that during this time the person establishes relationships with relatives. However, a person's identity—and consequently, the sense of self he or she may hold—encompasses more than relations with relatives. It is rooted in the person's relationships to the world at large. Consequently, the cultural interpretations of the social structure one lives in, of social relations, of neighboring societies, and of nature are crucial for any person's sense of self and thus for the personality that will be exhibited.

Before attacking directly the question of why the adult personalities of the FulBe and the RiimaayBe differ, let me discuss one way in which their childhood experiences do diverge, namely the simple fact that FulBe children are brought up in a FulBe milieu and RiimaayBe children in a RiimaayBe one. Given that the ways adults interact in these two groups contrast markedly, it is evident that the children's experience of what adults are like and what normal interaction is like will also vary. I mentioned before that FulBe and RiimaayBe women tend to do their household chores with company. Some women do prefer more solitude, but most of them do the bulk of their food preparation, laundry, and so on, in groups. With the RiimaayBe the group is often large, four or more women and many children all working, joking, and playing together. The spirit of the group is very lively, with loud talk, bantering, teasing, and frequent bursts of laughter. Among the FulBe, in contrast, one would only see such large groups at festive occasions or in wealthy households with many wives. Generally women work together in groups of two or three, and there—even in the larger groups—the tone is very different from that of the RiimaayBe. FulBe women seem very subdued by comparison, and though there is much banter, the overall feeling is one of calmness and tranquility rather than boisterousness and fun. In both social groups, however, the children play with equal liveliness. In neither group is there much effort, though there is a little, on the part of adults to get the children to play with them or react to them.

Could this be the difference we are looking for? Can growing up in a boisterous social environment as opposed to a sedate one explain why RiimaayBe turn out to be more boisterous than the FulBe? I think it does have something to do with the adult personality differences. These behaviors affect the children of the two groups, not in a direct formative sense, but rather by means of two crucial, intervening factors: first, the child's knowledge of the overall social system and of his or her place in it, and second, the meanings which these different patterns of behavior express within the cultural framework.

These two factors are interrelated in that for any identity people will consider only a certain range of qualities appropriate, and they may severely sanction a person whose qualities do not fit the range of identity that person has or claims. It follows from this that the task of understanding why members of a particular society exhibit certain common personality characteristics does not involve focusing on the possible shaping effects of early childhood experience. Rather it requires that we study how people perceive themselves to be located in the social contexts they live in, what factors influence this perception of themselves, and how the choice and performance of acts from the cultural repertoire express this sense of self. This expression occurs on two levels at once, for the manners one adopts are both like a badge by which everyone can locate you in the realm of possible cultural identities, and they portray in the cultural language of gestures the meaning of that identity in the society's value system. It is not necessary for this notion of personality that one be fully conscious of what one is doing, but it is necessary that one be a fairly sophisticated human being.

One of the key questions we must ask, then, is: What is being expressed by the behavior patterns of each group? In describing these two social groups I have emphasized self-restraint versus self-expression as a major contrast. The cultural code of the FulBe, I have argued, places supreme importance on controlling the public expression of "natural" urges and needs, like eating and defecating and, more uniquely, of powerful emotions such as weeping, crying out, or even laughing. Not only do the FulBe usually restrain themselves in the way they express emotions, but they also hold back in the very expression of meaning itself. In general, they do not like to make things explicit. This is true in their personal relations and also in their expression of their total culture—such as parts of their kinship system—but it goes beyond that. As compared with both the RiimaayBe and ourselves, the FulBe are indirect, vague, and discreet even about things that are not actually vague. Although the RiimaayBe share in some of these behavioral ideals—they, too, for instance, would think it cowardly to give in to physical pain—they generally express emotions of joy, sadness, and anger more immediately in response to situations and more openly. They are also more aggressive and outgoing than the FulBe in their interpersonal behavior. Rather than being reserved and dignified like the FulBe, they give the overall impression of being hearty and down-to-earth.

In describing these differences between adult FulBe and adult RiimaayBe I am, of course, attempting to categorize these peoples' behavior in our own terms, according to dimensions of personality *we* consider to be meaningful. While the FulBe and RiimaayBe themselves clearly distinguish between the qualities each group has, it is important to realize that they do not perceive or emphasize these differences in quite the same way as I have. For example, I have never heard FulBe or RiimaayBe invoke concepts of "restraint" versus "expression," or "suspicious" versus "open" to describe themselves or each other. The fact that they recognize, and in fact highlight, contrasts in character and behavior between the two groups confirms my own finding of differences, yet it raises only more clearly the following question: What is the relation between my interpretations and theirs concerning the meaning of their characteristic behaviors? We can see from this discussion that to explain personality differences amounts to finding causes in the culture under study for features that I have partly constructed myself. This is not to say that my constructs have no validity, but it does imply that the explanation I seek will require relating those constructs to the FulBe's and the RiimaayBe's own ways of describing and experiencing their personalities.

To understand the social meanings expressed by these differences we have to rely primarily on what people say about their different ways of acting—both how they describe them and how they react when people either follow them or fail to do so. It is important to recall, for instance, that not only are FulBe and RiimaayBe aware of differences in what their behavioral patterns express, but also that they are constantly calling attention to them in everyday conversations. These everyday references serve not only to keep certain images constantly in people's minds, but also have the weight of sanctions: FulBe who act like RiimaayBe degrade themselves, while a Diimaajo who acted like a Pullo would in many contexts be considered uppity.

And yet, the FulBe and the RiimaayBe do not characterize the differences between themselves in terms of the self-restraint versus self-expression contrast I have invoked here. For them the most important difference is between being free and being slave, that is, between being one's own master and not. This English expression I have just used is fairly close in meaning to the usual Fulfulde phrase that describes the responsible citizen, the normal adult, namely "to own one's own head." When you say, "So-and-so owns his own head," you mean that he is free and in control of himself, and that the acts he engages in are chosen, not forced. When you say of someone that he doesn't own his own head you mean that he is not in control of himself; this might be a temporary condition caused by powerful emotions or a burdensome obligation, or it might be more long-term, due to being mad, seriously ill, or a child, or it might be permanent, due to being owned by somebody else.

We can infer from this that, in FulBe thought, emotions and appetites are capable of jeopardizing one's "ownership of one's own head." People do not see the contrast as free expression of self versus restraint, but as being mastered by one's emotions versus being master of them. Subjectively speaking, acts that demonstrate "ownership of one's own head" are ones that do not directly express an emotion, a need, or a purpose; they are also not direct responses to a need, purpose, or emotion perceived in the other(s) whom one is with at the time. In other words, what distinguishes those acts I have characterized as "restrained" from other sorts of acts is that the sense they make—if any—is entirely social and quite radically independent of any utilitarian purpose. In contrast to Americans who often see working for utilitarian ends as supremely meaningful, the FulBe do not think of themselves or others as consciously directing individual self-interest into socially valuable channels. On the contrary, they seek to express the very value of the social by means of gestures which are devoid of, or purified of, personal interest.

Current ideas about the nature of language are helpful in attempting to understand the FulBe ideal of social action. What gives language its power to convey meanings is precisely its disjunction from purely phatic communication, that is, the signalling of emotional states. As Suzanne Langer has written, words "in themselves . . . are completely trivial. . . . A symbol which interests us *also* as an object is distracting. It does not convey its meaning without obstruction" (1951:73). She goes on to argue that a peach cannot successfully express an unambiguous message, such as the idea of abundance, because it is already good to eat. In the same way, any act loses its "self-controlled" quality and its ability to mean if it is something you do anyway. Thus a man who cannot obtain food is also unable to fast, and a man who has a nervous twitch in his eye cannot wink. So, too, the FulBe would not be able to express their sharing of values, their mutual respect, if they felt that they were acting under compulsion or for ulterior motives.

In striving to embody their behavioral ideals, the FulBe are thus conveying a double message. Not only are they identifying themselves as members of a particular social group but, more significantly, they are indicating to other members of that group that they are participating actively in maintaining the group's shared meanings, come what may. From this perspective, needs, desires, and feelings are neither parts of the personality nor influences that shape it—roughly a contemporary Western view. Rather, the fact that one has these feelings, and so on, has meaning in the cultural code and can thus be used by people to express and validate major social distinctions, to create and affirm identity. One expresses and validates one's nobility by acting as one's own master with respect to bodily needs and so on, while one expresses one's condition of servitude by appearing not to be master of those needs.

Thus the FulBe actor strives to approximate a socially defined ideal for all situations, regardless of the feelings, health, and idiosyncracies of the people involved. One must continually demonstrate in public and before certain categories of kin that one is stronger than one's needs, discomforts, and impulses. Needs and emotions are points of weakness for the FulBe because in their experience it is through these qualities that people are dependent on nature and dependent on other people, and this is an unpleasing fact. It is not exactly that they try to conceal this fact from themselves, but rather that they resist it and, to the extent that they engage in "restrained" behavior, succeed. The ideal the FulBe strive to represent, therefore, is that of a person who transcends all physical and emotional determinants. The reason that embodying this ideal is so important for FulBe is that people who are not in control of their own needs and emotions are not in control of themselves, and people who are not in control of themselves need to be controlled by others. Self-control is thus an absolute prerequisite for being on an equal footing with other members of society.

Self-control is closely related to another concept used by the FulBe and RiimaayBe to describe the differences between themselves: the notion of shame, *semteende*. FulBe behavior can be seen as expressing the deep FulBe sense of shame, while the RiimaayBe are more "shameless." Shame and "owning one's head" are not alternate concepts for the same thing but are related to each other in a complex way. Linguistic analysis of the morphology and use of the Fulfulde word for "shame" reveals that its root meaning is "to be weak" (Riesman 1977:129–134). To be in a state of shame is to expose one's weakness, while to have a sense of shame is to *fear* exposing one's weakness. Consequently, one's social honor, one's *pulaaku*, depends directly on one's abilities to avoid what comes "naturally" to one's lips, and to avoid the "natural" outcome of bodily needs. In actuality, of course, both the FulBe and the RiimaayBe have a sense of shame in that both feel shame when certain things happen. For the FulBe, however, situations that might cause shame are common and normal in daily life, such that concern about it figures far more in their mental life than in that of the RiimaayBe. It is easy to see that there is a connection between fear of exposing one's weakness and wanting to appear master of one's own head.

But there is an important implication of this fear that is even more significant, namely that a group of people exists for whose sake weakness must be kept hidden. Significantly, the term pulaaku is a cognate of Pullo. It can refer not only to "the qualities appropriate to a Pullo" but to "the group of FulBe persons possessing these qualities" as well. To demonstrate one's pulaaku is thus to behave as a proper Pullo. And this means especially, and before all else, to act in such a way that the other members of the group can detect no difference between the actor and themselves. This group is first and foremost one's own family of origin, but it ultimately includes in ever-widening expansion all those FulBe with whom one feels related. Any deviation from these ideals would be seen as a lack of pulaaku, bringing shame not only upon the individual actor but also all others with whom the actor is closely identified.

However, it would be a serious mistake to view the twin forces of pulaaku and semteende in daily social life as purely restrictive in nature. In the experience of the FulBe, they are also powerful liberating forces insofar as they require individuals to achieve a certain freedom before their being and their action can be socially validated. From this perspective, the rules and restrictions on behavior in different social contexts and with different categories of kin, which sustain their social structure, may be understood—and are understood by the FulBe—as furnishing a person with opportunities to manifest self-control, that is to say, freedom with respect to the forces acting on one. This suggests that the FulBe regard the public demonstration of this freedom as a necessary condition for full participation in social life and, hence, for the very existence of their social life and order. Any Pullo feels like a Pullo by virtue of having been born one, but at the same time, since FulBe must manifest their nobility through characteristics such as those we have been discussing, each Pullo is constantly being tested just by living in society and must always be able to validate this membership by behaving appropriately. Not only does this involve mastering oneself, but also to some extent mastering the world around one, so that one's words correspond to the way things are and one's resources suffice to fulfill one's needs.

What is more, the group with which a Pullo senses kinship includes illustrious ancestors whose deeds and qualities are known to
everyone and often recited in stories or referred to in everyday
conversation. It is their actions that must be continually reflected
in one's own.

For the RiimaayBe, in contrast, a group with which to identify
simply does not exist. Consequently, the twin forces of pulaaku
and semteende are far less powerful in the everyday social life of
the RiimaayBe than in that of the FulBe. Though RiimaayBe grow
up in families whose internal structure shares similarities with
FulBe families, they do not have lineages, they do not have gene-
alogies, and they do not have ancestors. They do have networks of
kin, but these networks are nothing more than that: they are not
corporate groups with a shared identity and a shared history. Although two generations have passed since slavery officially came
to an end in this region, this aspect of social structure has changed
little despite significant economic and political transformations.
The only group with which the RiimaayBe can identify is that of
their masters and ex-masters. In the past, and in a few cases today,
RiimaayBe could take pride in being associated with this or that
FulBe family, yet their identification with it could never lead to
imitation of FulBe but only to support of their superiority through
maintenance of the distinctions between FulBe and RiimaayBe
characteristics.[3]

Thus the RiimaayBe do not have a past in which they can take
pride. Even when great deeds of slaves are celebrated in stories, no
Diimaajo alive can consider such a hero one's own because slaves,
by the very condition of their being, do not found a line: they
merely leave offspring who belong, as do the offspring of cattle, to
the owners of the mother. RiimaayBe today express a whole gamut
of thoughts and feelings about the FulBe, but I think that the majority accord them some sort of ineffable superiority. The previously described conversation I had with the young Diimaajo
Koranic student about why he considered the FulBe to be "whiter"
than the RiimaayBe is exemplary. His response suggested that it
was "the rope"—or captivity—that effectively cut the RiimaayBe
off from their past, making them nobodies. Even if by their own
efforts they are able to become somebodies, there is no way, he
implied, for this self-worth to be stored, so to speak, as a patri-

mony for the next generation. For them, the concept of *suudu baaba* (father's house), and all it represents simply does not exist.

We can see from these considerations that FulBe would have a very different sense of self from the RiimaayBe. For the Pullo self includes in some measure the selves of relatives, both past and present, and one's own sense of worth is enhanced by the very admiration felt toward those relatives and ancestors. One's behavior expresses esteem for this group by portraying through the cultural code a certain notion of nobility. The RiimaayBe, on the other hand, are prevented from having this enhanced sense of self because it is impossible for them to see themselves as more than individuals. In other words, though people in both groups live and work surrounded by persons related to them in known ways, FulBe culture defines the idea of kinship in such a way that the sense of relatedness is greatly expanded for the FulBe while it is greatly curtailed for the RiimaayBe. What remains to be explored, however, is how these very different notions of self are conveyed to and incorporated by maturing RiimaayBe and FulBe children.

We have seen that one of the most important sources of feeling at one with other people, and thereby of participating in larger selves, is the feeling that certain persons are direct extensions of oneself. Accordingly, one of the primary goals of parenting for both the RiimaayBe and the FulBe is for parents to convince their children that they are one with them and that their future lies together with that of other family members. However, the fact of the matter remains that FulBe parents have powerful material and symbolic means of cultivating this sense of we-ness in their children that the RiimaayBe do not have, including their noble ancestry, their lineage ideology, and their cattle wealth. By far the most important of these is their cattle. For not only are cattle a source of daily nourishment and a source of capital in emergencies for the FulBe but, more importantly, they are the indispensable means by which FulBe maintain their social structure, their forms of interpersonal relations, and the values they consider supreme and most characteristic of themselves, especially independence.

Of course, from a purely ecological point of view, it could be argued that cattle confer on the FulBe certain benefits that nonpastoral agriculturalists like the RiimaayBe do not have. There are two main benefits of this type. First is better health, because of their having more protein in the diet and because of the seasonal movements of the villages that lead to more sanitary conditions in the settlements. Second is the ability to survive on milk during a crop-growing season, since the mobility of a herd allows a man to cultivate a field in an area he has never been in before and thus take advantage of, rather than suffer from, the great micro-regional fluctuations in rainfall that characterize the Sahel ecological zone. And yet, real as these ecological advantages may be, they do not enter at all into FulBe thinking on why they keep cattle, nor do they appear to be causal factors in their maintenance of a pastoral way of life. In fact, the connection between having cattle and getting food is less direct among the FulBe than might appear. During the rainy season, for instance, when the cows have the most milk to give, FulBe herds are often split up for transhumance, and thus the people staying at home do not necessarily have milk in abundance. During the dry season the cows give little or no milk, so for at least half the year most people get at most a few sips of milk per day. Furthermore, there is no commercialization of milk and very little selling of butter. Cattle are sold occasionally to get money for taxes, clothes, and other necessities, but not to buy grain unless there has been crop failure. What sustains the FulBe is not their cattle but rather their millet, for it is this that they eat far more than anything else. And yet, they do not normally view millet as being either a staff of life or a source of spiritual values. If the opinions expressed by the FulBe elders I overheard debating the relative merits of "farming for oneself" are indeed representative of wider fields of FulBe opinion, it seems that most FulBe would willingly abandon their hoes in favor of purchased grain, if only they had the means. Although FulBe suffer willingly for their cattle and take a lively satisfaction in seeing them quench their thirst, it is my impression that they deeply resent work in the fields as a task imposed by the sheer necessity of having to eat. And to act merely in order to fulfill one's needs is a character trait that FulBe, not surprisingly, consider more appropriate to the RiimaayBe than to themselves.

Viewed in this light, our earlier observations about the somewhat tenuous linkage between cattle wealth and the satisfaction of physical needs takes on added meaning. It is precisely because cattle are not *merely* the basis of subsistence—and actually make a small and apparently inessential contribution to the food supply for many families—that the FulBe are able to dissociate their love of cattle from their basic survival needs. We may think of milk as an excellent food to satisfy hunger and thirst, but for the FulBe it is akin to divine ambrosia. They experience the very availability of milk not as a matter of having enough to eat but as a symbol of having cattle and thus of belonging to a superior class of people. In the FulBe view, cattle wealth has nothing to do with mere survival or even with having a better standard of living; rather, it allows one to act with "a touch of class," with munificence and pizzazz. At the same time, this wealth which "goes on its own" imposes certain conditions on those who possess it or covet it.

First, the cattle care itself is often exhausting since it may involve late night searches for stray animals and long and difficult treks to distant salt licks, as well as many arduous hours wandering in the bush under a hot sun or standing over a well hoisting heavy buckets to the surface. Herdsmen on transhumance are especially conscious of accomplishing a difficult task (cf. Riesman 1977:157). Given the cows' taste for young millet stalks, the variability of the soil, and the scarcity of water in the dry season, separations of herd and field are seasonally necessary. This in itself requires of FulBe a degree of labor differentiation and group coordination that is unprecedented among the RiimaayBe. The FulBe must also constantly adjust the size of their domestic groups in accordance with herd size, a readjustment which consists in including other relatives (father or brothers) and their animals in case of need, and in separating from them and from one's own sons when the number of persons and of cattle allows it. Indeed, the success of a generation—as measured by the proliferation of its cattle and its members—means its geographical dispersion, but that does not automatically mean the weakening of its social ties. These centripetal forces, built as they are into the very structure of the FulBe socioeconomic order, are counterbalanced by a shared consciousness of an enduring connection between dispersed family and lineage members—which is to say a consciousness of and respect for suudu baaba. Geographical distance for the FulBe has no pre-established significance but may be considered, according to the circumstances, as an obstacle to be surmounted in reaffirming ties or as a means of escaping from a disagreeable situation.

The cow, being a moveable object and a mortal one, can also be lost to the group in a variety of ways. It can die from disease, animal attack, or old age, and it can be captured by another person. In fact, before the colonial period, there was constant cattle rustling going on between different FulBe groups and between the FulBe and other ethnic groups. A central part of owning cattle thus became the ability to defend them. The story I recounted of the young FulBe man who was rejected by his own mother after having failed to defend the family herd with his life illustrates this well. His loss of cattle was considered a disgrace because it implied that he was not man enough to stand up to their attackers. Just as one cannot live as a Pullo without cattle, if one has no cows it is assumed by the FulBe that one has not acted like a Pullo. The equation of poverty with cowardice was particularly direct prior to colonization and to the suppression of cattle raiding. Though there is currently little need for FulBe to defend their cattle against thieves and warriors, or even wild animals, the temptations to cash in on the market value of the animals in return for comfort and luxury have increased tremendously in recent years. However, most FulBe, as I explained, continue to view the reward of the new economic and political order with disdain. Not only is the acquisition of such goods interpreted among FulBe as a form of personal weakness—that is, as a "need" for creature comforts—but, more pointedly, as a shameful abandonment of one's Pullo responsibilities. For it is assumed that anyone who has managed to acquire these luxuries has behaved in a fundamentally non-Pullo fashion either by abandoning his herding responsibilities or, worse yet, by brazenly cashing in on the market value of his animals to the detriment of his immediate dependents and extended familial group. For all of these reasons, the forms of wealth in which the RiimaayBe take such pride have been largely rejected by the FulBe as antithetical to their cattle-herding ethos. On the psychological level, moreover, the feeling still persists among the FulBe that it would be demeaning for them to enter into competition in this sphere with the RiimaayBe and other neighboring peoples whom they perceive as social inferiors.

Now, it can be readily seen that a Pullo's willingness to defend his cattle and his willingness to defend his honor are practically the same thing. FulBe superiority, then, consists in having something that is uniquely theirs and yet which can be lost. This something is the three-part complex I have been exploring: namely, their cattle, their honor, and their character (an essential component of which is the readiness to defend honor and cattle). A loss of any of these, it can easily be seen, implies destruction of the whole. From a sociological perspective, it could easily be argued that the ownership of cattle is the key factor in the FulBe's sense of superiority and the psychological complex revolving around honor and character follows from this. But from the point of view of the FulBe, it is the FulBe character which is fundamental, for it is this that gives them a strong sense of honor and justifies the fact that they and no others in their geographical region herd cattle. Unlike the Riimaay-Be, who need not justify the fact that they are farmers nor the reasons why they live where they do, the FulBe feel that they must defend their cattle as well as their right to own them. The implications of this are far-reaching. The FulBe think, like many other peoples, that their culture is superior to all others—and, in particular, superior to that of their ex-slaves, the RiimaayBe. But this is not enough; they must also demonstrate this superiority through their behavior and honor code. The struggle to be a person is thus built right into the FulBe cultural code, since adherence to its values and behavioral ideals presupposes the existence of those unruly needs and impulses that individuals are trying to master. Thus to become human is, for the FulBe, to become something which one in a sense is not.

From the perspective of the maturing FulBe child, this triple-value relationship—together with the principles of hierarchy and possibilities of autonomy it entails—is incorporated, at least initially, through feelings of oneness with, and of love for, cattle. For it is through his relations with cattle that the FulBe boy gradually becomes conscious, in a highly concrete way, of the existence and the personal relevance of the broader social groups into which he has been born. As the scope of his social world gradually expands beyond the limits of his immediate family, he begins to realize the extent to which his daily associations with cattle are a quintessential aspect of his Pullo identity. This identity derives both from the hierarchical relations of the patrilineage, and from the network of more egalitarian matrilateral relationships. Awareness of this latter aspect of identity is enriched and deepened by the association of cattle with women.

At about the age of seven years, after a child has gained enough social sense to understand the important role that cattle are going to play in life, the father will show the child the herd, pointing out the heifer or heifers that were given to the child at birth. Although a boy does not manage his own herd before his majority, he feels from that moment on intimately tied to the herd, for his fortune in life depends directly on the health and fertility of his cattle. In the case of a girl, her cattle will be held in trust by her father until some time after her marriage, whereupon they will join her husband's herd. While the child's cows are merged with the herd of the father or an older brother, they are subject to the same fate as the other cattle. The father or older brother may take one of the child's animals and sell it when he deems necessary, without being responsible for its replacement. The husband retains similar rights over his wife's cattle. And thus, two brothers who each begin life with a cow may have at the time of their marriages, at about twenty-five years, entirely different herds: it is not rare that one of the two will own one or two cows or even none while the brother finds himself the owner of ten. He who is destitute has no recourse; it is God who has given luck to the one and not to the other. Of course, while he lives with his parents he can be fed from their herd, but the reconstitution of his herd depends on the generosity of his relatives: his father, above all, and his maternal uncle. Giving in such circumstances is a matter of helping one's dependent, one's relative, to maintain his humanity and to remain master of himself in the face of life's difficulties. "May you have children to give to" is the FulBe attitude toward parenthood expressed commonly in blessings.

These observations draw attention to a major difference in parental responsibilities between the FulBe and the RiimaayBe. Whereas parents in both social groups strive to forge enduring, mutually respectful relationships with their children so that they will remain together, FulBe parents must do something more: they must also hand over a certain amount of livestock to their offspring so that the children can get their own start in life. Significantly, there is no parallel for this transgenerational gift of independence among the RiimaayBe since the RiimaayBe father has little or nothing to confer on his children that the latter could not obtain through their own efforts upon their maturity. Moreover, the kinds of wealth that RiimaayBe might obtain from their parents would not be self-reproducing like cattle. Thus, such wealth would not confer on the RiimaayBe child the possibility of a durable independence. In contrast, it is precisely this possibility that the FulBe father (and sometimes other relatives as well) confers on the child, symbolically and materially, in the form of a cow during the naming ceremony shortly after birth.

One might say that it is because mature FulBe men retain the right to dispose of their wives' and children's livestock that they can exercise authority over them. But it is equally true to say that it is their authority over their dependents that permits them to claim rights over their property. This latter perspective is, I have shown, much closer to FulBe understandings of this situation in that their cultural system of social stratification is premised on the idea of dominance through relative self-mastery rather than on the direct mastery of others. And it is precisely this principle of hierarchy that the maturing FulBe boy explores and learns through his relationships with cattle.

As a boy's general competence in the care of cattle increases, he will begin to release his father and/or older brothers from their day-to-day cattle-care responsibilities, while spending in the process far more time in the company of his peers. And this transformation in his daily routine directly supports the extended social hierarchy in three important ways. First, it is in the company of peers that adolescent FulBe boys begin to explore their abilities and limitations with regard to the behavioral code. The boy's father and senior kinsmen will thus learn of his bravery and leadership primarily through contacts with his peers. Peer relations are of utmost importance to the social system as whole in that they strengthen solidarity at the same time as they blur lines of descent. This in itself greatly enhances the sense of self a FulBe youth has within his immediate family by broadening the social group with which he identifies. Furthermore, it is among his peers that any gaps in his education, bad habits, or other peculiarities in his behavior traceable to his immediate family will be called to his attention and gradually reshaped through pointed insults, teasing, mocking, challenges, and the like until his bearing is the same as all FulBe. For ultimately, every Pullo must be something other than just the product of a father and a mother, demonstrating as well both connectedness with ancestors and a sense of belonging to ever-broadening circles of relatives. This is done by modeling oneself on ideals of comportment shared by all adult FulBe. It is thus primarily during adolescence, and not during early childhood, that the ideal social self that adults strive to portray through their actions and personality is forged.

Second, the cattle-tending responsibilities FulBe youths increasingly assume during adolescence directly contribute to their fathers' (and other senior kinsmen's) authority within the domestic group as well as to the latter's abilities to influence wider networks of kin. Within the family, the relationship between authority and leisure is direct. For to be able-bodied and not to work means that there is someone who works for one, and that between oneself and that person there exists a relation of authority based on inequality of status. It is for this reason that mature FulBe men see themselves as competing in leisure rather than in work (Riesman 1977:71-73).

Last, the leisure time FulBe youths confer on their fathers and senior kinsmen is crucial to the continuance of the social order in that it enables the latter group to devote its energies more fully to broadening relations between people and maintaining them in particular forms. Since mature men always feel true kinship to be a lineage community that is larger than the one experienced by the youths, and since it is the mature men who maintain the political order, these ties can remain alive despite the continual dispersal of the families that make up the lineage group.

It is in light of these remarks that the full meaning of the fact that there is no able-bodied RiimaayBe man who does not work becomes clear. There is no point at which an able-bodied RiimaayBe father can step back from his subsistence tasks and rely on the productive labor of his sons. And thus the father's authority over his sons is, comparatively speaking, very weak. Just as there is little division of labor among the RiimaayBe with respect to subsistence tasks, so too, everyone is in a sense responsible for forging and maintaining his own networks of kinship relations. The RiimaayBe son simply cannot assume that the extra-familial relations his father builds will endure beyond the latter's death. Without a lineage ideology in which to ground them, there is little way for him to extend the "social labor" of his seniors. I will return to this point shortly.

But FulBe boys, on reaching adolescence, gain more than a deepened appreciation for the behavioral ideals and status differentials upon which their society is based. They also gain an added arena of personal autonomy. This newfound freedom is experienced on several planes. First, in spending greater amounts of time in the company of peers deep within the bush, an adolescent FulBe boy is able to escape to some degree the pressures and status differentials governing daily life within the village. He is always freer in the sense that his peers cannot boss him around. Indeed, some youths prefer to remain herding their cattle far away from the village for months at a time. Second, the growing cattle responsibilities of the Pullo youth entail a more direct relationship between him and the bush in that he must enter and live in the bush in order to look after his herd. The bush is a powerful symbol among the FulBe of the "unknown" both within individuals and within the world at large (Riesman 1977:247–57). Furthermore, it is from the bush that people obtain their necessary subsistence, and to do this they must bow to its demands. This necessity has a double consequence: it makes people aware of their weakness in relation to it, while it also gives each person the possibility of individualization insofar as responsibility is taken for one's own needs. And thus, a person's entry into the bush, whether in the pursuit of cattle or for the satisfaction of pressing personal needs, signifies for the FulBe solitude, separation from society, and the individuation of the person.

Paradoxically, it is precisely the idea that FulBe are weak in relation to the bush that makes it possible for the individual male to free himself from the hold of his peers. This is because, from the individual's point of view, freedom in society is founded on the possibility of each person's entering into a direct relation with the bush, that is nature, without the mediation of another person or of any social institution. It thus seems legitimate to conclude that FulBe society, by placing a high value on the association of adolescent youths and their cattle, is encouraging them to forge a more personal relationship with the bush, with the "unknown," and thereby establish themselves as independent individuals able to meet their peers on an equal footing.

Nowhere was the sense of freedom and joy FulBe youths experience in their relationships with cattle and with the bush made more clear to me than when I accompanied a number of young men on transhumance. I had the distinct impression at that time that I was in some way looking at "the true FulBe life," which is to say a life of actions expressing more clearly than any others the values that FulBe consider most characteristic of themselves. The love of cattle, the interdependence between man and animal, the tending of the herd, and considerations concerning its well-being and its increase dominated our existence. Our needs and, of course, our comfort, took second place. Our moments of rest and the hours of our departure, as well as the speed of our traveling, were largely determined by the animals. To be so completely at the mercy of cattle is not an agreeable thing in itself, and those who go on transhumance unceasingly emphasize these difficulties. The feeling of the FulBe in this situation is truly ambiguous. For on the one hand the activities of the herdsman do not depend on himself; he cannot do what he wants. But on the other hand, he escapes almost totally from the habitual pressures of the social life of the community. This sense of escape is reflected in the feeling of oneness and the lack of hierarchy that often characterize relations between fellow herders. Thus the transhumance experience rounds out a different dimension of the male Pullo's place in suudu baaba—equality rather than hierarchy. The cattle embody the highest values for FulBe society, but they are not integrated into it in the same way as human beings are. They play a role in it, but they remain beyond people's influence. For a FulBe youth the fact of submitting to cattle, which are outside human society, liberates him from the influence of that society and at the same time makes people admit the incontestable value and legitimacy of his action. One of the kinds of men most admired among the FulBe is one who "loves cows."

In many ways, one might view the symbolic role played by cattle in FulBe social life as something akin to that of the succulent peach in Suzanne Langer's linguistic example: maturing FulBe boys are usually far too interested in cattle themselves to notice all the principles of differentiation and interdependence that cattle embody and convey. These principles derive in large part from the fact that an individual's access to cattle wealth is controlled in some measure by others—most notably, by that person's father, older brothers, and other senior kinsmen or, in the case of married

women, by their husbands. Consequently, there is far greater stratification on the basis of age, sex, and descent among the FulBe than
is the case among the RiimaayBe, whose wealth, as we have seen,
is generally acquired individually. This stratification is evident, for
instance, in the profound importance FulBe attach to primo-
geniture and birth order in their families and to generation in their
lineages. Whereas social mobility in the parent–child relationship
is guaranteed for FulBe and RiimaayBe men alike (virtually all
children will one day become parents), there is no mobility between the status of younger brother and older brother among the
FulBe while the older brother is alive. All important family decisions, including those governing the fate of collectively held cattle,
devolve upon the oldest son after the father's death. Although this
principle of seniority may be plainly annoying at times for younger
sons—and especially for those who have reached maturity—it
would be difficult for them to challenge their older brother's authority directly. To do so would be interpreted by others as demonstrating personal weakness—that is, as a failure on the younger
brother's part to model himself on an ideal recognized by all as that
of a good Pullo. The compliance of the younger brother, therefore, may be understood more as deference to culturally shared
ideals than as deference to the will of his older brother.

Interestingly, the importance FulBe attach to birth order sometimes takes on strange twists within the generational structure of
specific lineages. The basic principle that all lineage men of the
generation of one's father are in some way identified with him and
may thus exercise power over one is greatly complicated by the
fact that many men, by the system of multiple marriages, have
children over the course of many years and thus establish enormous gaps between oldest and youngest children. And these gaps
continue to widen over successive generations. Consequently, descendants of a younger son of the founding ancestor may sometimes assert seniority over descendants of the oldest son on the
basis that fewer generations separate them from the common ancestor. The FulBe must thus keep track of far more complex patterns
and principles of identity and of authority than the RiimaayBe, for
whom seniority is based solely on age. The socioeconomic system
of the FulBe contains both the possibility for greater domination
of some people by others, and at the same time the possibility for

greater personal independence—and both of these are realized through the ownership of cattle. Indeed, one could argue that FulBe are able to express their sharing of values and mutual respect in daily life through behavioral ideals that emphasize unity over diversity and equality over hierarchy precisely because the status differences inherent in their socioeconomic order are asserted and achieved indirectly, as it were, through control over cattle.

Among the RiimaayBe, in contrast, the influence any particular person will exercise on the life of the community is totally unpredictable on the basis of sociocultural data about the person's family or location in the birth order. The power and social influence individual RiimaayBe achieve within their communities depend less on identity than on strength of personality and on the kinds of personal relationships formed with surrounding individuals. From this perspective, the senses of self that RiimaayBe develop share characteristics with those developed by many middle-class Americans. In both cases, personality overshadows identity as the primary source of a person's sense of self.

The very fact that the RiimaayBe lack a lineage identity, of course, disqualifies them in the eyes of the FulBe from positions of authority within Fulani society at large. Nevertheless, it does not preclude their seeking leadership positions within their own communities. But the "social labor" that goes into the creation and maintenance of social networks among the RiimaayBe is based on premises very different from those characteristic among the FulBe. Whereas the FulBe, as we have seen, assert their oneness through conformity with a socially shared ideal of self, the RiimaayBe, at once freer from social pressures and less responsible to others, are more alone. They may direct their communicative energies to the constant creation of feelings of social intimacy through emotional expressiveness, but at the same time these expressions reaffirm their inferiority in the larger system of meaning they and the FulBe share.

Significantly, the split between village life and life in the bush is experienced less intensely by the RiimaayBe. The productive activities of RiimaayBe youths do not require that they spend long periods alone, or in the company of their peers, deep in the bush. Rather, they are expected to work side by side with their fathers and senior kinsmen in the fields. Accordingly, the day-to-day relations between RiimaayBe fathers and their children are much more relaxed than those of their FulBe counterparts. There is no expectation among the RiimaayBe, for instance, that sons will continually defer to their fathers' authority through acts of avoidance and self-restraint. Nor is there any single social ideal of self shared by all RiimaayBe that the youths are expected to emulate in their own behavior and encourage in the behavior of others. The heterogeneity of the RiimaayBe, with respect to both what people do and where they have come from, has precluded the possibility of constructing of such a social ideal. Whatever oneness the RiimaayBe may feel as an abstract social community is based not on a core of socially shared values and ideals passed down from one generation to the next, but derives rather from an historically grounded and contemporarily reinforced opposition between themselves and their ex-masters, the FulBe.

It is in light of these remarks that the absence of a lineage concept among the RiimaayBe begins to take on its full significance. Among the FulBe, the concept suudu baaba indicates not only one's patrilineage but, beyond this in the abstract, all of the customs and rules which one must observe in relations with one's fellow members. But, as is true of most FulBe kinship terms, only the context indicates whether it refers just to close relatives, to an immediate group, or to a widely dispersed and loosely affiliated group of people who are as much as seven or eight generations removed from their founding ancestor. Common expressions of solidarity used to affirm the unity of the particular group in question include "We are all of the same corral" or, alternately, "We are all the same belt." The first of these envisages the unity of the group in terms of a common herd which members draw upon in order to marry and thereby expand the group, while the second evokes the image of the cord with which men hold their trousers around their waists—a euphemism, then, for the genitals. Although these expressions thus conceive of the unity of the group from different angles both draw attention to its procreative core—which is to say, its potential for transgenerational continuity and expansion. It is precisely this concept and this capability that the RiimaayBe lack.

This difference was brought out clearly in our comparative examination of the wedding rites and the meaning of marriage in these two social groups. RiimaayBe marriage focuses mainly on the bride and groom as individuals. Both the symbolism of RiimaayBe

wedding ceremonies and the speed with which they are carried out
suggest that marriage among them is viewed primarily as a personal rite of passage, a coming of age or gaining of adulthood (for
both the bride and groom in the case of first marriages). In the case
of the bride, moreover, this transformation is conceived and experienced by all the participants as involving the severing of her
kinship ties with her first family. The elaborate praises she receives
from her mother and other female relatives while lying, quiet and
still, beneath a cloth covering her entire body signify this rupture through images of death. It will be recalled that both adult
RiimaayBe and FulBe equate a parent's praising of a child to its
face with its death. Significantly, no such death imagery nor implications of a permanent break in kinship relations are evident in
FulBe marriage ceremonies. On the contrary, FulBe marriages are
frequently used to intensify lineage connections. Ideally, every
Pullo man selects his first wife from within his own suudu baaba.
And few things make a Pullo grandfather happier than to see two
of his grandchildren marry, for if it is not a guarantee against dis-
aggregation of the lineage, it is like a pledge that the fight against it
will be continued. The striking decorum and reserve with which
FulBe wedding ceremonies are completed also draw attention to
the fact that the bride and groom represent something more than
themselves as individuals, and that something is suudu baaba.

Nevertheless, it is important to realize that the significance of
lineage for the FulBe is not that of a vital corporate institution interacting with like institutions. There are no rites which call the
lineage together; its members do not meet and they do not act in
common with a collective goal. However, belonging to a lineage
gives an individual a clear identity or sociogeographic base from
which to operate: a man will have a territory, even if quite vaguely
delimited and sometimes discontinuous, where he will be able to
pasture his herd and cultivate his field; other members of the lineage will not be strangers but suudu baaba. However, the genea-
logical hierarchy of the lineages within a specific territory has no
real effect on the political and social life of that region. Rather, the
concept of suudu baaba is crucial because it helps to establish, in
what remains a society with strong anarchic tendencies, the notion
of an order in which each individual has a place. It follows that
individual FulBe are able to conceptualize the social order, and
their relative places within it, in a much more specific and compre-

hensive way than is possible among the RiimaayBe. The sense of self individual FulBe develop is thus strengthened and enhanced accordingly.

Some Comparative Reflections

My analysis of the Fulani case reveals, I think, some features of the process of creating an identity that are obscured in the United States by the extreme complexity and diversity of the environments in which people grow up.[4] In both societies the wider community as well as the immediate family convey messages to the child about who he or she is, and this is accepted and encouraged by the parents. But in America the sheer number of people children meet, both other children and adults, is very large, and they present them with contradictory messages. A very large percentage of these individuals will be unimportant to them, or will completely disappear from their lives within a few months or years, regardless of their impact at the time of contact.

The Fulani child, in contrast, finds the wider context beyond the family very homogeneous, and the messages received from those others concerning who the child is by and large reinforce what has been learned at home. The Fulani child getting to know the world discovers that it is a world of people who remain pretty much the same during the time the child is growing up. For most American children what remain the same are objects, institutions, and functions—like towns, streets, schools, telephones, policemen, Coca-Cola, and so on—but the people are constantly changing. Another way of describing the quality of the Fulani world from the child's point of view would be to say that persons and institutions are the same thing, since the major institutions of the society are in fact the enduring relationships between people. Thus in a sense the child always feels like the "same" person in his early years. It is only in adolescence and then adulthood that a variety of relationships are experienced in which very different kinds of behavior are called forth (e.g., highly restrained and decorous as opposed to expressive or even crude).

With these thoughts in mind, I would like to return now to the question of why Western popular thought and scholarship have placed so much importance on childhood as the crucial period for the formation of the adult. If the theory of self, identity, and personality I have developed in this book is correct, it should be possible to understand our view of childhood as arising out of the sense of self that is prevalent in our cultural milieu rather than the other way around. Put as a question, does the sense of self we have explain why we believe that we are largely formed and determined by our childhood? Let me illustrate briefly why I think it does. It will help to start with an experience we all know both as children and as adults: children act differently at home from the way they do in school, or with friends or other people. For instance, a child might even be a sort of crybaby at home yet quite stoical and tough in relations outside the home. The reason for this difference in comportment is not just that the home is perceived as safer, but more importantly that in the family the child is known both as an individual with a history and as a participant in particular relations with each family member, especially those of dependence on the parents. Thus the child at home is not a representative of the family but is merely an individual, with particular relationships with each other family member, and the child's self is constituted in those relations. But when childen step outside the family something is added to who they are as family members, namely the awareness that they are more than just individuals: they embody and represent their families in the world and for that reason their senses of self will be greatly influenced by how their families are perceived to be situated therein. The personality which the child exhibits outside the family will thus be a portrayal of that complex sense of self.

The notion that our selves are actually made up of the selves of the people we live with clashes with much of the history, ideology, and experience of life in our society, which all affirm that each person is at bottom a separate self and that relations are not fundamental to our existence but are means each person can use to satisfy and further personal needs and interests. Although an examination of why we have this ideology is beyond the scope of this book, I do want to mention one of this ideology's consequences, namely a dulling or repression of any awareness that we mutually participate in one another's selves. These points help explain why people find it so difficult, though not impossible, to change. First, we are not in fact isolated selves, so any attempt to alter oneself involves change in more than just one person. Second, because we have repressed the fact that we are not isolated selves we find it all the more difficult to get access to ourselves. With this observation we come back to the problem of the role of childhood in our lives.

Given that as we grow up and live in this society we are taught that we *are* isolated individuals, we feel we cannot look to those to whom we are related for our sense of who we are. We are thrown back on ourselves. In practical terms this means that we learn who we are by way of that which we can call ours, namely our property, our deeds, and our experiences. Interestingly enough, even though we normally look to childhood to begin our quest for self-understanding, few adults, I expect, could actually point to ways in which experiences they had before the age of five made them what they are now.[5] Rather, it is later experiences that we remember as formative for us. From the point of view of parents, however, early childhood is considered important for another reason altogether, but still one that derives from our social life. In contrast to Fulani society, where parents expect that most of the children they are raising will, if they do not die, remain with them or nearby for life, in middle-class Western culture, especially the United States, the expectation is just the opposite. Parents not only expect their children to move out of the house, but also to follow careers that will take them too far away to make close association possible. We seem to assume that in order to be independent we have to be separate, and many middle-class people feel that grown children who stay around home are not fully grown because they have not cut the apron strings, have not become their own people. There is a strong sense in much of modern literature that you somehow cannot really begin to live your own life until you have found yourself, that is to say found some kernel or essence of self that is independent of all other selves. Once this self has been found, then it is possible to enter intimate relationships. But if you enter such relationships before finding yourself you have missed something. It is as if for us the social contract depended on the assumption that each person enters relationships as a totally free and independent individual, and so we feel that people who appear not to do this have somehow not achieved the full personhood that our society offers.

It seems paradoxical, given these values, that parents live

through their children as much as they do. This is not paradoxical, however, when we assume that everyone's self is in fact constituted in part by the selves to which one feels in relation. My hunch is that middle-class parents are ready to think childhood is important for the simple reason that it is all the time they expect they will get with their children. This expectation not only impinges on the simple pleasure of being together with them, but also evokes the haunting feeling they have that now—childhood—is the only chance they are going to have to influence their children. Thus we as parents want to believe both that we can influence children when they are young, and also that the influence will be perma- nent, for it is only these beliefs that allow us to imagine that we are still related to our children in the face of minimal or no interaction with them.

Another reason why we find childhood's importance so com- pelling is that the effect of childhood experiences may indeed be more pronounced in our culture than in some others. In part for the reasons given above, and for a number of others as well, par- ents begin training their children in a variety of areas, including toilet habits, very early, and they perceive much of the care they bestow, as I have said, as training or molding. I see this as having two results, neither of them good. In the worst cases these at- tempts can be pathogenic and the children can end up neurotic or psychotic. Now, since "overtraining" as well as neglect, abuse, and other factors can be a cause of later psychopathologies, we tend to draw an inference that does not necessarily follow, namely that childhood experiences in general are the cause of adult person- ality. Secondly, from the child's point of view, even in the more normal family situation, this constant attempt by the parents to mold, shape, and direct is usually interpreted, I believe, as a kind of rejection.[6] The child senses that whatever he or she is is some- how not good because the parents seem to want something else. In Erik Erikson's terms, these experiences would make the child feel shame and doubt as opposed to autonomy and inner goodness (Erikson 1963:151–58). Notice here that the child's experience of rejection is warranted insofar as the parents think they are prepar- ing the child for separation, which is very much akin to rejection.[7]

Now, if psychoanalysts are right in asserting that children com- pensate for loss of parental love or closeness by internalizing the parents,[8] that is by trying unconsciously to become more like them, this process would constitute an additional means by which Western adults affect their children's sense of self. Yet the results of internalization are not at all predictable, for they depend on what image of the person the child internalizes and the child alone knows that. Perhaps because internalization *is* a compensation, however, it can be said never fully to succeed at replacing what is lost, namely a living relationship; neither can work or achievement, which are adult ways of trying to fill up the detached, and hence empty, self.

In contrast, then, to the situation among the FulBe and the RiimaayBe, where people tend to be living and working with their relatives and where the sense of self they have is maintained through those ongoing relations, middle-class Americans tend to live their adult lives quite isolated from their relatives. Hence the influence of those relatives on them, such as it is, does in fact derive from the period of childhood when that influence was not only strong but also internalized because of the sense of inadequacy and rejection I have just mentioned (cf. Loewald 1962, 1973).

Thus we can see that our widespread belief that childhood experience shapes the personality of the adult in no way corresponds to a law of human development that applies universally. Instead, that belief corresponds to important aspects of middle-class experience in our society (I restrict myself here to middle-class experience because that is what I know from the inside). The key factor in this experience is the sense of self we have, which is isolated and individual. We get this sense of self in part from the ideology of our society and in part from the actual separations we undergo throughout our lives. In addition, however, there is a circular effect of this sense of self on children that makes this effect difficult to change and thus sets up a relationship between childhood experience and adult personality that may be fairly regular in our culture. Even if we solidly established that relationship, however, it would not be evidence for an unvarying influence of childhood on the adult personality, but would further confirm the power that our ideologies have to shape the way in which we make sense of our experience.

THEORETICAL
IMPLICATIONS

Carol Trosset

First Find Your Child a Good Mother has several distinctive features that give it the potential to make major contributions to the development of psychological anthropology. By simultaneously examining two different communities within the same cultural milieu, it addresses the problem of situational comparability that habitually plagues both culture-and-personality and cross-cultural psychology. By showing in detail how theories were examined and developed as part of the ethnographic process, it adds to our understanding of the role of theory in the study of both social and psychological processes. In addition, this grounded quality of Paul Riesman's new theory makes it possible to infer and work with many of his concepts even though the book is incomplete. He states in chapter 8 that his ultimate objective is "to build on this case study to develop a more general theory that would describe the relations between self, personality, and society for all situations." It is impossible even to attempt the reconstruction of that intended final chapter. Instead, my purpose here is to situate his work in psychological anthropology and to reflect briefly on the implications of the theory he was developing.

Since contemporary psychological anthropology is somewhat fragmented in its approaches and its foci, it may be helpful to deal separately with three distinct "schools": culture-and-personality, cross-cultural psychology, and ethnopsychology.

Culture-and-Personality

Freudian psychoanalytic theory has always been the basis of the culture-and-personality school, which at one time was synonymous with psychological anthropology. Despite periodic claims that Freudian theory has been discredited, or has simply gone out of style, it is still widely perceived as central to psychological anthropology (White 1989). Paul Riesman's study is related to culture-and-personality in that the latter provided its initial problem: the book is most directly concerned with challenging the common notion that child-rearing practices determine adult personality. His investigation of a whole range of parenting behaviors leads him to argue not only against the influence of specific practices, but against the whole idea that infancy and childhood are a time of shaping a future adult. This extended study of two groups with identical child-rearing practices but very different adult personalities is important because it provides sound empirical evidence of a sort which has generally been lacking from attempts to argue that Freudian ideas are not cross-culturally applicable.

His challenges are much in line with those presented by Richard Shweder in the latter's articles "Rethinking culture and personality theory" (1979a,b, 1980); at the time the articles appeared in print Paul referred to Shweder as "so uncannily doing what I am doing" (personal communication). Riesman's theory of personality not only critiques classical ideas of personality formation, but also challenges the dominant notion of personality as a noncultural phenomenon (cf. Wallace 1961). Shweder's (1979a) argument in this connection is that "traits" are so context-dependent as to be virtually meaningless, and Riesman takes a similar position when he argues that a personality which one "has" or which is "made" of traits cannot be shown to exist. Culture-and-personality creates a conceptual gap that then needs to be bridged, when it claims that personality is fundamentally noncultural but is primarily determined by cultural conditioning. Riesman here replaces this inherently problematic notion with a social concept of personality as a process of cultural expression and interpretation of the self. This is generally in accord with Shweder's recommendation of an increasingly hermeneutic focus for culture-and-personality (1980).

Cross-Cultural Psychology

I mention this field because, though not a branch of anthropology, it is concerned with similar issues and is increasingly seeking a dialogue with psychological anthropology. Cross-cultural psychology was first mentioned in the Annual Review of Psychology in 1973, a year before Paul began the fieldwork for this study, and although since then there has been increasing acceptance "in theory" of the importance of culture, it has recently been argued that this idea still has little impact on the discipline (Kagitçibasi and Berry 1989). Literature on personality development is dominated by studies of the mother–child dyad, and Freudian causal models of the importance of child rearing are clearly fundamental, despite a general failure to find cross-cultural data in support of these theories. Most work on human infancy has been either retrospective (subject to the accuracy of the mother's memory) or experimental (focusing on responses to unusual stimuli provided by the researcher). Longitudinal studies do not appear to have been done cross-culturally. Paul Riesman's study presents a longitudinal, observational study in two cultures, that ultimately compares personality in three cultures. Segall (1986) argues that the ideal study format should include observations in at least three cultures, and notes a shift from a study of the effects of monolithic "culture" on "personality," to "an interest in the effects of particular cultural practices on both developmental processes and personality" (1986:531). This advance could be carried much further by an application of Riesman's very different approach to the relation between personality and culture. In the 1970s cross-cultural psychology was seeking a theoretical framework; in the 1990s it is seeking psychological universals which it is not finding in anthropology. In this book, Paul Riesman provides a theoretical framework for the cross-cultural study of personality, and one which, moreover, suggests where universals, as opposed to culturally variable elements, may be found.

Ethnopsychology

Paul Riesman's work was always in line with ethnopsychology's program of studying the indigenous processes of constructing social meanings, and the relation of culture to self and affect. He was a pioneer in the study of the cultural construction of person and self, and much of his work in this area predated the delineation of ethnopsychology as a subfield. He always worked in an observational, rather than an experimental, mode, focusing on naturally occurring behavior (an approach somewhat tentatively espoused by Kirkpatrick and White (1985) as something that should form a part of ethnopsychology's program), and some dimensions of his approach remain highly unusual (see Abu-Lughod's introductory discussion). Though his work does not display the linguistic focus common to many current ethnopsychological studies, it always shows great sensitivity to the meanings and uses of words. In the technical sense of "ethnopsychology" as "native conceptions of psychological issues," this was an important component of his analyses in *Freedom in Fulani Social Life,* and he focused increasingly on this approach in the last two years of his life. In one way, all of *First Find Your Child a Good Mother* is an ethnopsychological study. On another level, in terms of Paul's program for psychological anthropology, ethnopsychology becomes one essential component of a larger enterprise.

Paul Riesman's Theoretical Perspective

For the purposes of psychological anthropology, Riesman's theoretical discussion does three important and distinctive things. First, personality is redefined so that it is no longer opposed to society, a "thing" or a list of "traits" that one "has," but instead becomes a social process of expression and interpretation. This is quite different from the approaches that dominate personality psychology and psychological anthropology.

Second, a distinction is drawn between personality, identity, and self, and the relations between them are defined. A constant theme of Paul's writing and his teaching was that the self is made up of bonds with others. Here, in the last chapter he wrote, he specifies how this works. Identity, as one's location in a social structure, clearly has major implications for the differences in personality between the FulBe, who belong to lineages, and the RiimaayBe, who do not. Personality and sense of self, as interpretations and expressions of understandings of each other, appear to exist in a Bateson-style cybernetic feedback loop, suggesting that interpersonal interactions take on many of the qualities of "mind" (Bateson 1979: 102 ff.).

Third, Riesman suggests a culturally variable relationship between identity and personality. As a corollary to this, he also proposes (though these ideas do not appear to have been fully developed) which factors in personality may be universal (processes of attachment), as opposed to culturally variable (qualities perceived in the nature of attachments).

Paul Riesman had another theoretical program that he did not complete: to discuss the broader relationships between self, social structure, economy, and ideology. To situate his approach to the study of the self in a broader context of cultural anthropology, it would be helpful to know how he perceived these relationships. Considerations of power and hierarchy would clearly have been important to this formulation; an increased awareness of the significance of power in relationships is one of the most striking differences between this book and his earlier writings. Unfortunately, he wrote nothing about how power would fit into his theoretical scheme. It is possible, however, to draw some incomplete inferences about the placement of the self in relation to other dimensions of social life.

What is important about social structure is that people are located in it, and that perceptions of these locations give rise to identity and affect one's sense of self. Some features of identity change with age; others are comparatively stable, such as the identity of relatives, and are learned in childhood.

Economy apparently creates or restricts available locations within the social structure; the difference between owning and not owning cattle turns out to be crucial not only for the differences between FulBe and RiimaayBe, but also for individual differences within FulBe society. Also, it is largely the economy that provides or fails to provide an individual with the resources he or she needs to fulfill or achieve certain roles; for example, cattle are needed to marry, or to provide for one's children.

Ideology is never defined, but the term is used to refer to the culturally available symbolic meanings and values. In a particular culture, ideology limits the parameters for defining identity and provides the elements used in interpreting personality. It also appears to define the culture-specific relations between identity and personality in forming a sense of self. Specifying this relationship is given as one of the tasks of ethnopsychological analysis, as a part of the larger program of studying the self.

What are the wider implications of Paul Riesman's theoretical perspective? Let me approach this question by speculating about what he might have considered an appropriate program of ethnographic study. He seems to be arguing that to know about identity, one needs to know about social structure and the workings of the economy (what social roles exist in what relations to each other, and what their resources and requirements are); in what kinds of situations and for what purposes people interact with and act upon each other; and what elements of identity are deemed important by the culture's ideology. To know these things, and to understand personality, one needs an understanding of the culturally available symbolic meanings, the values placed on them, and the ways in which they are understood and manipulated. Understanding personality and sense of self further requires finding out how people interpret their own and each other's behavior (both the process by which they interpret, and the meanings that result from such interpretation); and a careful awareness of one's own (the ethnographer's) interpretations of people and the causes underlying these interpretations. Here Paul's method of reflexive introspection becomes more than a responsibly accurate methodology. It becomes theoretically *necessary*, for the ethnographer participates in the meaning-making cycle of personality and sense of self.

Because the sense of self is made up of identity interacting with personality, one must also know how the cultural ideology defines

the relationship between these two elements (what the native ethnopsychology of self and personality is); the native concepts of
personhood (what it means to them to be human and how people
get that way, a related ethnopsychological effort); and native attitudes toward agency and free will. I include this because of
Riesman's statement that an identity "is the conviction that it is . . .
oneself as a complete human being who is acting in the world,"
which seems to imply a need to pursue the sorts of questions examined in *Freedom in Fulani Social Life*.

Finally, to understand how all this works in a specific culture,
one must also sort out how all these perceptions and behaviors
vary: (a) from one social category to the next (FulBe–RiimaayBe,
age-groups, gender), (b) in the different types of situations that an
individual may be in, and (c) between individuals. Presumably,
these variations would then have to be accounted for, probably in
terms of differences in both social positioning (features of identity), and the culturally available meanings attributed to the categories and situations. Some parts of this last effort were completed
more fully than others; most would clearly have been worked out
in detail in the final chapters. The childless women and the old
men discussed in chapter 4 seem to provide the beginnings of an
analysis of individual differences.

This outline should give some idea of the kinds of questions
Paul Riesman felt psychological anthropology should be dealing
with, and tries to show how fully integrated he perceived them to
be. Some fall squarely within the domain of ethnopsychology, but
some are outside the usual range of psychological anthropology altogether. His is an approach in which psychology is truly integrated with culture, not because either one causes the other, but
because both are seen as interactive dimensions in an overall process
of constructing meanings. In a sense, it is not just ethnopsychology
that becomes part of a larger enterprise, but psychology itself.
From this perspective, it is clear that psychological anthropology
cannot be done apart from considerations of ideology, symbolic
meanings, and social organization, and that these things cannot, in
turn, be studied without an understanding of personality and self.

NOTES

Chapter 1

1 The opening section of this chapter was written by Paul Riesman. Lila Abu-Lughod added a few sentences near the end to provide a context for the following chapters.

2 This section was constructed by Paul Stoller to provide information on the cultural and historical background of the Fulani. Parts of the text were taken from Riesman (1984).

3 For general descriptions of Fulani life, see Hopen (1958), Stenning (1959), Dupire (1962), and Riesman (1977). For studies of Fulani character and the difference between FulBe and RiimaayBe, see Delmond (1952), Kane (1961), Seydou (1972), Dognin (1975), and Riesman (1977).

Chapter 9

1 This chapter was constructed by Sharon Hutchinson, drawing on Paul Riesman's outlines for the conclusions of the book, his discussions with various colleagues, material from earlier chapters, and segments and arguments from Riesman 1975, 1980, 1983, 1986, and 1990. Material on the RiimaayBe, and on women of both groups, was particularly scattered. What has been included often had to be teased or inferred from numerous sources and hints. She was also aided by her related research on the cattle-raising Nuer of the Sudan.

2 My thinking here is obviously close to the work of G. H. Mead (1964) and Erving Goffman (1961, 1967), though at the time of my first field trip, it should be clear by now, it was not their ideas but psychoanalytic ones that I was attempting to perceive and think with. Another important strand is the thinking of Suzanne Langer (1951, 1953), whose ideas about how artistic symbolism works are a mine of suggestions as to how we should understand the self. For current sociological work on the self, Gecas (1982) is a useful source.

3 J. P. Olivier de Sardan came to a very similar conclusion concerning the slaves of the Songhay in West Africa. He writes (my translation), "In essence, the captive, deprived of a family, is deprived of shame. For shame means not to be faithful to your name, not to live up to the prestigious image of your ancestors, and to pass on a deformed version of it to your descendants" (Olivier de Sardan 1973:431).

4   The following section was taken from Riesman (1983).

5   The psychoanalytic response to this point is that the formation of the Oedipus complex and the superego takes place around age five or six and involves repression of the memory of those early formative experiences. As I will argue below, however, this is not a universal psychological process, and the degree to which a superego is internalized varies considerably from culture to culture.

6   For a cross-cultural study of the psychological effects of rejections, which is interesting despite the inherent drawbacks of the Human Relations Area File (HRAF), see Rohner (1975).

7   Arthur Kleinman has suggested (personal communication) that the fact that the United States is a nation of emigrants and refugees would help to explain these concerns with separation and dependency. This is a thought-provoking idea, for it seems likely that people who had abandoned their own families of origin would in turn expect (out of guilt, perhaps), to be abandoned by their children. What would require investigation, however, is whether in Europe the movement from rural to urban, or from one social class to another, was any less productive of such feelings than was emigration to the New World.

8   Cf. this remark by Harry Guntrip (1973:10): "Freud observed that 'Identification is a substitute for a lost human relationship,' or indeed for one that was urgently needed and unobtainable. Thus a child who finds that he cannot get any satisfactory kind of relationship with a parent who is too cold and aloof, or too aggressive, or too authoritarian tends to make up for his sense of apartness and isolation by identifying with, or growing like, that parent, as if this were a way of possessing the needed person within oneself."

BIBLIOGRAPHY

Bateson, G. 1972. *Steps to an Ecology of Mind*. New York: Ballantine Books.
———. 1979. *Mind and Nature*. New York: Bantam Books.
Beckwith, C. 1983. *Nomads of Niger*. New York: Harry N. Abrams.
Bocquene, H. 1986. *Moi, un Mbororo: autobiographie de Oumarou Ndoudi, Peul nomade de Cameroun*. Paris: Karthala.
Clifford, J. 1988. *The Predicament of Culture*. Cambridge, Mass.: Harvard University Press.
Crapanzano, V. 1977. On the writing of ethnography. *Dialectical Anthropology* 2:69–73.
———. 1980. *Tuhami*. Chicago: University of Chicago Press.
D'Andrade, R. 1984. Cultural meaning systems. In *Culture Theory: Essays on Mind, Self, and Emotion*, edited by R. Shweder and R. LeVine. New York: Cambridge University Press.
Delmond, P. 1952. Essai de classification des Peul du Cercle de Dori. In *Conferencia International Dos Africanistas Ocidentais, Bissau, 1947*, vol. 5, pt. 2, pp. 27–52, Lisbon.
Devereux, G. 1967. *From Anxiety to Method in the Behavioral Sciences*. The Hague: Mouton.
Dognin, R. 1975. Sur trois ressorts du comportement peul. In *Pastoralism in Tropical Africa*, edited by Theodore Monod, 298–321. London: Oxford University Press (for IAI).
Dumont, J. P. 1978. *The Headman and I*. Austin: University of Texas Press.
Dupire, M. 1962. *Peuls nomades*. Paris: Institut d'Ethnologie.
Dwyer, K. 1982. *Moroccan Dialogues*. Baltimore: The Johns Hopkins University Press.
Erikson, E. 1953. Growth and crises of the "healthy personality." In *Personality in Nature, Society, and Culture*, edited by Clyde Kluckhohn, Henry A. Murray, with David M. Schneider. 2nd ed., 185–225. New York: Knopf.
———. 1963. *Childhood and Society*. 2nd ed. New York: W. W. Norton.
Gecas, V. 1982. The self-concept. *Annual Review of Sociology* 8:1–33.
Goffman, E. 1961. *Encounters: Two Studies in the Sociology of Interaction*. Indianapolis: Bobbs-Merrill.
———. 1967. *Interaction Ritual: Essays in Face-to-Face Behavior*. New York: Doubleday Anchor Books.
Guntrip, H. 1973. *Psychoanalytic Theory, Therapy, and the Self: A Basic Guide to the Human Personality in Freud, Erikson, Klein, Sullivan, Fairbarn, Hartmann, Jacobson, and Winnicott*. New York: Basic Books.

Hopen, C. 1958. *The Pastoral Fulbe Family in Gwandu*. London: Oxford University Press (for IAI).
Kagitçibasi, C., and Berry, J. W. 1989. Cross-cultural psychology: current research and trends. *Annual Review of Psychology* 40:493–531.
Kane, C. 1961. *L'Aventure ambigue*. Paris: Julliard.
Kirkpatrick, J., and White, G. 1985. Exploring ethnopsychologies. In *Person, Self, and Experience: Exploring Pacific Ethnopsychologies*, edited by White and Kirkpatrick. Berkeley: University of California Press.
Kracke, W. 1987. Encounter with other cultures: psychological and epistemological aspects. *Ethos* 15:58–81.
Langer, S. 1951. *Philosophy in a New Key: A Study in the Symbolism of Reason, Rite and Art*. 2nd ed. New York: New American Library.
———. 1953. *Feeling and Form: A Theory of Art*. New York: Charles Scribner's Sons.
Lee, D. 1959. *Freedom and Culture*. Englewood Cliffs, N.J.: Spectrum Books, Prentice-Hall.
———. 1976. *Valuing the Self*. Prospect Heights, Ill.: Waveland Press.
Loewald, H. 1962. Internalization, separation, mourning, and the superego. *The Psychoanalytic Quarterly* 31:483–504.
———. 1973. On internalization. *The International Journal of Psychoanalysis* 54:9–17.
Malinowski, B. 1948. *Magic, Science, and Religion and Other Essays*. New York: Doubleday.
Marcus, G., and Fischer, M. 1986. *Anthropology as Cultural Critique*. Chicago: University of Chicago Press.
Mead, G. H. 1964. *George Herbert Mead On Social Psychology*. Selected papers, edited and with an Introduction by Anselm Strauss. Chicago: University of Chicago Press.
Olivier de Sardan, J. 1973. Personnalité et structures sociales (À propos des Songhays). In *Colloques Internationaux du CNRS No. 544: La notion de personne en Afrique noire*, pp. 421–45. Paris: Éditions du CNRS.
Rabinow, P. 1977. *Reflections on Fieldwork in Morocco*. Berkeley and Los Angeles: University of California Press.
Riesman, P. 1971. Defying official morality: the example of Man's quest for Woman among the Fulani. *Cahiers d'études Africaines* 44:602–13.
———. 1974. *Société et liberté chez les Peul Djelgobe de Haute-Volta: Essai d'anthropologie introspective*. Paris–The Hague: Mouton.
———. 1975. The art of life in a West African community: formality and spontaneity in Fulani interpersonal relationships. *Journal of African Studies* 2(1): 39–63.
———. 1977. *Freedom in Fulani Social Life: An Introspective Ethnography*. Chicago: University of Chicago Press.
———. 1980. Aristocrats as subjects in a multi-ethnic state. In *Image and Reality in African Interethnic Relations: The Fulbe and their Neighbors*, edited by E. Schultz. 21–29. *Studies in Third World Societies*, Publication No. 11.
———. 1982. Fieldwork as initiation and as therapy. Paper presented at the Annual Meeting of the American Anthropological Association, Washington, D.C.
———. 1983. On the irrelevance of child rearing practices for the formation of personality: an analysis of childhood, personality, and values in two African communities. *Culture, Medicine and Psychiatry* 7:103–29.

————. 1984. The Fulani in a development context: the relevance of cultural traditions for coping with change and crisis. In *Life Before the Drought*, edited by E. Scott, 171–91. Boston: Allen and Unwin.

————. 1986. The person and the life cycle in African social life and thought. *African Studies Review* 29:71–138.

————. 1987. Power, action, and critique: comments on Nancy Scheper-Hughes's essay, "The madness of hunger: sickness, delirium and human needs." Paper presented at the Annual Meeting of the American Anthropological Association, Chicago, Ill.

————. 1990. Living poor while being rich: the pastoral folk economy. In *The Creative Communion: African Folk Models of Fertility and the Regeneration of Life*, edited by A. Jacobson-Widding and W. van Beek, 323–34. Uppsala Studies in Cultural Anthropology, Sweden.

Rohner, R. 1975. *They Love Me, They Love Me Not: A Worldwide Study of the Effects of Parental Acceptance and Rejection*. New Haven: HRAF Press.

Rosaldo, M. 1980. *Knowledge and Passion: Ilongot Notions of Self and Social Life*. New York: Cambridge University Press.

Rouget, G. 1985. *Music and Trance: A Theory of the Relations Between Music and Possession*. Chicago: University of Chicago Press.

Satir, V. 1972. *Peoplemaking*. Palo Alto, Calif.: Science and Behavior Books.

Segall, M. 1986. Culture and behavior: psychology in global perspective. *Annual Review of Psychology* 37:523–64.

Seydou, C. 1972. *Silamaka et Poullori, épopée peule du Massina*. Paris: Éditions A. Colin.

Shweder, R. 1979a. Rethinking culture and personality theory: Part 1. *Ethos* 7(3): 255–78.

————. 1979b. Rethinking culture and personality theory: Part 2. *Ethos* 7(4): 279–311.

————. 1980. Rethinking culture and personality theory: Part 3. *Ethos* 8(1): 60–94.

Stenning, D. 1959. *Savannah Nomads*. London: Oxford University Press (for IAI).

Tedlock, D. 1987. Questions concerning dialogical anthropology. *Journal of Anthropological Research* 43(4):325–37.

Tyler, S. 1987. On "writing-up/off" as "speaking-for." *Journal of Anthropological Research* 43(4):338–42.

Wallace, A.E.C. 1961. *Culture and personality*. New York: Random House.

White, G. 1989. Heartlands and borderlands: reflections on the first SPA conference. *Ethos* 17(4):504–12.

Winnicott, D. 1964. *The Child, the Family, and the Outside World*. Baltimore: Penguin Books.

INDEX

actions: individual responsibility for, 49, 50; significance of children's, 173; utilitarian, views of, 201, 206
adolescence: in boys, 20, 21, 44–51, 211–212; in girls, 74–75; and independence, 44, 213; and personality development, 212
adoption, 61, 96–97
adultery, 48, 50–51, 62
agriculture: 31, 37–38; as shameful, 64. *See also* millet
ancestors, 61, 155
anger: on behalf of relatives, 146; with children, 136–137, 166–167
artisans, 14
authority, 212. *See also* hierarchy; power

babies: attitudes toward, 118; care of, 106–129; holding of, 112, 113, 115–116; playing with, 113–114, 118, 123; sickness, 117, 128; spitting up, 112, 116; treatment of as adults, 113, 186; washing of, 108. *See also* defecation; nursing; weaning
basi (medicinal broth), 115, 116, 117, 153
bastardy, 29
Bateson, Gregory, 77, 228
beating: reasons for, 129, 134, 136, 138, 151, 152, 174; threats of, 135, 143, 144
beauty, female: importance of, 19–20, 89, 100; standards of, 95, 98
Beckwith, Carol, 11

beds, 108–109
Bella, 149
blessings: content of, 53, 140, 210; occasions for, 34, 85; sources of, 63–64, 172, 173
Bocquene, Henri, 178
breast feeding, *see* nursing
bush, 213

cattle: benefits of, 34–35, 62–63, 205–207; care of, 32–33, 154, 207–208; from ancestors, 155; from God, 65; importance of, 155, 156, 205, 206–207, 209, 214; ownership of, 156–157, 210; responsibility for, 208–209, 210, 214–215; use in marriages, 79
character, *see* personality
charms: as protection, 109, 110, 113, 172; as secret, 153; in weaning, 128
chief, intervention of, 52, 53, 134, 145
child care: by children, 35, 113, 138; degree of homogeneity in, 9, 111, 112, 158; frustrations of, 106; of infants, 106–129; initiative in, 117–118, 122, 124–125, 126–127; interaction between caretakers, 136
child rearing: as formative, 8, 160–161, 176, 179–180; Fulani views of, 170, 180–183
childbirth, 30, 75, 106–112
childhood: American beliefs about, 220–223; importance of for personality, 197, 222
childlessness: effects on men, 58, 59; effects on women, 94–99